EASY
Japanese

T0001476

Learn to Speak Japanese Quickly!

EASY
Japanese

EMIKO KONOMI

TUTTLE Publishing

Tokyo | Rutland, Vermont | Singapore

The Tuttle Story
"Books to Span the East and West"

Our core mission at Tuttle Publishing is to create books which bring people together one page at a time. Tuttle was founded in 1832 in the small New England town of Rutland, Vermont (USA). Our fundamental values remain as strong today as they were then—to publish best-in-class books informing the English-speaking world about the countries and peoples of Asia. The world has become a smaller place today and Asia's economic, cultural and political influence has expanded, yet the need for meaningful dialogue and information about this diverse region has never been greater. Since 1948, Tuttle has been a leader in publishing books on the cultures, arts, cuisines, languages and literatures of Asia. Our authors and photographers have won numerous awards and Tuttle has published thousands of books on subjects ranging from martial arts to paper crafts. We welcome you to explore the wealth of information available on Asia at **www.tuttlepublishing.com**.

Published by Tuttle Publishing, an imprint of Periplus Editions (HK) Ltd.

www.tuttlepublishing.com

Copyright © 2020 Periplus Editions (HK) Ltd.
Cover photo © liza5450/123rf.com
and Rawpixel.com/shutterstock.com
Illustrations by Suman S Roy

Library of Congress Control Number
2017956490

ISBN: 978-4-8053-1587-3

23 22 21 20   6 5 4 3 2 1
Printed in Malaysia   2001VP

Distributed by

North America, Latin America & Europe
Tuttle Publishing
364 Innovation Drive,
North Clarendon,
VT 05759-9436, USA
Tel: 1 (802) 773 8930
Fax: 1 (802) 773 6993
info@tuttlepublishing.com
www.tuttlepublishing.com

Japan
Tuttle Publishing
Yaekari Bldg., 3rd Floor
5-4-12 Osaki, Shinagawa-ku
Tokyo 141 0032
Tel: (81) 3 5437 0171
Fax: (81) 3 5437 0755
sales@tuttle.co.jp
www.tuttle.co.jp

Asia Pacific
Berkeley Books Pte Ltd
3 Kallang Sector #04-01/02
Singapore 349278
Tel: (65) 6280 1330
Fax: (65) 6280 6290
inquiries@periplus.com.sg
www.periplus.com

Contents

Introduction

Who is this book for?

Easy Japanese is designed for beginners who want to learn basic Japanese in order to travel, work or live in Japan. Besides helping you build a working foundation in the language and to develop a knowledge of the culture, an additional goal of this book is to enable readers to become lifelong Japanese learners.

This basic level self-study book includes many elementary sentence patterns (these correspond to the Japanese Language Proficiency Test Levels 5 and 4—see www.jlpt.jp/e/). The vocabulary and situations have been specifically tailored for adults and can be used in everyday conversations, whether in professional settings or when socializing with Japanese friends. Explanations are kept very concise so as to only cover the key points. The main focus is on oral communication.

What will you learn?

After finishing this book you will be able to handle most everyday interactions, avoid social blunders, answer the most frequently asked questions about yourself, and communicate well with native speakers. The topics, grammar patterns, and vocabulary in this book are selected on the basis of practicality and frequency of use.

How is the book structured?

This book is divided into ten lessons. Except for Lesson 1, which introduces greetings and common expressions, each lesson consists of four brief dialogues, each one followed by a vocabulary list, grammar and cultural notes, drills and exercises, and review questions. Make sure you can answer the review questions correctly before moving on to the next lesson as each lesson builds on top of the previous one. For this reason, it is imperative that you progress in order and not skip lessons or parts of lessons.

Reading and writing Japanese

Modern Japanese is written using a combination of *kanji* (characters borrowed from China) along with *hiragana* and *katakana* (two independent alphabets with 46 letters, each representing a Japanese sound). While authentic Japanese script is included in the dialogues and vocabulary lists, no reading or writing instruction is included. There are other books you can buy to learn the writing system, for example *Japanese Hiragana and Katakana for Beginners* and *Japanese Kanji for Beginners*.

Japanese pronunication

Japanese words and sentences are presented in phonetic romanized form (that is, using the Roman alphabet to represent Japanese pronunciation). Dialogues and vocabulary lists are also presented in authentic Japanese script along with

romanization. Romanization is not meant to be an accurate representation of Japanese pronunciation but rather just a convenient tool for reference. Be particularly mindful not to pronounce romanized Japanese as if you were reading English but try to learn the correct Japanese way of pronuncing the words and sentences.

It is highly recommended that you listen to the audio recordings of all the dialogues, vocabulary lists and practice drills so you can learn to mimic the native speaker pronunciations. When using the audio, try not to look at the written scripts. For many of us, visual input will interfere with accurately perceiving the audio input. You should refer to the written scripts only when you need help with particular parts of the audio. After peeking at the script, go back to the audio again.

How should you use this book?

Dialogues: The dialogues present frequently used exchanges that are part of a longer conversation. It is important to memorize these to the point where you can recite them automatically and naturally without referring to the text, while integrating body language. You can expand each dialogue by adding elements before and after it to create a longer conversation, or change parts of the dialogue to fit different contexts. Either way, each dialogue serves as a basis to explore other possibilities.

Pattern Practices: Each dialogue has at least two drills that target key grammar patterns and vocabulary. These are meant to develop quick and automatic formation skills. The recommended procedure for these drill practices is to 1) listen to the two model exchanges and understand what changes to make in responding to the cues.and only look at the scripts for the model answers if you are not sure what to do. 2) Listen to the first cue, insert your response during the following pause, listen to the model answer, and repeat the model answer during the second pause. 3) Repeat this procedure for the following cues. It is recommended that you loop back to the beginning of the drill frequently. Always give yourself a chance to respond to the cues before you listen to the model answer. Be sure that you understand the meaning of what you are saying, and not merely repeating the sounds.

Exercises: Two additional types of exercises follow the drills. The first is "Say it in Japanese", which is a translation activity. The other is "Role Play", in which learners can freely respond to each other within the given context and expand the suggested interchange into a longer interaction. For this exercise, learners are encouraged to perform the roles as naturally as possible while integrating body language, facial expressions, etc.

Review questions: By answering the review questions at the end of each lesson, you will be able to assess your understanding of the chapter before moving onto the next one. If you are unsure of the answers, simply refer back to the grammar notes in that chapter.

Practice using what you learn

Make a clear distinction between knowing the material and using the material in actual real-life conversations. You may learn the grammar and vocabulary quickly, but it takes practice to develop the skills to speak Japanese in real-life situations. You should aim to be able to verbally respond to a native speaker in a culturally appropriate way. For this reason, the book contains drills and exercises for oral practice. Use the online audio recordings to practice on your own without a Japanese speaker being present.

Japanese syllables

A Japanese syllable is constructed in one of the following four ways.
1. one vowel alone can be a syllable (*a*, *i*, *u*, *e*, *o*)
2. one consonant + one vowel (62 possible combinations)
3. one consonant alone (*n*, *t*, *s*, *k*, *p*)
4. one consonant + *y* + one vowel (33 combinations)

All syllables have the same spoken duration or beat length. The pronunciation of the letters are similar to English.

The Japanese Vowels

a	like the "a" in "dark"	*asa* "morning"
i	like the "i" in "pit", slightly longer	*inu* "dog"
u	like the "u" in "pull"	*ureshī* "happy"
e	like the "é" in "café"	*Eigo* "English"
o	like the "o" in "bowl"	*oishī* "delicious"

Long Vowels

There are five long vowels in Japanese: *aa*, *ii*, *uu*, *ee*, and *oo*. They are "long" in terms of spoken duration, e.g., *aa* is twice as long as *a*.

aa	long "aa" written as *ā*, pronounced like "Ah!"	*rāmen* "ramen"
ii	long "ii" written as *ī*, like the "ee" in "keep"	*bīru* "beer"
uu	long "uu" written as *ū*, like the "oo" in "coop"	*kyū* "nine"
ee	long "ee" written as *ē*, like the "ere" in "where"	*mēru* "email, text"
oo	long "oo" written as *ō*, like the "ow" in "bowl"	*dō* "how"

The Japanese Consonants

Most consonants are pronounced similar to English.

b	like the "b" in "book"	*ban gohan* "dinner"
ch	like the "ch" in "chocolate"	*chotto* "a little"
d	like the "d" in "day"	*denwa* "phone"
f	like the "f" in "food"	*fuyu* "winter"
g	like the "g" in "gift"	*gohan* "rice"
h	like the "h" in "hope"	*ha* "leaf"

j	like the "j" in "**j**og"	*jikan*	"hour"
k	like the "k" in "**k**ing"	*kitte*	"stamps"
m	like the "m" in "**m**at"	*miseru*	"to show"
n	like the "n" in "**n**ut",	*natsu*	"summer"

at the end of the word, closer to "ng" as in "thi**ng**"   *ringo* "apple"

p	like the "p" in "**p**et"	*purezento*	"present"
r	like "r" in "ca**r**" (not rolled)	*raigetsu*	"next month"

between the English "r", "l" and "d",

s	like the "s" in "**s**oot"	*suru*	"to do"
sh	like the "sh" in "**sh**ook"	*shoku-gyō*	"profession"
t	like the "t" in "**t**ip"	*tenki*	"weather"
ts	like the "ts" in "hi**ts**"	*tsuma*	"wife"
w	like the "w" in "**w**att"	*watashitachi*	"we"
y	like the "y" in "**y**ou"	*yon*	"four"
z	like the "z" in "**z**oo"	*zutsū*	"headache"

Long Consonants

The consonants *t*, *s*, *k*, and *p* can also be long. They should be pronounced like so:

kk	like "kk" in "boo**kk**eeper"	*yukkuri*	"slowly"
tt	like "tt" in "fla**t-t**op"	*wakatta*	"I understand"
pp	like "pp" in "to**p-p**erforming"	*ippai*	"to be full"
ss	like "ss" in "mi**ss**tatement"	*zasshi*	"magazine"

When these consonants constitute an entire syllable without a vowel, they are not pronounced but take a full syllable length.

three syllables: *ki-t-te*	"stamps"
four syllables: *ma-s-su-gu*	"straight"
five syllables: *sho-p-pi-n-gu*	"shopping"

The consonant *n* can also take up an entire syllable by itself, as in *sho-p-pi-N-gu* above. In this book, *n* with an apostrophe—*n'*—is used where there is a need to distinguish a syllabic *n*. Compare the following:

kinen	"commemoration"	three syllables	*ki-ne-N*
kin'en	"no smoking"	four syllables	*ki-N -e-N*

(The syllabic *n* is indicated by the capital here.)

Pitch Accent

Japanese speech has a rise and fall in pitch, changing from syllable to syllable in order to distinguish meaning. For example, there is a fall in pitch in *hai* "yes", while there is a rise in *hai* "ash", distinguishing these two words. This is called pitch accent, and this can be represented using capital letters as follows:

   HA-i "yes" as compared to *ha-I* "ash"

On the other hand, in English a difference in volume, i.e., loud vs soft serves this function. This is called stress accent. Compare the following (the capital indicates the louder syllable).

INsult (noun) as compared to inSULT (verb)

All Japanese words have one of the following three pitch patterns:

Falling: *JAa* "well then"
DŌmo "thanks"

Rising: *maTA* "again"
saYONARA "goodbye"
oHAYŌ "good morning"

Rising then Falling:
aRIgatō "thanks"
suMIMASEn "sorry"

If a word has only one syllable, a fall or a rise occurs with the following word.

HA desu. "It's a tooth."
ha DEsu. "It's a leaf."

In the rest of this book, pitch accent is not provided in either romanization or Japanese scripts. Please refer to the audio for correct pitch.

A note on the cultural significance of pitch is in order. As you learn Japanese, pay attention to pitch at the sentence level as well as the word level. A slight change in pitch may indicate a subtle but significant change in meaning or mood. It is observed in many, if not all, languages that speakers tend to raise their pitch when talking to babies or when trying to sound gentle. Japanese is no exception. Talking in a high pitch is generally associated with politeness in Japanese. Women tend to talk in a higher pitch, but regardless of the gender, sales and customer service personnel, receptionists, waiters, etc., speak with an overall higher pitch. Just to be safe, bow, smile, and talk gently.

Review Questions

1. a) What is romanization? b) What should you be cautious of regarding romanization when studying Japanese pronunciation?
2. What is recommended when using dialogues?
3. How should one use the Pattern Practice Drills?
4. How many vowels are there in Japanese?
5. What are the five long consonants?
6. a) How many syllables are in *kin'en* "no smoking"? b) How about *hai* "yes"?
7. What are the pitch accents and stress accents?
8. What three pitch accent patterns are there in Japanese?
9. When speaking Japanese, what is the significance of pitch?

LESSON 1

Greetings and Everyday Expressions

A journey of a thousand miles begins with a single step
千里の道も一歩から　***Senri no michi mo ip-po kara***

In this lesson, greetings and some common expressions are introduced. To learn each item and pronounce it like a native speaker, use the accompanying audio.

Greetings

Ohayō	おはよう	Good morning
Ohayō gozaimasu	おはようございます	Good morning (polite)
Kon'nichiwa	こんにちは	Hello
Kon'ban'wa	こんばんは	Good evening

Gozaimasu indicates politeness and formality. People who know each other well (e.g., family members, good friends) can use just ***Ohayō***. You should never use the short form with your superiors (e.g., customer, teacher, supervisor). ***Kon'nichiwa*** and ***kon'ban'wa*** cover both formal and informal situations. ***Kon'nichiwa*** and ***kon'ban'wa*** are not used among family members but ***Ohayō*** is.

Addressing Someone and Responding

Satō-san	佐藤さん	Mr/s. Sato
Satō-sensei	佐藤先生	Prof./Dr. Sato
hai	はい	that's right; I'm here; here you are

The ending ***-san*** is a title indicating deference that is usually attached to a person's given name or a family name, and even some job titles. Never attach it to your own name or the names of people in your group when speaking about yourself or your group.

The ending ***-sensei*** is a title that can be attached to teachers, professors, doctors, lawyers or someone else who is a "master" in their field (generally a very senior person). You should not use ***-san*** to refer to people in these roles.

Hai means "that's right", "present" (in roll call), or "here you are" (handing something over).

Requesting and Offering

Onegai-shimasu	お願いします	I cordially request...
Dōzo	どうぞ	go ahead; help yourself

Onegai-shimasu is a polite expression asking for help or requesting for things and actions. It is also equivalent to "Thank you in advance" for a requested favor. *Dōzo* is used to offer things or invite people to go ahead and help themselves.

Thanking and Apologizing

A(a)	あ(あ)	oh; ah
Dōmo	どうも	thank you; I'm sorry
Arigatō	ありがとう	thank you
Arigatō gozaimasu	ありがとうございます	thank you (polite)
Arigatō gozaimashita	ありがとうございました	thank you for what you've done
Ie, i'ie (formal), *iya* (casual)	いえ、いいえ、いや	no; that's wrong
Dō itashimashite	どういたしまして	you're welcome; don't mention it

Dōmo expresses gratitude or apology. When combined with *arigatō* (*gozaimasu*) or *sumimasen*, it intensifies the meaning—"Thank you very much".

    Arigatō (*gozaimasu*) expresses thanks in general. You should never use the short form with your superiors because it is too casual.

    Gozaimashita is used when the act is completed while *gozaimasu* indicates that the act is ongoing.

    I'ie and its variations indicate negation. When used as a response to "thank you" or an apology, repeating it twice—*i'ie, i'ie*—is common.

Sumimasen	すみません	thank you; I'm sorry
Sumimasen deshita	すみませんでした	thank you; I'm sorry for what I've done

Sumimasen expresses apology or gratitude when you are about to trouble or have troubled someone. It is also commonly used to get attention from or address someone whose name you do not know such as store clerks or strangers. *Sumimasen deshita* expresses apology or gratitude when you have troubled someone.

Gomen	ごめん	sorry; excuse me (casual)
Gomen nasai	ごめんなさい	sorry; excuse me (casual, gentle)
Shitsurei-shimasu	失礼します	excuse me
Shitsurei-shimashita	失礼しました	excuse me for what I've done

Shitsurei-shimasu literally means "I'm going to do something rude" and is used when entering a room, interrupting someone, or leaving. *Shitsurei-shimashita* is used for what you've already done. *Gomen* and *gomen nasai* are both casual, and therefore should not be used with a superior. *Gomen nasai* is gentle and typically used by female speakers.

Expressions for Eating and Drinking

Itadakimasu	いただきます	ritual expression before eating
Gochisō-sama	ごちそうさま	ritual expression after eating
Gochisō-sama deshita	ごちそうさまでした	formal version of *gochisō-sama*

Itadakimasu literally means "I'll humbly accept it" and is used before eating or receiving a gift. *Gochisō-sama* (*deshita*) shows gratitude for the food or drink one has been offered. Even when alone, Japanese people tend to whisper *itadakimasu* and *gochisō-sama* before and after eating.

Leaving and Coming Back to Home or the Office

Itte kimasu	行ってきます	ritual expression when leaving home
Itte rasshai	行ってらっしゃい	ritual response to *itte kimasu*
Tadaima	ただいま	ritual expression upon coming home
Okaeri nasai	お帰りなさい	ritual response to *tadaima*

Itte kimasu is used when leaving home or stepping out the office for an errand. It implies that you are coming back within a few hours.

Acknowledging Hard Work

Otsukare(-sama)	おつかれ(さま)	thanks for your work
Otsukare-sama desu	おつかれさまです	(formal) (on going)
Otsukare-sama deshita	おつかれさまでした	(the work is over)

The above are common greetings between co-workers. They are also used to thank service personnel or acknowledge anyone's hard work.

Ja(a)   じゃ(あ)   then; bye

Ja is used to follow up on what has been said, to switch topic, etc.

Ja, mata	じゃ、また	see you
Sayonara, sayōnara	さよなら、さようなら	Goodbye

Going to Sleep at Night

Oyasumi	おやすみ	Good night (casual)
Oyasumi nasai	おやすみなさい	Good night (formal)

SAMPLE DIALOGUES

The dialogues below provide sample exchanges for the greetings and common ritual expressions introduced above. Practice expressions using the dialogues along with appropriate body language rather than by memorizing them in isolation.

First listen to the accompanying audio and practice each line **aloud**. After you can say the phrase naturally, add on another and practice those two lines together. Imagine the context, take a role, then switch roles. Practice alternatives for different contexts.

A: *Ohayō.* おはよう。 Good morning.
B: *Ohayō gozaimasu.* おはようございます。 Good morning.

A: *Dōzo.* どうぞ。 Go ahead. (Please take it)
B: *Ā, dōmo.* ああ、どうも。 Oh, thanks.

A: *A, sumimasen.* あ、すみません！ Oh, sorry!
B: *Ie, ie.* いえ、いえ。 No, no.

A: *Shitsurei-shimasu.* 失礼します。 Excuse me.
B: *Hai, dōzo.* はい、どうぞ。 Yes, come in.

A: *Dōzo.* どうぞ。 Please (have some).
B: *Jā, itadakimasu.* じゃあ、いただきます。 Well, then I'll have some.
  Gochisō-sama ごちそうさまでした。 Thank you (That was
  deshita.   delicious).

A: *Ja, shitsurei-shimasu.* じゃ、失礼します。 Well then, I'll go (excuse me).
B: *Ā, otsukare-sama* ああ、お疲れさま Ah, thanks for the good
  deshita. でした。 work.

A: *Dōmo shitsurei-* どうも失礼しました。 I'm sorry. It was rude of
  shimashita.   me.
B: *Ie, ie. Dō* いえいえ、どういた No, no. Please don't
  itashimashite. しまして。 mention it.

| A: *Ja, mata.* | じゃ、また。 | Well, see you. |
| B: *Sayonara.* | さよなら。 | Goodbye. |

| A: *Ja, oyasumi.* | じゃ、おやすみ。 | Well, then good night. |
| B: *Ā, oyasumi nasai.* | ああ、おやすみなさい。 | Oh, good night. |

| A: *Itte kimasu.* | 行ってきます。 | See you later. |
| B: *Itte rasshai.* | 行ってらっしゃい。 | See you later. |

A: *Tadaima.*	ただいま。	I'm home.
B: *Okaeri nasai.*	おかえりなさい。	Welcome back.
Otsukare-sama deshita.	お疲れさまでした。	Thanks for your work.

EXERCISE 1
Say it in Japanese

First, say the Japanese equivalent of the English phrase, listen to the audio for the model answer, and then repeat the model. Work in loops. After finishing a few lines, go back to the ones above and see if you still remember them. If you do, proceed to the next few and repeat this procedure until you can confidently and naturally say all the phrases in Japanese.

1. Good evening.
2. Good morning. (to a friend)
3. Good morning. (to a boss)
4. Thanks. (to a friend)
5. Thank you. (to a stranger)
6. You are welcome!
7. Thank you very much (for what you did). (to a customer)
8. I'm sorry. (to a stranger)
9. I'm very sorry. (to a boss)
10. I'm very sorry (for what happened). (to a customer)
11. Please (help me). (Thank you in advance.)
12. I'll start eating.
13. Thank you for the delicious treat. (politely)
14. Good morning. See you later. (heading out)
15. Goodbye.
16. I'm back.
17. Welcome back.
18. Good night! (to a friend)
19. Good night. (politely)

20. Good work! (Thank you for the hard work)
21. Good work. Good night. (to a co-worker)
22. Excuse me (for what I am about to do—to a stranger).
23. Excuse me (for what I did—to a stranger).

EXERCISE 2
Role Play
Imagine the situation and role-play with a partner, if possible, in Japanese. Use appropriate gestures and facial expressions.

1. Greet your coworkers in the morning.
2. Greet a neighbor in the afternoon.
3. Offer a seat to a visitor.
4. Accept a gift from a visitor.
5. Leave your office to attend a meeting outside.
6. Say "Thank you" to a delivery person.
7. Hand a report to the assistant to make copies.
8. You are late. Apologize to a friend.
9. At a restaurant, get the waiter's attention.
10. Thank a coworker for making copies for you.
11. Visit the office of a supervisor.
12. Leave the office of a supervisor.
13. At a store, get a sales clerk's attention and ask for help.
14. Thank a supervisor for treating you to a meal at a restaurant.
15. You stepped on a stranger's foot. Apologize.
16. Ask a coworker to pass a document to you.
17. Say goodbye to a coworker who is about to go home.
18. Say goodbye to coworkers as you leave the office to go home.
19. Say good night to friends as you part after a night out.
20. Say goodbye to coworkers as you leave the office party.

REVIEW QUESTIONS

1. What is the difference between *ohayō* and *ohayō gozaimasu*?
2. What is the difference between *arigatō gozaimasu* and *arigatō gozaimashita*?
3. Which is more polite, *arigatō* or *dōmo*?
4. a) What is the difference between *gomen* and *gomen nasai*?
   b) Who typically uses the latter?
5. What are three ways to use *hai*?
6. a) When do you use *ā*?
   b) How about *jā*?
7. What is the difference between *sayonara* and *itte kimasu*?
8. What is the Japanese equivalent of "Thank you in advance" for the job you've just requested?
9. Many Japanese equivalents for "thank you" have been introduced so far.
   a) How many can you list?
   b) Can you describe a typical situation where each can be used?

LESSON 2
Meeting People

Cherish every encounter as a once-in-a lifetime opportunity.
一期一会　*Ichi-go ichi-e*

⊙ DIALOGUE 1 How do you do?

Michael Hill has been transferred by his company to the Japan office in Tokyo. He meets Ms. Sato at the office and she introduces herself.

Sato:　　How do you do? I'm Sato.
　　　　Hajimemashite. Satō desu.
　　　　はじめまして。 佐藤です。
Michael:　You're Ms. Sato? I'm Hill.
　　　　Satō-san desu ka. Hiru desu.
　　　　佐藤さんですか。 ヒルです。
　　　　Nice to meet you.
　　　　Dōzo yoroshiku onegai-shimasu.
　　　　どうぞよろしくお願いします。
Sato:　　You speak Japanese well!
　　　　Nihongo, o-jōzu desu nē.
　　　　日本語、 お上手ですねえ。
Michael:　No, no, (I) still (have) a long way to go.
　　　　Ie, ie, mada mada desu.
　　　　いえいえ、 まだまだです。

VOCABULARY

Hajimemashite.	はじめまして。	How do you do?
Satō	佐藤	Sato—a common Japanese family name
X desu	Xです	it is/I'm/you're/they are X, etc.
ka	か	question-marker
Hiru	ヒル	Hill—a family name
yoroshiku	よろしく	ritual expression when meeting someone or when needing a favor
Nihongo	日本語	Japanese
(o)jōzu	（お）上手	good at

*O is a prefix that is added to certain nouns to indicate politeness. This alternative will be shown in parentheses ( ) in front of the noun from here on.

nē　　ねえ　　Particle of empathy
mada　　まだ　　still, (not) yet

ADDITIONAL VOCABULARY

Eigo　　英語　　English
heta　　下手　　bad at
meishi　　名刺　　business card

Common Japanese Surnames

1. Satō	8. Nakamura	15. Saitō
2. Suzuki	9. Kobayashi	16. Matsumoto
3. Takahashi	10. Katō	17. Inoue
4. Tanaka	11. Yoshida	18. Kimura
5. Watanabe	12. Yamada	19. Hayashi
6. Itō	13. Sasaki	20. Shimizu
7. Yamamoto	14. Yamaguchi	

GRAMMAR NOTE **Japanese Sentence Types and Predicates**

There are three types of sentences: noun, verb, and adjective sentences. Nouns, verbs, and adjectives occurring at the end of a sentence are collectively called predicates and they are the core element of the sentence. Other elements such as subject, object, time expression, etc., are all optional. When they do occur, they occur before the predicate and you can order these rather freely. However, the following is the most neutral and common order. To give extra emphasis to any item, place it in the front of the sentence.

Time—Subject—Object—Quantity/Degree—Predicate

A predicate can comprise a complete sentence by itself. Unlike English, where a subject is required, the subject and other elements are usually not mentioned in Japanese if they are understood from the context. So, in the dialogue above, Ms. Sato simply says *Sato desu* "Sato am" in order to introduce herself. She does not mention "I", which is obvious from the context. Noun predicates are explained below and verb and adjective predicates will be introduced in Lessons 2 and 3, respectively.

GRAMMAR NOTE Noun Predicate—X *desu*. "(It) is X."

A noun sentence ends with a noun plus *desu* (Affirmative) or *ja nai desu* (Negative). X *desu* means "is X" and X *ja nai desu* means "is not X".

Satō desu.	I'm Sato.
Eigo ja nai desu.	It's not English.

Japanese uses a two-way tense system: Past or Non-past. Non-past covers both present and future. These noun predicates X *desu* and X *ja nai desu* are Non-Past, and they are in the Formal form as opposed to the Casual form, which will be introduced later. The Formal (or courteous) form is typically used when speaking to superiors, people you are meeting for the first time, or strangers. It is a safer form that should be first used by learners.

GRAMMAR NOTE Questions with *Ka* and *Ne(e)*

Sentence particles such as *ka* and *ne(e)* occur after a predicate. *Ka* is a question marker. *Ne*, when used with a rising intonation, checks if your assumption is in fact correct. *Ne(e)* with a falling intonation indicates that you assume the addressee shares your feelings. It is culturally preferred, probably more so in Japan than in other cultures, to feel that everyone involved is in harmony, and therefore you will frequently hear *nē* either at the end of a sentence or all by itself. Compare the following.

Jōzu desu ka.	Is he good at it?
Jōzu nē.	He is good at it, isn't he?
Jōzu desu ne.	He is good at it, right?
Jōzu ja nai desu ne.	He is not good at it, right?

A question in the negative form is also used 1) to show some uncertainty, and 2) to politely correct someone.

1)	*Eigo desu ka.*	Is it English?
	-Nihongo ja nai desu ka.	Isn't it Japanese?
2)	*Heta desu ne.*	I'm bad at it, right?
	-Iya, jōzu ja nai desu ka.	No. You are good, aren't you?

CULTURAL NOTE **Introductions**

It is important to know the ritual expressions and use them when meeting people for the first time in Japan. *Hajimemashite*, literally meaning "for the first time", and *Dōzo yoroshiku onegai-shimasu*, "please treat me favorably", are the most commonly used expressions when making introductions. After a person tells you his/her name, confirm it by asking *X-san desu ka* "Are you Mr./Ms. X?" Repetition may seem unnecessary, but it's customary to do so during introductions.

In business situations, you'll need to exchange business cards or *meishi*, so make sure you have an ample supply with information in Japanese on the back (or get a native Japanese speaker to provide a translation on the back). As you present your card (Japanese side up, with both hands with palms up), bow and turn it so that the other person can read it. As you receive the other person's card, take a moment to read/acknowledge it. During the meeting, carefully place their business cards in front of you to refer to. Don't write on them or leave them behind. If you have any questions—such as how to read the Kanji on the card, inquiring about the person's first name (usually the family name precedes the first name), the address, division's name and its function—it's best to ask for clarification at the beginning.

Self-introductions, where a person gets up in front of a group and explains who he/she is, are very common in Japan. These follow a formula, which starts with *hajimemashite*, followed by your name (even if it has already been mentioned) and other information like your hometown, the college you have attended, and ends with *dōzo yoroshiku onegai shimasu*.

Shaking hands and other physical contact are not customary in Japan, although they are becoming more common these days. Remember to bow as you introduce yourself, and nod when others bow. When in doubt, bow!

PATTERN PRACTICE 1

Pattern Practices are to train fast oral response, so the correct phrase will instinctively come to mind when having a conversation with a Japanese speaker. Using audio is essential. Do **NOT** read the script as you do drills. Following the first two model exchanges, respond to each cue. Make sure you do all four steps:
1. Listen to the cue.
2. Insert your response.
3. Listen to the model response.
4. Repeat the model.

Cue: *Hiru desu.*
                 I'm Hill.
Response: *Hiru-san desu ka. Hajimemashite.*
                 Mr. Hill? How do you do?

Cue: *Honda desu.*
              I'm Honda.
Response: *Honda-san desu ka. Hajimemashite.*
              Ms. Honda? How do you do?

*Repeat this drill adding your surname plus *desu*. *Dōzo yoroshiku onegai-shimasu.* Then repeat the drill with these Japanese surnames:

1. *Tanaka desu.*
2. *Yamada desu.*
3. *Kimura desu.*
4. *Itō desu.*
5. *Suzuki desu.*
6. *Yamamoto desu.*
7. *Nakamura desu.*
8. *Watanabe desu.*
9. *Sasaki desu.*
10. *Kobayashi desu.*

EXERCISE 1
Say it in Japanese
You are meeting someone for the first time. Say the following in Japanese.

1. I'm (your full name). Nice to meet you.
2. Are you Ms. Sato? How do you do? Here is my card. Nice to meet you.
3. Are you Mr. Ito? How do you do? I'm (your full name). Nice to meet you.
4. You are good at English, aren't you?
5. My Japanese is bad. I'm sorry.

EXERCISE 2
Role Play
1. Meet Ms. Honda, a business associate, for the first time.
2. Exchange your business cards. Confirm her name.
3. You've been complimented on your Japanese speaking ability. Respond humbly.
4. You hear a co-worker speaking English. Compliment his English.
5. Ask Ms. Sato if Mr. Suzuki, a co-worker, is good at English and if Ms. Sasaki, a boss, is good at English.

🔘 DIALOGUE 2 Are you American?

Mei Wong, a transfer student from Seattle, meets Tanaka Yūki[*] , a fellow student at Waseda University. Yuki and Mei greet each other first, and then he asks Mei where she's from.

Yuki: Are you an American?
         Amerika-jin desu ka.
         アメリカ人ですか。

Mei: Me? Yes, I am.
         Watashi desu ka. Hai, sō desu.
         私ですか？はい、そうです。

Yuki: Are you a freshman?
         Ichi-nen-sei desu ka.
         一年生ですか。

Mei: No, I'm not. I'm a junior.
         Ie, ichi-nen-sei ja nai desu. San-nen-sei desu.
         いえ、一年生じゃないです。三年生です。
         How about you?
         Tanaka-san wa?
         田中さんは？

Yuki: I'm also a junior.
         Boku mo san-nen-sei desu.
         僕も三年生です。

Mei: I see.
         Ā, sō desu ka.
         ああ、そうですか。

VOCABULARY

Amerika-jin	アメリカ人	American
watashi	私	I, me
sō	そう	so (as in, "Is that so?")
ichi-nen-sei	一年生	first-year student; freshman
san-nen-sei	三年生	third-year student; junior
X ja nai desu	Xじゃないです	is not X
Tanaka-san	田中さん	Mr/s. Tanaka
X wa?	Xは？	How about X?
boku	ぼく	I; me (male speaker)
mo	も	too; either

---

[*] See Grammar Note: Addressing a Person (page 28)

sō	そう	so
sō desu ka	そうですか	Is that so?; I see
ni-nen-sei	二年生	second-year student; sophomore
yo-nen-sei	四年生	fourth-year student; senior
nan-nen-sei	何年生	what year student
gakusei	学生	student

ADDITIONAL VOCABULARY

COUNTRIES	NATIONALITIES (-JIN)	LANGUAGES (-GO)
Foreign country *Gaikoku*	Foreigner *Gaikoku-jin/Gaijin*	Foreign language *Gaikoku-go*
Australia *Ōsutoraria*	Australian *Ōsutoraria-jin*	English *Eigo*
Cambodia *Kanbojia*	Cambodia *Kanbojia-jin*	Cambodian *Kanbojia-go*
Canada *Kanada*	Canadian *Kanada-jin*	English *Eigo*
China *Chūgoku*	Chinese *Chūgoku-jin*	Mandarin Chinese *Chūgoku-go*
France *Furansu*	French *Furansu-jin*	French *Furansu-go*
Germany *Doitsu*	German *Doitsu-jin*	German *Doitsu-go*
Great Britain *Igirisu*	British *Igirisu-jin*	English *Eigo*
India *Indo*	Indian *Indo-jin*	Hindi *Hindu-go*
Indonesia *Indoneshia*	Indonesian *Indoneshia-jin*	Indonesian *Indoneshia-go*
Ireland *Airurando*	Irish *Airurando-jin*	English *Eigo*
Italy *Itaria*	Italian *Itaria-jin*	Italian *Itaria-go*
Japan *Nihon*	Japanese *Nihon-jin*	Japanese *Nihon-go*
Korea *Kankoku*	Korean *Kankoku-jin*	Korean *Kankoku-go*
Malaysia *Marēshia*	Malaysian *Marēshia-jin*	Malay *Marē-go*
Myanmar *Myanmā*	Burmese *Biruma-jin*	Burmese *Biruma-go*
New Zealand *Nyūjīrando*	New Zealander *Nyūjīrando-jin*	English *Eigo*
Philippines *Firipin*	Filipino *Firipin-jin*	Tagalog *Tagarogu-go*
Russia *Roshia*	Russian *Roshia-jin*	Russian *Roshia-go*
Scotland *Sukottorando*	Scottish *Sukottorando-jin*	English *Eigo*
Singapore *Shingapōru*	Singaporean *Shingapōru-jin*	English *Eigo*
Spain *Supein*	Spanish *Supein-jin*	Spanish *Supein-go*
Taiwan *Taiwan*	Taiwanese *Taiwan-jin*	Mandarin Chinese *Chūgoku-go*
Thailand *Tai*	Thai *Tai-jin*	Thai *Tai-go*
USA *Amerika*	American *Amerika-jin*	English *Eigo*
Vietnam *Betonamu*	Vietnamese *Betonamu-jin*	Vietnamese *Betonamu-go*
What country *Doko no kuni*	What nationality *Nani-jin*	What language *Nani-go*

GRAMMAR NOTE Addressing a Person

In Japanese name order, one's surname is followed by his/her given name. So, if a person introduces himself as Kimura Yūki, Kimura is his surname, although many people switch the order when speaking English.

Refer to yourself with the most common *watashi* "I". *Boku* is only used by male speakers, and is less formal than *watashi*.

In Japanese, use the person's name to refer to or address the person you are talking to, as seen in the dialogue (*Tanaka-san wa?* "How about you, Mr. Tanaka?"). The Japanese pronoun *anata* "you" is limited to anonymous addressees, and is inappropriate if you know the person's name or title.

To decide how to address a person, you need to consider your relationship with the person and the circumstances. Surname + *san* is most common, but *sensei* "teacher" and other titles are required to address and refer to people in such positions. Using -*san* instead of the title can be rude, as is using the surname alone. The given name, with or without -*san*, is more informal and is used among friends or to refer to those in subordinate positions.

Be conservative and start with "surname -*san*" or a title such as *sensei*. If a person expresses a preference for how he/she wishes to be called, abide by that.

Another thing to note is to not overuse personal references, which is one of the most common errors made by foreigners who are used to using these in sentences. Recall that the subject is not mentioned in Japanese when clearly understood from the context, thus you would say *Amerika-jin desu* or literally, "American person am" instead of *Watashi wa Amerika-jin desu* "I am an American" if it's obvious that you are talking about yourself. Remember that Japanese has its own way of saying things and directly translating words and structures from a foreign language rarely works.

GRAMMAR NOTE Affirmation and Negation

Hai means "what you said is right" and *i'ie* means "what you said is incorrect" regardless of whether the sentence is affirmative or negative. *Ee* and *iya* are less formal versions of *hai* and *i'ie*. Note how they work in 2) below, where the question is in the negative form.

1) *Gakusei desu ka.*   Are you a student?
   -*Hai, sō desu.*   Yes, I am.
   -*I'ie, gakusei ja nai desu.*   No, I'm not.
2) *Gakusei ja nai desu ne?*   You are not a student, right?
   -*Hai, gakusei ja nai desu.*   That's right. I'm not a student.
   -*I'ie, gakusei desu.*   No, I am.

GRAMMAR NOTE Echo Questions

While it's common for things that are clear from the context to be left unsaid in Japanese conversations, sometimes the context may not be understood by everyone

involved. In such cases, people use echo questions (echoing back all or part of what has just been said) for clarification. In Dialogue 2, Mei uses the echo question "Do you mean me?" to check if Yuki is referring to her.

While echo questions are not unique to Japanese, they occur a lot more frequently in Japanese conversations. This is because echo questions are not only used for clarification, but also to slow down the pace of conversation or soften the tone. When an echo question is used for this purpose, an answer is not necessarily expected.

GRAMMAR NOTE The Phrase Particle *Wa*

As mentioned in Japanese Sentence Types and Predicates on page 22, the subject and other elements of the sentence, all of which are optional, come before the predicate. So, all of the following sentences can be used to mean "I'm bad at English". The difference is what is already understood from the context and therefore left unsaid.

Heta desu.	(I'm) bad at (it).
Eigo, heta desu.	(I'm) bad at English.
Watashi, heta desu.	I'm bad at (it).
Watashi, Eigo, heta desu.	I'm bad at English.

Particle *wa* follows nouns and implies a contrast between that noun and others in the same category. Thus, it may carry the meaning of "at least". *Wa* can be attached to the subject noun or other elements (the object noun, time expressions, etc.)

Watashi wa heta desu.	(As for me) I'm bad at (it.)
	(Someone else may be good.)
Eigo wa heta desu.	(I'm) bad (at least in) English.
	(I may be good at other things.)

When particle *wa* attaches to a noun with a question intonation, it means "how about X?" So, *Tanaka-san wa?* means "how about Mr. Tanaka?" in the dialogue. Refrain from using "yes" or "no" to answer, since it's not a yes-no question.

A sentence such as *Tanaka-san wa Nihon-jin desu* is usually translated as "Tanaka is Japanese". However, unlike the English translation, where X equals Y (Y is the identity of X—in this case that *Tanaka-san* is Japanese), the interpretation of the Japanese sentence is more open and flexible. Consider *Honda-san wa Amerika desu*. This sentence does not mean "Ms. Honda is the U.S.", but rather that what is under discussion for Ms. Honda is the U.S. So, there are numerous possible interpretations depending on the context. For example, she is in America; she is in charge of the business operations with the U.S.; her trip is to the U.S.; her favorite country is the U.S., etc. So, be aware of the context and be imaginative. Now, what can *Sato-san wa Eigo desu* possibly mean?

GRAMMAR NOTE **The Phrase Particle** *Mo*

The particle *mo* indicates similarities and performs the opposite function of that performed by the particle *wa*. The particle *mo* means "too" or "also" with an affirmative predicate (nouns, verbs and adjectives) and "either" when used with a negative predicate. It can be attached to a subject, or other elements like the object, time expressions or locations that will be introduced in Lesson 3.

Satō-san mo heta desu.	Ms. Sato is bad at (it), too. (Someone else is bad.)
Eigo mo jōzu ja nai desu.	(I'm) not good at English, either. (There are other things I'm bad at.)

CULTURAL NOTE **Foreign Words in Japanese**

Japanese has borrowed words and phrases from other languages. The majority of Japanese loanwords these days come from English. When words are borrowed, they go through some changes. First, their pronunciations change to fit the Japanese sound system, i.e., Mr. Hill becomes *Hiru-san*. Make sure you learn how your name is pronounced in Japanese. Second, these words usually become nouns in Japanese, regardless of what they were in their original language. Third, their meaning in Japanese may be different. Fourth, they are written in *Katakana* with a few exceptions using the English alphabet, i.e., "Wi-Fi" in Japanese is still "Wi-Fi".

If the original words or phrases are long, they get abbreviated and become very different words from the original (*sumaho* for "smartphone"). It's common to abbreviate two-word phrases by taking the first two syllables from each and combine them to make four syllable words (*pasokon* for "personal computer"—*n* is a syllable on its own).

CULTURAL NOTE *Aizuchi*: **How to be a Good Listener**

When you participate in a Japanese conversation you are expected to give frequent feedback and show that you are engaged and paying attention. Feedback includes nodding, making appropriate facial expressions, and using short expressions such as *Hai, Ā, sō desu ka*, and others. All these are called *Aizuchi*.

You will hear Japanese speakers using *hai* and see them nodding equally frequently. Nodding means "I'm listening", but it doesn't necessarily mean "I agree." So, don't just stare and listen with a poker face. Nod, smile, and say, "*Ā, sō desu ka.*"

PATTERN PRACTICE 2

Cue:	*Ichi-nen-sei desu ne.*
	You are a freshman, right?
Response:	*Hai, sō desu. Ichi-nen-sei desu.*
	Yes, that's right. I'm a freshman.

Cue: *Amerika-jin desu ne.*
             You are an American, right?
Response: *Hai, sō desu. Amerika-jin desu.*
             Yes, that's right. I'm an American.

Repeat the drills using the following information:
1. *Gakusei desu ne.*
2. *Chūgoku-jin desu ne.*
3. *Furansu-go desu ne.*
4. *Yo-nen-sei desu ne.*
5. *Kankoku desu ne.*

PATTERN PRACTICE 3

Cue: *Amerika-jin desu ka.*
             Is he an American?
Response: *Iya, Amerika-jin ja nai desu. Nihon-jin desu.*
             No, He is not an American. He is Japanese.
Cue: *Furansu desu ka.*
             Is it France?
Response: *Iya, Furansu ja nai desu. Nihon desu.*
             No, it's not France. It's Japan.

Repeat the drill using the following information.
1. *Gaikoku-jin desu ka.*
2. *Igirisu desu ka.*
3. *Supein-go desu ka.*
4. *Betonamu-jin desu ka.*
5 *Eigo desu ka.*

EXERCISE 3
Say it in Japanese
Yuki has asked you if that person is an American. Answer as follows:

1. Yes, she is. How about Ms. Wang?
2. No, she is not. She is a Chinese.
3. Isn't she a Korean?
4. Yes, she is an American. She is a freshman.
5. Do you mean Ms. Wang? She is an American (while others may not be).

EXERCISE 4
Role Play

1. At a party for new students, approach a person called Ms. Sato and introduce yourself.
2. Find out her nationality.
3. Find out if she is a student.
4. Mention that you are a junior and then find out if she is, too.
5. Comment on Ms. Sato's excellent English skills, and then ask if she is good at French, too.

DIALOGUE 3 Introducing yourself

Michael attends a business conference. He checks in at the registration desk.

Staff: Excuse me. Your name (please)?
            Sumimasen. Onamae wa?
            すみません。お名前は？

Michael: I'm Michael Hill.
            Maikeru Hiru desu.
            マイケル・ヒルです。

Staff: I'm sorry. (I didn't catch it.)
            Hai?
            はい？

Michael: I'm Michael Hill from Google.
            Anō…Gūguru no Maikeru Hiru desu.
            あのう、グーグルのマイケル・ヒルです。

The staff hands out something to Michael.

Michael: Umm…what is this?
            Anō…kore nan desu ka.
            あのう、これ何ですか。

Staff: Do you mean that (what you are holding)?
            Sore desu ka.
            それですか。
            It's today's schedule (program).
            Kyō no sukejūru desu.
            今日のスケジュールです。

At the reception of the international club, Mei has been asked to go to the stage and introduce herself.

Staff: Please introduce yourself.
         Jiko-shōkai, onegai-shimasu.
         自己紹介、お願いします。
Mei: Hello. I'm Mei Wang.
         Hajimemashite. Mei Wan desu.
         はじめまして。メイ・ワンです。
         I'm an exchange student at Waseda University.
         Waseda-Daigaku no ryūgakusei desu.
         早稲田大学の留学生です。
         I'm from Seattle, USA.
         Shusshin wa Amerika no Shiatoru desu.
         出身はアメリカのシアトルです。
         Thank you (nice meeting you).
         Dōzo yoroshiku onegai-shimasu.
         どうぞよろしくお願いします。

VOCABULARY

(o)namae	お名前	name
Maikeru Hiru	マイケル・ヒル	Michael Hill
Hai?	はい？	Excuse me?; I missed what you've just said
Anō	あのう	Umm (hesitation noise)
Gūguru	グーグル	Google
kore	これ	this
nan	何	what
sore	それ	that (an object or place near you)
kyō	今日	today
no	の	of (See Note "Connecting Two Nouns with *no*" on page 34)
sukejūru	スケジュール	schedule; program of events
jiko shōkai	自己紹介	self-introduction
Mei Wan	メイ・ワン	Mei Wang
Waseda	早稲田	Waseda (University)
daigaku	大学	university
ryūgakusei	留学生	foreign student
shusshin	出身	hometown; where you are from
Shiatoru	シアトル	Seattle

ADDITIONAL VOCABULARY

Etto	えっと	Let me see…(hesitation noise)
kaisha	会社	company
(o)shigoto	仕事	work
are	あれ	that (object or place that is further away)
dore	どれ	which one
ashita	明日	tomorrow
kinō	昨日	yesterday
doko	どこ	where

GRAMMAR NOTE **Connecting Two Nouns with** *no*

Particle *no* connects two nouns to make a noun phrase. X *no* Y is similar to saying X's Y, e.g., *tomodachi no kaisha*, "my friend's company". Multiple nouns can be connected, but the last noun is always the main noun. Consider the following:

tomodachi no kaisha	my friend's company
kaisha no tomodachi	a friend from work
Amerika no tomodachi no kaisha	my American friend's company
Amerika no kaisha no tomodachi	a friend from an American company

The relationship between the main noun and the modifying noun(s) varies greatly depending on their meaning. The following are some examples.

Location	*Nihon no daigaku*	colleges in Japan
Affiliation	*Gūguru no Hiru*	Mr. Hill from Google
Possession	*watashi no kaisha*	my company
Time	*kyō no sukejūru*	today's schedule
Subgroup	*Amerika no Shiatoru*	Seattle, US
	daigaku no ichi-nen-sei	college freshman
Status	*Ichi-nen-sei no Wan-san*	Ms. Wang, a freshman

When the main noun in these phrases is already known from the context, it can be dropped. For example, if you are asking if this is Ms. Sato's cellphone or *kētai denwa*, you don't have to say "cellphone". Just show it to her and say:

Kore, Satō-san no desu ka.	Is this yours?
-Hai, watashi no desu.	-Yes, it's mine.
-I'ie, watashi no ja nai desu.	-No, it's not mine.

GRAMMAR NOTE Referring to Things in Japanese

When referring to things in English, a two-way distinction between this (close to the speaker) and that (away from the speaker) is made. In Japanese, a three-way distinction is made:

kore this thing (close to me) or this thing I just mentioned

sore that thing (close to you) or that thing which was just mentioned

are   that thing (away from both of us) or that thing we both know about

dore which one

There are more sets based on the same distinction. In Dialogue 4 on page 38, the second set *kono*, *sono*, *ano*, and *dono* is introduced. The difference between the two sets is that the first is a set of nouns and the second is a set of modifiers that require a following noun and cannot be used alone. For example, you can say *kore* on its own but not *kono*. *Kono* must be followed by a noun like *kaisha* "this company". Note that when translated into English, both *kore* and *kono* are translated as "this".

kore	this
kono kaisha	this company
kono Nihon no kaisha	this Japanese company

Other sets include the following and will appear in later lessons. *Sō* in *sō desu* comes from this last group.

koko, soko, asoko, doko	"here, there, over there, where"
kochira, sochira, achira, dochira	"this direction" etc.
konna X, sonna X, anna X, donna X	"this kind of X" etc.
kō, sō, ā, dō	"this manner" etc.

GRAMMAR NOTE Hesitation Noises

In general, Japanese conversations tend to favor less direct and less confrontational exchanges. For this reason, hesitation noises are very common. Without them, a conversation may sound too mechanical and abrupt. "Beating around the bush" may not be such a bad thing when speaking Japanese. One way to do it is to use hesitation noises. A lot of them!

Anō and *etto* are two of the most common hesitation noises in Japanese. *Anō* is the almighty hesitation noise while *etto* indicates that you are searching for the right answer. So, when asked what your name is, for example, *anō* is fine, but not *etto*. *Anō* is also used to get attention from a person, but not *etto*.

Besides hesitation noises, you will also hear Japanese speakers elongating the last vowel of each word, or inserting *desu ne* between chunks of words to slow down speech.

Imaa anoo Honda-san waa Amerika desu.

Honda is in the U.S. now.

Ano hito wa desu ne, daigaku no desu ne, tomodachi desu.

She is a friend from college.

PATTERN PRACTICE 4

Cue: *Daigaku wa Nihon desu ka.*
              Is your university in Japan?
Response: *Hai, Nihon no daigaku desu.*
              Yes, it's a Japanese university.
Cue: *Kaisha wa Amerika desu ka.*
              Is your company in America?
Response: *Hai, Amerika no kaisha desu.*
              Yes, it's an American company.

Repeat the drill using the following information.
1. *Shigoto wa Betonamu desu ka.*
2. *Meishi wa Eigo desu ka.*
3. *Hiru-san wa Gūguru desu ka.*
4. *Wan-san wa Waseda desu ka.*
5. *Jiko-shōkai wa Nihon-go desu ka.*

PATTERN PRACTICE 5

Cue: *Kore, kyō no sukejūru desu ka.*
              Is this today's schedule?
Response: *Sore desu ka. Hai, kyō no desu.*
              Do you mean that? Yes, it is today's.
Cue: *Kore, Chūgoku no kaisha desu ka.*
              Is this a Chinese company?
Response: *Sore desu ka. Hai, Chūgoku no desu.*
              Do you mean that? Yes, it's a Chinese one.

Repeat the drill with the following information:
1. *Kore, Satō-san no meishi desu ka.*
2. *Kore, ashita no shigoto desu ka.*
3. *Kore, gaikoku-jin no Nihon-go desu ka.*
4. *Kore, Igirisu no Eigo desu ka.*
5. *Kore, Kankoku-jin no namae desu ka.*

EXERCISE 5
Say it in Japanese
1. Ask a new member of the international club the following questions. Use hesitation noises.
   1) What is your name?
   2) Where are you from?
   3) What is your job?
   4) Where is your company?
   5) Are you a student? What grade are you?

2. You've been asked to identify something/someone. Answer as follows.
   6) Do you mean this? It's Mr. Ito's business card.
   7) Do you mean that? It's an American company.
   8) Which one do you mean? Do you mean that near you? It's today's schedule.
   9) This is the name of Ms. Suzuki's company.
   10) Do you mean me? I'm an exchange student at Waseda University. I'm from China.

EXERCISE 6
Role Play
1. At a welcome party of your office, you've been asked to introduce yourself.
2. At an event, ask a person at your table for his/her name, as well as where he/she is from, which university he/she went to, and what his/her job is. Remember to use hesitation noises and *hai* if you didn't get what he/she said.
3. Ms. Sato is carrying a big bag. Ask what is in it.
4. You've been asked if this is your phone. It's not. You think it might be Ms. Sato's.

◉ DIALOGUE 4 Who is That Person?

At the reception for the new international students, Mei spotted someone.

Mei: Who is that person?
      Ano hito, dare desu ka.
      あの人、だれですか。

Yuki: Do you mean that woman?
       Ano onna no hito desu ka.
       あの女の人ですか？
       Isn't she Professor Kimura?
       Kimura-sensei ja nai desu ka.
       木村先生じゃないですか。

Mei went to find out and then came back.

Yuki: Was she the professor (Kimura)?
       Sensei deshita ka.
       先生でしたか。

Mei: No, she wasn't the professor.
      Ie, sensei ja nakatta desu.
      いえ、先生じゃなかったです。

Michael is talking to someone he has met at the business conference.

Michael: What do you do (for a living)?
          Oshigoto wa?
          お仕事は？

Woman: I was with NTT before, but now I'm with Apple.
        Mae wa NTT deshita kedo, ima wa Appuru desu.
        前はNTTでしたけど、今はアップルです。

VOCABULARY

ano X	あのX	that X over there
hito	人	person
dare	だれ	who
onna	女	female; woman
Kimura	木村	Kimura
sensei	先生	teacher; professor; doctor
X deshita	Xでした	was X
X ja nakatta desu	X じゃなかったです	was not X
mae	前	before; front
NTT	NTT	a telecommunication company

kedo	けど	but
ima	今	now
Appuru	アップル	Apple

ADDITIONAL VOCABULARY

kono X	このX	this X
sono X	そのX	that X near you
dono X	どのX	which X
donata	どなた	who (polite)
otoko	男	man; male
senpai	先輩	senior member; upper classman
kōhai	後輩	junior member; lower classman
jōshi	上司	boss; person in a higher position
dōryō	同僚	co-worker; colleague
(o)tomodachi	友だち	friend
(o)shiriai	知り合い	acquaintance
kodomo	子供	child
ko	子	child

GRAMMAR NOTE Past Form of Noun Predicates

As seen above, *X desu* and *X ja nai desu* are the Non-past form of the noun predicate. Their Past versions are *X deshita* and *X ja nakatta desu*. They are all Formal forms and are shown below. Make sure you do not use *deshita* in Past Negative form.

Noun Predicates

	AFFIRMATIVE	NEGATIVE
Non-past	*X desu.* It's X.	*X ja nai desu.* It's not X.
Past	*X deshita.* It was X.	*X ja nakatta desu.* It wasn't X.

The Past forms are also used to express recollection of information, even when this information is about an event scheduled in the future.

> *Ano shigoto wa ashita deshita ne.*   That work was (is due) tomorrow, right?
> *-Iya, kyō ja nakatta desu ka.*   No, wasn't it today?

GRAMMAR NOTE The Conjunction *Kedo* "But"

Kedo "but" connects two sentences to make one. The two sentences typically contain contrasting ideas. In some instances, the first sentence simply serves as an introduction and prepares the listener for the second sentence.

Kore wa Nihon-go desu kedo, are wa Eigo desu.
This is in Japanese, but that is in English.
Sumimasen kedo, kore, onegai-shimasu.
I'm sorry but please give this to me.
Ano hito desu kedo, nani-jin desu ka.
It's about that person; what is his nationality?

In some cases, the second sentence is left unexpressed. Either the second sentence is clear from the context or the speaker hesitates to mention it for some reason.

Mae wa NTT deshita kedo…   I worked for NTT before, but …

There are several variations of *kedo* such as *keredo*, *kedomo*, and *keredomo*, which are more formal than *kedo*. An alternative is *ga*, which is more formal and is common in writing and formal speech.

CULTURAL NOTE *Senpai-Kōhai* "Senior–Junior" Relationship

The *senpai-kōhai* relationship is a strong mentoring relationship in many areas in the Japanese society including in school, in team sports, and at work. Usually the relationship is determined by who became a member of the group first rather than by the individual's merits and abilities. If the person you're conversing with does not have any group affiliation, use age to determine your relative ranking and address the person appropriately.

Once someone is your *senpai*, you are expected to treat the person as such for a lifetime. A *senpai* is also expected to take care of *kōhai* members for a lifetime. This relationship can be one of the most reliable connections in one's social network long after one leaves the group, company or school.

PATTERN PRACTICE 6

Cue: *Satō-san wa gakusei desu ka.*
             Is Ms. Sato a student?
Response: *Mae wa gakusei deshita kedo, ima wa gakusei ja nai desu.*
             She was a student before, but she is not a student now.
Cue: *Satō-san wa Appuru desu ka.*
             Is Ms. Sato with Apple?
Response: *Mae wa Appuru deshita kedo, ima wa Appuru ja nai desu.*
             She was with Apple before, but she is not with Apple now.

Repeat the drill using the following information.
1. *Satō-san wa tomodachi desu ka.*
2. *Dōryō wa gaikoku-jin desu ka.*
3. *Jōshi wa otoko no hito desu ka.*
4. *Ano ryūgakusei wa jōzu desu ka.*
5. *Senpai wa Nihon-go no sensei desu ka.*

PATTERN PRACTICE 7

Cue:	*Satō-san wa Igirisu deshita ka.*	Was Sato in England?
Response:	*Ie, Igirisu ja nakatta desu.*	No, she wasn't.
Cue:	*Jōshi wa Nihon-jin deshita ka.*	Was your boss Japanese?
Response:	*Ie, Nihon-jin ja nakatta desu.*	No, she wasn't.

Repeat the drills using the following:
1. *Kinō wa shigoto deshita ka.*
2. *Kaisha wa NTT deshita ka.*
3. *Eigo wa jōzu deshita ka.*
4. *Are wa Kankoku no kaisha deshita ka.*
5. *Mae wa tomodachi deshita ka.*

EXERCISE 7
Say it in Japanese
You've been asked what something was. Answer in Japanese.
1. That was a Japanese company.
2. They were computers from American companies.
3. That was yesterday's schedule.
4. Wasn't that Mr. Honda's smartphone?
5. Wasn't it a job in a Chinese computer company?

EXERCISE 8
Role Play
1. Someone is knocking on your door. Ask who it is.
2. You've been told that someone was absent yesterday. Ask who it was.
3. You caught sight of Prof. Kimura at a party. Confirm with a co-worker if that person is not Prof. Kimura.
4. You are discussing someone's language ability. Mention that:
   1) it was good before, but it is bad now;
   2) it was bad before but good now;
   3) it was not good before. It is still not good;
   4) it was not bad before, but it is now.

REVIEW QUESTIONS
Answer the following questions. Review your answers in the Grammar Notes.
1. a) What does X *desu* mean?
   b) How about X *deshita*?
2. a) What is the Non-Past Negative form of the Noun predicate?
   b) How about the Past Negative?
3. a) Give two examples of Japanese hesitation noises.
   b) What is the difference between them?
   c) How are they used?
4. a) Which is the main noun in the noun phrase X *no* Y, X or Y?
   b) What is the relationship between the two nouns?
5. What four changes may happen when a word is borrowed into Japanese from another language?
6. What is the difference in meaning between the following?
   1) *Satō-san desu ka.*
   2) *Satō-san desu ne?*
7. What is the difference between *sore* and *sono*?
8. What is the difference in meaning between the following?
   1) *Satō-san, gakusei desu.*
   2) *Satō-san wa gakusei desu.*
   3) *Satō-san mo gakusei desu.*
9. a) What is an echo question?
   b) How do you use it?
10. How is *Hai?* used?

11. What possible questions have been asked to elicit the following answers?
    1) *Hai, Nihon-jin ja nai desu.*
    2) *I'ie, Nihon-jin desu.*
12. How do you make the polite versions of *namae* and *shigoto*?
13. What is the difference in meaning between the following:
    1) *Nihon-jin ja nakatta desu.*
    2) *Nihon-jin ja nakatta desu ka.*
14. What should beginner Japanese students be aware of regarding using personal references?

LESSON 3
Schedule and Daily Activities

Strike while the iron is hot. (Hurry when doing good.)
善は急げ　***Zen wa isoge***

DIALOGUE 1 Taking a Bus Tour

Mei and Yuki are checking the schedule of the bus tours that they reserved. They're planning to travel around Tokyo over the weekend.

Mei:　What day is it today?
　　　Kyō wa nan-yōbi desu ka.
　　　きょうは何曜日ですか。

Yuki:　Isn't it Tuesday?
　　　Ka-yōbi ja nai desu ka.
　　　火曜日じゃないですか。

Mei:　When are the reservations for?
　　　Yoyaku wa itsu desu ka.
　　　予約はいつですか。

Yuki:　They are (for) 9:30 on Saturday and Sunday.
　　　Do-yōbi to Nichi-yōbi no ku-ji-han desu yo.
　　　土曜日と日曜日の九時半ですよ。

On the day of the tour, Mei and Yuki have arrived at the pick-up point for the bus tours to Tokyo…

Mei:　What time is it now?
　　　Ima nan-ji desu ka.
　　　今何時ですか。

Yuki:　Let's see…it's 9:20.
　　　Etto…ku-ji ni-jup-pun desu.
　　　えっと、九時二十分です。

Mei:　It will soon be time, won't it?
　　　Mōsugu jikan desu ne.
　　　もうすぐ時間ですね。

VOCABULARY

nan-yōbi	何曜日	what day of the week
Ka-yōbi	火曜日	Tuesday
yoyaku	予約	reservation
itsu	いつ	when
Do-yōbi	土曜日	Saturday
X to Y	XとY	X and Y
Nichi-yōbi	日曜日	Sunday
ku-ji	九時	9 o'clock
han	半	half
yo	よ	I tell you; you know (sentence particle)
nan-ji	何時	what time
nan-pun	何分	how many minutes
jup-pun	十分	ten minutes
mōsugu	もうすぐ	soon
jikan	時間	time; hours

ADDITIONAL VOCABULARY

mainichi	毎日	every day
yasumi	休み	break; day off; holiday; absence
kaigi	会議	meeting; conference
apo	アポ	appointment
uchiawase	打ち合わせ	(preliminary/organizational) meeting
jugyō	授業	class
shiken	試験	exam
shukudai	宿題	homework
shimekiri	締め切り	deadline
X ya Y	XやY	X, Y, and others
X toka Y	XとかY	(casual) X, Y, and others
X ka Y	X かY	X or Y

GRAMMAR NOTE Days of the Week

Yōbi indicates days of the week. There are three variations for each day of the week. The variations for Monday, for example, are *Getsu*, *Getsu-yō*, and *Getsu-yōbi*. The longer, the more formal. Abbreviations like the following are also very common.

Getsu-sui-kin	Monday-Wednesday-Friday
Kā-moku	Tuesday-Thursday
Do-nichi	Saturday-Sunday

Note that the question word *nan-yōbi* "what day of the week" CANNOT be used to ask "what day of the month", which will be introduced later in Lesson 8 (page 160).

Days of the Week

Nichi-yōbi	日曜日	Sunday
Getsu-yōbi	月曜日	Monday
Ka-yōbi	火曜日	Tuesday
Sui-yōbi	水曜日	Wednesday
Moku-yōbi	木曜日	Thursday
Kin-yōbi	金曜日	Friday
Do-yōbi	土曜日	Saturday
Nan-yōbi	何曜日	what day of the week

GRAMMAR NOTE Japanese Numbers and Telling Time

Japanese numbers up to 100 are shown below. Note that numbers four, seven and nine (underlined) have alternating forms: *yon, yo* and *shi* for four, *nana* and *shichi* for seven and *kyū* and *ku* for nine. The form depends on what is counted, such as 4 o'clock or *yo-ji* and four minutes or *yon-pun*. Japanese numbers are usually followed by a classifier, which indicates what is counted or numbered. Use of "bare" numbers (counting the number of push-ups, etc.) is rather limited.

Numbers Through 100

1	*ichi*	11	*jū-ichi*	21	*ni-jū-ichi*	40	*yon-jū*
2	*ni*	12	*jū-ni*	22	*ni-jū-ni*	50	*go-jū*
3	*san*	13	*jū-san*	23	*ni-jū-san*	60	*roku-jū*
4	*shi/yo/yon*	14	*jū-shi/yon*	24	*ni-jū-shi/yon*	70	*nana-jū*
5	*go*	15	*jū-go*	25	*ni-jū-go*	80	*hachi-jū*
6	*roku*	16	*jū-roku*	26	*ni-jū-roku*	90	*kyū-jū*
7	*shichi/nana*	17	*jū-shichi/ nana*	27	*ni-jū-shichi/ nana*	100	*hyaku*
8	*hachi*	18	*jū-hachi*	28	*ni-jū-hachi*		
9	*kyū/ku*	19	*jū-kyū/ku*	29	*ni-jū-kyū/ku*		
10	*jū*	20	*ni-jū*	30	*san-jū*		

Recall the classifier *-nen-sei* for grade in school. Similarly, *-ji* is the classifier for hours and *-fun/-pun* for naming and counting minutes. Note that *-fun* becomes *-pun* after the numbers one, three, six, ten and the question word.

In telling time, the hour precedes minutes. So, 9:10 is *ku-ji jup-pun*. You can also attach *han* "half an hour", e.g., *ku-ji-han* for 9:30. Note which alternating forms are used for the numbers four, seven, and nine when *-ji* or *-fun/pun* is attached.

4:04   *yo-ji yon-pun*
7:07   *shichi-ji nana-fun*
9:09   *ku-ji kyū-fun*

To ask what time it is, *ima* "now" is commonly used in Japanese, as shown in the dialogue.

Clock Time

	Hours	Minutes		Hours	Minutes
1	*ichi-ji*	*ip-pun*	9	*ku-ji*	*kyū-fun*
2	*ni-ji*	*ni-fun*	10	*jū-ji*	*jup-pun*
3	*san-ji*	*san-pun*	11	*jū-ichi-ji*	
4	*yo-ji*	*yon-pun*	12	*jū-ni-ji*	
5	*go-ji*	*go-fun*	midnight	*rei-ji*	
6	*roku-ji*	*rop-pun*			
7	*shichi-ji*	*nana-fun*			
8	*hachi-ji*	*hachi-fun*			

GRAMMAR NOTE Connecting Multiple Nouns

X *to* Y means "X and Y". While "and" in English can connect various elements including adjectives, verbs, or sentences, the Japanese particle *to* only combines nouns or noun phrases.

X *ya* Y and its casual version X *toka* Y mean "X, Y, and others", e.g., *Getsu-yōbi toka Sui-yōbi* "Monday, Wednesday and others". These expressions allow you to list a few samples from a group instead of exhaustively listing all possibilities in the group, e.g., *Eigo ya Furansu-go ya Supein-go* "English, French, Spanish, etc". These expressions are also used to soften the statement. X *ka* Y means "X or Y".

There is no limit to the number of nouns connected by these particles, but it's rare for an adult speaker to list more than three or four. The particles must occur between all the nouns listed.

GRAMMAR NOTE Using *Yo* to Share New Information

Unlike the particle *ne(e)*, which indicates shared information, the particle *yo* indicates that the speaker thinks the information presented is new to the listener. So, it is often used to correct or assure someone. In the dialogue above, Yūki presents the reservation times as new information to Mei.

Since *yo* assumes the listener is not aware of the information presented, take extra care to note when and with whom you can safely use it.

CULTURAL NOTE The Japanese Sense of Time

Many foreigners find that the Japanese sense of time is very meticulous and resolute. Most Japanese always like to know exactly how things will proceed. As little as possible is left to chance in order to avoid any unexpected turn of events.

Travel itineraries and event schedules are much more detailed for this reason. It's also not a surprise that pocket planners are still very popular in Japan despite the abundance of digital devices.

When meeting someone, most Japanese arrive five minutes before the scheduled time. There is no such notion in Japan as "being fashionably late". If you arrive at a meeting just on time, you may find you are the last person to arrive. Yes, "on time" is late in Japan. Be sure to adjust your schedule accordingly, since being late in Japan for business-related meetings is a sure-fire way to lose your credibility. Once a deadline is set, failing to make it is out of the question. If you are likely to be late, inform all involved as soon as possible. Short notice is not welcome, but definitely better than last-minute surprises or no notice at all.

It is sometimes difficult to determine a finish time, due to the consensus-based decision making process in Japan. Be sure to factor this in and add more time (perhaps a month or a few weeks) to make sure the project is finished on schedule.

PATTERN PRACTICE 1

Cue: *Kyō wa Getsu-yōbi desu ne?*
              Today is Monday, right?
Response: *Iya, Ka-yōbi ja nai desu ka.*
              No, isn't it Tuesday?
Cue: *Kyō wa Moku-yōbi desu ne?*
              Today is Thursday, right?
Response: *Iya, Kin-yōbi ja nai desu ka.*
              No, isn't it Friday?

Repeat the drill using the following:
1. *Kyō wa Nichi-yōbi desu ne.*
2. *Kyō wa Do-yōbi desu ne.*
3. *Kyō wa Ka-yōbi desu ne.*
4. *Kyō wa Kin-yōbi desu ne.*
5. *Kyō wa Sui-yōbi desu ne.*

PATTERN PRACTICE 2

Cue: *Yoyaku wa, go-ji desu ne?*
              The reservation is at five, right?
Response: *Yoyaku desu ka. Iya roku-ji desu yo.*
              Reservation? No, it's at six.
Cue: *Kaigi wa yo-ji jup-pun desu ne?*
              The meeting is at 4:10, right?

Response: ***Kaigi desu ka. Iya go-ji jup-pun desu yo.***
            Meeting? No, it's at 5:10.

Repeat the drill using the following:
1. *Apo wa ichi-ji desu ne.*
2. *Jugyō wa jū-ichi-ji desu ne.*
3. *Kaigi wa, hachi-ji han desu ne.*
4. *Uchiawase wa, jū-ni-ji jū-go-fun desu ne.*
5. *Shiken wa ku-ji to ni-ji desu ne.*

EXERCISE 1
Say it in Japanese
You are talking about last week's meeting. Ask the following:
1. When was it?
2. What day of the week was it?
3. What time was it?
4. Where was it?
5. In what language was it conducted?

Tell a co-worker/fellow student about the schedule.
6. The organizational meeting is on Tuesday and Thursday.
7. The exam is either on Monday or Tuesday.
8. Wasn't Wednesday the deadline for the English homework?
9. Chinese, Korean, etc., classes are held every day.
10. The appointment was for 10:30 before, but now it is for 10:45.

EXERCISE 2
Role Play
1. You are at the registration office. Ask when the Japanese class is scheduled. Who is the instructor? Where is it held?
2. Warn co-workers that the deadline is approaching. Time is up. Announce it to your group.
3. You assume that you are off on Saturday. Confirm it with a boss.
4. Using a world time zone map or the world clock on your smartphone, tell a friend what time it is in different parts of the world.
5. Using an airline schedule (you can find one online), discuss the departure times, for different destinations.

DIALOGUE 2 Practicing Your Japanese

Ms. Sato is teaching Michael some useful business Japanese phrases.

Sato: Do you understand this?
            Kore, wakarimasu ka.
            これ、わかりますか。
Michael: I'm sorry. I don't understand very much.
            Sumimasen. Amari wakarimasen.
            すみません。あまりわかりません。
Sato: Then, why don't we practice a little bit?
            Jā, chotto renshū-shimasen ka.
            じゃあ、ちょっと練習しませんか。
Michael: Yes. Thank you (in advance).
            Hai, onegai-shimasu.
            はい、お願いします。
After some practice…
Sato: Did you get it?
            Wakarimashita ka.
            わかりましたか。
Michael: Yes, I got it (now).
            Hai, yoku wakarimashita.
            はい、よくわかりました。

VOCABULARY

wakarimasu	わかります	understand
amari	あまり	(not) very much
wakarimasen	わかりません	do not understand
chotto	ちょっと	little
renshū	練習	practice (noun)
renshū-shimasu	練習します	practice (verb)
renshū-shimasen	練習しません	do not practice
wakarimashita	わかりました	understood
yoku	よく	well; a lot; often

ADDITIONAL VOCABULARY

zenzen	ぜんぜん	(not) at all
shimasu	します	do
dekimasu	できます	can do; is completed

Useful Verbs

hanashimasu	話します	talk; speak
yomimasu	読みます	read
kakimasu	書きます	write
kikimasu	聞きます	listen; ask
mimasu	見ます	look; watch
tsukaimasu	使います	use
benkyō	勉強	study (noun)
benkyō-shimasu	勉強します	study (verb)
denwa-shimasu	電話します	call
mēru-shimasu	メールします	send emails or text messages
tsuīto-shimasu	ツイートします	tweet

IT and Social Media

konpyūtā	コンピューター	computer
pasokon	パソコン	PC; laptop
denwa	電話	telephone
kētai	ケータイ	cellphone
sumaho	スマホ	smartphone
apuri	アプリ	application
taburetto	タブレット	tablet
mēru	メール	email; text message
Rain	ライン	Line
Feisubukku	フェイスブック	Facebook
Tsuittā	ツイッター	Twitter
Yūchūbu	ユーチューブ	YouTube
Insuta(guramu)	インスタ(グラム)	Instagram
manga	まんが	comics
anime	アニメ	animation
shinbun	新聞	newspaper
zasshi	雑誌	magazine
hon	本	book
terebi	テレビ	TV
nyūsu	ニュース	news
Netto	ネット	Internet
gēmu	ゲーム	game
shashin	写真	photography
bideo	ビデオ	video
eiga	映画	movie
dōga	動画	video (on Internet)

GRAMMAR NOTE Verb Predicates

A Japanese verb ends in *-masu, -masen, -mashita* and *-masen deshita*. A Non-past verb refers to an act that is performed regularly or will be performed in the future. It does NOT refer to an act that is currently being performed. See below for how a statement like *Wakarimasu* "I understand" is changed.

Tense	Affirmative		Negative	
Non-past	*Wakarimasu.*	I understand.	*Wakarimasen.*	I don't understand.
Past	*Wakarimashita.*	I understood.	*Wakarimasen deshita.*	I didn't understand.

Negative questions are sometimes used to suggest or invite somone to do something.
Kore, mimasen ka.   Won't you watch this? or Why don't we watch this?
Renshū-shimasen ka.   Won't you practice? or Shall we practice?

When turning down an invitation, avoid saying no directly. It's best to instead leave things ambiguous by saying *chotto* and sound hesitant by speaking slowly and elongating vowels.
Kore tsukaimasen ka.   Would you like to use this?
Accepting: *Arigatō gozaimasu. Ja…*   Thank you. Then…
Turning down: *Iyā, chotto…*   Well, it's just …

GRAMMAR NOTE Compound Verbs

Noun + *shimasu* and Noun + *dekimasu* combinations are compound verbs. Many nouns that mean actions such as *benkyō* "study" appear in this pattern.
Benkyō-shimasu.   I'll study.
Renshū-dekimashita.   I was able to practice.

When verbs in English are borrowed into Japanese, *-shimasu* is attached to them and they become Japanese verbs. Make sure you pronounce it the Japanese way.
Mēru-shimasu yo.   I'll email (or text) you.
Getto-shimasu.   I'll get/obtain it.
Kyanseru-shimasu.   I'll cancel it.

GRAMMAR NOTE Expressing Frequency

Expressions such as *chotto* "little" indicate how much, how often, or in what manner something happens. They usually appear right before the verb. *Amari* "very much" and *zenzen* "at all" combine with a negative form of a predicate.
Amari wakarimasen.   I don't understand it very well.
Zenzen hanashimasen.   I do not speak it at all.

Yoku means "well", "a lot", or "frequently" depending on the context.

Yoku wakarimasu. I understand very well.

Yoku tsukaimasu. I use it often.

CULTURAL NOTE **Virtue of Ambiguity**

Japanese culture is marked by a preference for ambiguity over precision, particularly in less-than-favorable situations. It is often the result of an effort to avoid negativity and save face. For example, *chotto* "a little" is used to reject an invitation rather than bluntly saying "No, thank you."

Although the language may seem to be ambiguous, what is meant is usually unmistakably clear. It is a challenge at first for new learners of Japanese to figure out what is really meant, but you'll soon find that this linguistic ambiguity is a fact of life in Japan and an integral part of many customs. It's just the way the language works!

PATTERN PRACTICE 3

Cue: **Eigo wakarimasuka.**
Do you understand English?

Response: **Eigo desu ka. Ie, amari wakarimasen.**
English? No, I don't understand (it) very well.

Cue: **Gēmu, shimasu ka.**
Do you play games?

Response: **Gēmu desu ka. Ie, amari shimasen.**
Games? No, I don't play a lot.

Repeat the drill with the following:
1. **Manga, yomimasu ka.**
2. **Kētai, tsukaimasu ka.**
3. **Terebi, mimasu ka.**
4. **Chūgoku-go hanashimasu ka.**
5. **Pasokon, dekimasu ka.**

PATTERN PRACTICE 4

Cue: **Chūgoku-go, wakarimasu ka.**
Do you understand Chinese?

Response: **Mae wa yoku wakarimashita kedo, ima wa zenzen wakarimasen.**
I used to understand it well before, but now I don't understand it at all.

Cue: **Denwa, shimasu ka.**
Do you make phone calls?

Response: *Mae wa yoku shimashita kedo, ima wa zenzen shimasen.*
I called a lot before, but now I don't call at all.

Practice this drill with the following:
1. *Manga, mimasu ka.*
2. *Supein-go benkyō-shimasu ka.*
3. *Shinbun yomimasu ka.*
4. *Pasokon, tsukaimasu ka.*
5. *Shigoto, shimasu ka.*
* Repeat this drill by switching *mae* and *ima* (Past and Non-past):
Ima wa yoku wakarimasu kedo, mae wa zenzen wakarimasen deshita.
Now I understand it well, but I didn't understand at all before.

EXERCISE 3
Say it in Japanese
1. You've been asked if you use something. Answer in Japanese.
   1) Yes, I use it every day.
   2) No, I do not use it very much.
   3) Yes, I use it a little every day.
   4) I used it a lot before, but now I don't use it at all.
   5) I didn't use it very much before, but now I use it a lot.

2. Ask a co-worker about his current and past activities.
   6) Do you watch TV? Did you watch TV yesterday?
   7) Do you play online games? Did you play yesterday?
   8) Do you read the newspaper every day? Did you read the newspaper yesterday?
   9) Do you use a cellphone, smartphone, etc.?
   10) Do you study Japanese a lot? Did you study yesterday?

EXERCISE 4
Role Play
1. Ask a co-worker if she speaks foreign languages.
2. Someone took your cellphone by mistake. Politely tell her it's yours.
3. Describe how you get news, whether it's from watching television, newspaper, or online.
4. You've found an interesting/funny video on YouTube. Invite your co-workers to watch it.
5. Discuss what activities you do regularly and what you did yesterday.

🔘 DIALOGUE 3 It's Lunch Time

Ms. Sato and Michael want to have lunch and they need to check the restaurant's business hours.

Sato: Why don't we have (lit., eat) lunch?
            Hiru-gohan o tabemasen ka.
            昼ご飯を食べませんか。

Michael: From what time is lunch served?
            Ranchi wa nan-ji kara desu ka.
            ランチは何時からですか。

Sato: It's from 11 to two every day.
            Mainichi jū-ichi-ji kara ni-ji made desu.
            毎日１１時から２時までです。

Michael: What time do you go?
            Nan-ji ni ikimasu ka.
            何時に行きますか。

Sato: I go around 12, but come back by one.
            Jū-ni-ji goro ikimasu kedo, ichi-ji made ni kaerimasu.
            十二時ごろ行きますけど、一時までには帰ります。

VOCABULARY

gohan	ご飯	cooked rice; a meal
(o)hiru	お昼	noon; lunchtime; lunch
hiru-gohan	昼ご飯	lunch
ranchi	ランチ	lunch (typically at a restaurant)
kara	から	from
made	まで	until
ni	に	at
-goro	ごろ	about
ikimasu	行きます	go
made ni	までに	by
kaerimasu	帰ります	return; go home

ADDITIONAL VOCABULARY

asa	朝	morning
asa-gohan	朝ご飯	breakfast
ban	晩	evening; night
ban-gohan	晩ご飯	dinner

Daily Activities

kimasu	来ます	come
ikimasu	行きます	go
kaerimasu	帰ります	return; go home
tabemasu	食べます	eat
nomimasu	飲みます	drink
hatarakimasu	働きます	work
yasumimasu	休みます	rest; sleep; take time off
asobimasu	遊びます	play
nemasu	寝ます	sleep
okimasu	起きます	wake up; get up
sanpo-shimasu	散歩します	go for walk
ryōri-shimasu	料理します	cook
sentaku-shimasu	洗濯します	do laundry
sōji-shimasu	掃除します	clean
kaimono-shimasu	買い物します	do shopping

GRAMMAR NOTE Object of a Verb and Particle *o*

An object precedes the verb and is marked by particles *wa* (contrast), *mo* (addition), *o* (focus is on the object) or no particle at all, depending on the context.

Hiru-gohan tabemasu.	I'll eat lunch.
Hiru-gohan wa tabemasu.	I'll eat lunch at least (I didn't eat breakfast).
Hiru-gohan mo tabemasu.	I'll eat lunch, too.
Hiru-gohan o tabemasu.	It's lunch that I'll eat.

Particle *o* typically follows question words (what, whom, which, etc.) while *wa* or *mo* doesn't. This is because question words represent the focus of the sentence.

Nani o tabemasu ka.	What will you eat?
-Kore o tabemasu.	I'll eat this. (This is the one I'll eat.)
Pasokon o tsukaimasu ka.	Is it a laptop that you use?
-Iya, pasokon wa tsukaimasen.	No, I don't use a laptop.
Sumaho o tsukaimasu.	I use a smartphone.

Note that in the answer above *pasokon* takes particle *wa*, while *sumaho* takes particle *o*. This is because *sumaho* is the focus item being presented for the first time. On the other hand, *pasokon* has already been mentioned in the question and the particle *wa* here indicates that *pasokon* is in contrast to *sumaho*.

When the entire sentence presents new information, which has not yet been mentioned in the conversation, the object takes particle *o*, as well.

Nemasu ka.	Are you going to bed?
-Iya, terebi o mimasu.	No, I'll watch TV.
Kaigi desu yo.	It's a meeting.
-Ja, taburetto o tsukaimasen ka?	Then why don't we use the tablet?

GRAMMAR NOTE Time Expressions

Use a time expression with the particle *ni* "at" to indicate the time when something happens or has happened, except when statements include *kyō* "today", *ashita* "tomorrow", *kinō* "yesterday", *ima* "now" and *-goro* "about".

Nichi-yōbi ni kaerimasu.	I'll return on Sunday.
Shichi-ji goro kaerimasu.	I'll go home around seven.

GRAMMAR NOTE The Particles *ni* "At", *kara* "From", *made* "Until", and *made ni* "By"

The particle *kara* "from" indicates when something starts, the particle *made* "until" indicates when something ends, and the particle *made ni* "by" indicates the time limit within which something happens.

San-ji ni shimasu.	I'll do it at three.
San-ji kara shimasu.	I'll do it from three.
San-ji made shimasu.	I'll do it until three.
San-ji made ni shimasu.	I'll do it by three.

The particles *wa* (contrast) and *mo* (addition) can be added to these particles.

Ka-yōbi ni shimasu. Sui-yōbi ni wa shimasen.
I do it on Tuesday. I don't do it on Wednesday.
Ka-yōbi ni shimasu. Sui-yōbi ni mo shimasu.
I do it on Tuesday. I do it on Wednesday, too.

Kara and *made* can be also used with expressions other than time expressions.

Waseda made onegai-shimasu.	To Waseda, please. (in a taxi)
Amerika kara kaerimasu.	I'll be coming back from America.

Note: *Desu* can directly follow *kara* and *made* phrases, e.g., *Kaigi wa san ji kara yoji made desu.* "The meeting is from three to four." When these phrases modify another noun, particle *no* is required between them, e.g., *Amerika kara no ryūgakusei* "an exchange student from America".

PATTERN PRACTICE 5

Cue:	*Ikimasu yo.*	I'll go.
Response:	*Nan-ji ni ikimasu ka.*	What time will you go?
Cue:	*Ranchi o tabemasu yo.*	I'll eat lunch.
Response:	*Nan-ji ni tabemasu ka.*	What time will you eat?

Practice the above drill using the following information:
1. *Terebi o mimasu yo.*
2. *Sanpo-shimasu yo.*
3. *Nihon-go o renshū-shimasu yo.*
4. *Nemasu yo.*
5. *Shigoto o shimasu yo.*

PATTERN PRACTICE 6

Cue:	*Ranchi wa jū-ni-ji kara desu ka.*	Is lunch served from 12?
Response:	*Ee, jū-ni-ji kara ichi-ji made desu.*	Yes, from 12 to one.
Cue:	*Kaigi wa hachi-ji kara desu ka.*	Is the meeting from eight?
Response:	*Ee, hachi-ji kara ku-ji made desu.*	Yes, from eight to nine.

Practice the above drill using the following information:
1. *Jugyō wa ku-ji kara desu ka.*
2. *Yasumi wa san-ji kara desu ka.*
3. *Nyūsu wa shichi-ji kara desu ka.*
4. *Renshū wa roku-ji han kara desu ka.*
5. *Uchiawase wa ichi-ji jū-go-fun kara desu ka.*

PATTERN PRACTICE 7

Cue:	*Go-ji ni ikimasu ka.*
	Do you go at five?
Response:	*Ee, go-ji goro ikimasu kedo, shichi-ji made ni kaerimasu.*
	Yes, I go around five, but return by seven.
Cue:	*Getsu-yōbi ni ikimasu ka.*
	Do you go on Monday?
Response:	*Hai, Getsu-yōbi goro ikimasu kedo, Sui-yōbi made ni kaerimasu.*
	Yes, I go around Monday, but return by Wednesday.

Use the following information to practice the above drill.
1. *Ni-ji ni ikimasu ka.*
2. *Moku-yōbi ni ikimasu ka.*
3. *Ku-ji-han ni ikimasu ka.*
4. *Jū-ji ni ikimasu ka.*
5. *Ka-yōbi ni ikimasu ka.*

EXERCISE 5
Say it in Japanese
You've been asked about your daily activities. Answer in Japanese.
1. I get up at 7:00.
2. I work from nine to five.
3. I eat lunch around 12.
4. I go home by 7:00.
5. I go for a walk around 6:30.
6. I sleep from 11:30 to 6:00.

EXERCISE 6
Role Play
1. At a restaurant, ask a co-worker what she will eat.
2. Ask a waiter from what time to what time lunch is served.
3. A co-worker is going to a meeting. Ask her what time she is returning.
4. The tour bus leaves this site at 11. Tell the guide that you will be back by 10:45.
5. A new restaurant has opened. Invite Ms. Sato to go either on Saturday or Sunday.
6. Discuss your typical weekday schedule and your weekend.

DIALOGUE 4 Texting Someone

Michael is texting someone.

Sato: Do you always email in English?
       Itsumo Eigo de mēru-shimasu ka.
       いつも英語でメールしますか。

Michael: Yes, but I sometimes write in Japanese.
          Ee, demo tokidoki Nihon-go de kakimasu.
          ええ、でも時々日本語で書きます。

Sato: Why is that?
       Dōshite desu ka.
       どうしてですか。

Michael: It's because he is a Japanese friend.
          Nihon-jin no tomodachi desu kara.
          日本人の友だちですから。

Sato: That explains it.
       Naruhodo.
       なるほど。

VOCABULARY

itsumo	いつも	always
de	で	by means of
mēru-shimasu	メールします	email (verb), text
demo	でも	but; however
tokidoki	時々	sometimes
kakimasu	書きます	write
dōshite	どうして	why
naruhodo	なるほど	that makes sense; I see

ADDITIONAL VOCABULARY

taitei	たいてい	usually; most of the time
tamani	たまに	every now and then; sometimes
naze	なぜ	why (formal)
nande	なんで	why (casual)

GRAMMAR NOTE The Particle *de* "By Means Of"

A noun followed by particle *de* indicates how something is done. Note that there are a number of ways in which this might be translated into English.

Supūn de tabemasu.   I'll eat with a spoon.

Takushī de ikimasu.   I'll go by a taxi.

Nihongo de hanashimashita.   I spoke in Japanese.

Note: You can request someone to speak in English by saying: *Sumimasen. Eigo de onegai-shimasu.* "Excuse me. In English, please."

GRAMMAR NOTE Asking and Explaining Why Using
kara "Because"

In the sequence of /Statement A *kara* Statement B/, Statement A represents the cause and Statement B the effect. *Kara* here means "because" rather than "from".

Eigo-go desu kara wakarimasen. Because it's (in) English, I don't understand.

Wakarimasen kara kikimasu.   Because I don't understand it, I'll ask.

Statement B can be left unsaid when it is understood from the context.

Ikimasen ka.   You are not going?

Ee, Nichi-yōbi desu kara.   Right. Because it's Sunday.

The clause particles *kara* and *kedo* "but" are opposites of each other. Compare the following.

Nichi-yōbi desu kara, hatarakimasen.   Because it's Sunday, I'll not work.

Nichi-yōbi desu kedo, hatarakimasu.   It's Sunday, but I'll work.

GRAMMAR NOTE Asking Questions with "Why"

There are three Japanese words for "why". *Dōshite* is most common, *naze* more formal, and *nan de* is casual. *Desu ka* can directly follow them if the rest of the sentence is understood from the context.

Dōshite ikimasen ka.   Why don't you go?

Dōshite desu ka.   Why is it (that you are not going)?

PATTERN PRACTICE 8

Cue: *Itsumo mēru-shimasu ka.*
            Do you always email him?

Response: *Taitei mēru-shimasu kedo, tokidoki shimasen.*
            Most of the time I do, but sometimes I don't.

Cue: *Itsumo Eigo desu ka.*
            Is it always (in) English?

Response: *Taitei Eigo desu kedo, tokidoki Eigo ja nai desu.*
            Most of the time, it is, but sometimes, it isn't.

Repeat the drill using the following information.
1. *Itsumo sanpo-shimasu ka.*
2. *Itsumo Ka-yōbi desu ka.*
3. *Itsumo renshū-shimasu ka.*
4. *Itsumo go-ji made desu ka.*
5. *Itsumo ranchi tabemasu ka.*

PATTERN PRACTICE 9

Cue: *Nichi-yōbi desu ne.*
             It's Sunday, isn't it?
Response: *Ee, Nichi-yōbi desu kara, shitsurei-shimasu.*
             Yes, it's Sunday, so excuse me. (I'll get going.)
Cue: *Dekimashita ne.*
             It's done, isn't it?
Response: *Ee, dekimashita kara shitsurei-shimasu.*
             Yes, it's done, so excuse me.

Repeat the above drill using the following information.
1. *Go-ji desu ne.*
2. *Kaimono-shimasu ne.*
3. *Mōsugu jikan desu ne.*
4. *Denwa desu ne.*
5. *Wakarimasen ne.*

EXERCISE 7
Say it in Japanese
1. You've been asked if you engage in some activities. Answer in Japanese.
   1)   I often go for a walk.
   2)   I always eat breakfast but sometimes do not eat lunch.
   3)   I usually get up at 7:00, but on weekends I sleep until around 12:00.
   4)   I usually work from 9:00, but every now and then I work from 10:00.
   5)   I studied Japanese all the time before, but now I don't do so very much.

2. You've been asked why you are not going to a gathering. Answer in Japanese.
   6)   Because I'll be doing my homework.
   7)   Because I went yesterday.
   8)   Because I am not a freshman.
   9)   Because I work until six.
   10) Because I'll play video games.

EXERCISE 8
Role Play
1. Ask a co-worker what time he usually gets up.
2. Politely ask a store clerk to speak in English.
3. You've been told to go home now. Ask why, since it's only 3:00.
4. You've just been given an explanation. Let the person know that you got it; it makes sense.
5. Discuss what language you use to do certain activities: to email; to call; to read; to tweet.

REVIEW QUESTIONS
Answer the following questions. Review the answers in Grammar Notes.
1. a) What classifier is used to express clock time in Japanese?
   b) How about the days of the week?
2. a) How do you ask what time it is in Japanese?
   b) How about what day of the week it is today?
3. How are the following statements different from one another?
   1) *Eigo to Nihon-go*
   2) *Eigo ya Nihon-go*
   3) *Eigo ka Nihon-go*
4. What four endings of the Japanese verbs were introduced in this lesson?
5. What activity does a Non-past verb form refer to?
6. What is a compound verb?
7. a) Give four examples of frequency expressions.
   b) Where in a sentence do they usually appear?
8. How is the object of a verb indicated in a Japanese sentence?
9. How are the following statements different from one another?
   1) *Shinbun yomimasu.*
   2) *Shinbun wa yomimasu.*
   3) *Shinbun mo yomimasu.*
   4) *Shinbun o yomimasu.*
10. How are the following statements different from one another?
   1) *Go-ji ni shimasu.*
   2) *Go-ji kara shimasu.*
   3) *Go-ji made shimasu.*
   4) *Go-ji made ni shimasu.*

11. How are the following statements different from one another?
    1) *Kore, kakimasu.*
    2) *Kore de kakimasu.*
12. How do you ask for a reason in Japanese?
13. How are the following statements different from one another?
    1) *Nichi-yōbi kara desu.*
    2) *Nichi-yōbi desu kara.*

LESSON 4
Eating and Drinking

Different strokes for different folks (Ten people, ten colors)
十人十色　*Jū-nin to-iro*

⏺ DIALOGUE 1 Visiting an Izaka-ya Restaurant

Michael and Ms. Sato have decided to go to an *Izaka-ya* (restaurant bar) after work.

Waitress: Hello (Welcome to our business).
Irasshaimase.
いらっしゃいませ。

Michael and Ms. Sato nod in acknowledgment.

Waitress: How many people in your party?
Nan-mei-sama desu ka.
何名様ですか。

Michael: Two.
Futa-ri desu.
二人です。

Waitress: This way, please.
Kochira e dōzo.
こちらへどうぞ。
What would you like to order?
Go-chūmon wa?
ご注文は？

Michael: Two beers to start, please.
Toriaezu, bīru o ni-hon kudasai.
とりあえず、ビールを二本ください。

Sato: And what are today's recommendations?
Sore kara, kyō no osusume wa?
それから、今日のおすすめは？

Waitress: They are these.
Kochira desu.
こちらです。

Sato:	Then, two of these, please.
	Ja, kore o futa-tsu onegai-shimasu.
	じゃ、これを二つお願いします。
Waitress:	Certainly.
	Kashikomarimashita.
	かしこまりました。

Michael and Ms. Sato wait for their drinks. The waitress returns shortly after.

Waitress:	Thank you for waiting. (Here they are.)
	Omatase-itashimashita.
	お待たせいたしました。

Michael and Ms. Sato get their beers and toast each other.

Michael:	Then, cheers!
	Ja, kanpai!
	じゃ、乾杯。
Sato:	Cheers!
	Kanpai!
	乾杯。

After eating their dinner, Michael signals the waitress to get the check.

Michael:	Excuse me. Check, please.
	Sumimasen. Kaikei, onegai-shimasu.
	すみません。会計お願いします。

VOCABULARY

Irasshaimase.	いらっしゃいませ。	Welcome to our business.
-mei	名	counter for people (formal)
-mei-sama	名様	counter for people (formal, polite)
nan-mei-sama	何名様	how many people
-ri/nin	～人	counter for people
futa-ri	二人	two people
kochira	こちら	this way; these
(go)chūmon	注文	order
toriaezu	とりあえず	to start; for now
bīru	ビール	beer
-hon	本	counter for long things
ni-hon	二本	two (long things)
kudasai	ください	give me please
sore kara	それから	and
osusume	おすすめ	recommendation

-tsu	〜つ	unit (classifier)
futa-tsu	二つ	two units
Kashikomarimashita.	かしこまりました。	Will do; Certainly, sir/madam
Omatase-itashimashita.	お待たせいたしました。	Thank you for waiting.
Kanpai!	乾杯!	Cheers!
chūmon-shimasu	注文します	order (verb)
kanpai-shimasu	乾杯します	toast
susumemasu	すすめます	recommend; urge
nomimono	飲み物	drinks; beverages

Drinks and Beverages

bīru	ビール	beer
nama	生	draft beer
(o)sake	酒	Sake
wain	ワイン	wine
mizu	水	water
ocha	お茶	green tea
kōcha	紅茶	black tea
ūron-cha	ウーロン茶	oolong tea
kōhī	コーヒー	coffee
hotto	ホット	hot coffee (when ordering)
aisu kōhī	アイスコーヒー	iced coffee
jūsu	ジュース	juice
miruku, gyūnyū	ミルク、牛乳	milk
kōra	コーラ	cola

Popular Dishes

(o)sushi	寿司	sushi
(o)sashimi	さしみ	sashimi
tempura	天ぷら	tempura
(o)miso-shiru	みそ汁	miso soup
yaki-tori	焼き鳥	skewered chicken BBQ
yaki-niku	焼き肉	Korean BBQ beef
yaki-soba	焼きそば	stir-fried noodles
tonkatsu	とんかつ	pork cutlet
kara-age	唐揚げ	fried chicken
edamame	枝豆	edamame (soybeans in a pod)
furai	フライ	deep-fried items
hanbāgu	ハンバーグ	Salisbury Steak (hamburger without buns)
sutēki	ステーキ	steak
karē	カレー	curry

GRAMMAR NOTE Counting People and Things using Classifiers

When counting items in Japanese, numbers are combined with classifiers that are conventionally used for the particular nouns being counted. This is similar to English expressions like "ten sheets of paper", or "a loaf of bread" (not "a bread").

There are two numerical systems in Japanese: one of Chinese origin, which was introduced in Lesson 3, and another system of Japanese origin, which only goes up to the number ten.

1 *hito*, 2 *futa*, 3 *mi*, 4 *yo*, 5 *itsu*, 6 *mu*, 7 *nana*, 8 *ya*, 9 *kokono*, 10 *tō*

The classifiers *-ri/nin*, *-mei*, and *-mei-sama* are used to count people. The *-ri* plus the Japanese number is used for the number one and two (*hito-ri*, *futa-ri*), and *-nin* is used for three and above with Chinese numbers (*san-nin*, *jūichi-nin*, *hyaku-nin*, etc.) The question word is *nan-nin* "how many people".

The classifier *-mei*, used with Chinese numbers, is a formal version and *-mei-sama* is its polite version (raising the person you're talking to), commonly used by service people. Make sure you do not use *-mei-sama* to refer to your own group.

The classifier *-tsu* is the most generic classifier, which can be used for both tangible and intangible items such as opinions, meetings, etc. It may be a safe choice when you are not sure what classifier to use. The classifier *-tsu* is combined with Japanese numerals and for quantities over ten, Chinese numerals without a classifier are used: *jū-ichi*, *jū-ni,* etc.

The classifier *-hon* is combined with Chinese numerals and is used to count long cylindrical objects such as bottles, pens, umbrellas, bananas, etc. Note the alternatives for *-hon*: *-pon* for one, six, eight, ten and *-bon* for three and "how many".

	-ri/nin	*-mei; mei-sama*	*-tsu*	*-hon/pon/bon*
1	*hito-ri*	*ichi-mei*	*hito-tsu*	*ip-pon*
2	*futa-ri*	*ni-mei*	*futa-tsu*	*ni-hon*
3	*san-nin*	*san-mei*	*mit-tsu*	*san-bon*
4	*yo-nin*	*yon-mei*	*yot-tsu*	*yon-hon*
5	*go-nin*	*go-mei*	*itsu-tsu*	*go-hon*
6	*roku-nin*	*roku-mei*	*mut-tsu*	*rop-pon*
7	*shichi-nin*	*nana-mei*	*nana-tsu*	*nana-hon*
8	*hachi-nin*	*hachi-mei*	*yat-tsu*	*hap-pon*
9	*kyū-nin/ku-nin*	*kyū-mei*	*kokono-tsu*	*kyū-hon*
10	*jū-nin*	*jū-mei*	*tō*	*jup-pon/jip-pon*
11	*jū-ichi-nin*	*jū-ichi-mei*	*jū-ichi*	*jū-ip-pon*
12	*nan-nin*	*nan-mei*	*ikutsu/o-ikutsu*	*nan-bon*

Other common classifiers include *-ko* for relatively small units, *-mai* for thin flat objects, and *-satsu* for bound volumes such as books and magazines and *-hiki/piki/ biki* for small animals.

The classifier *-ko* is used for counting pieces—everything from pieces of cake to apples to packets of sugar. The classifier *-ko* overlaps in many respects with *-tsu*. One difference is that *-tsu* can be used for abstract things like ideas, meetings, or items in a list, while *-ko* is used only for concrete items. Note that the sound changes with certain numbers. The classifier for counting (small) animals like dogs, cats, insects, fish, etc.is *-hiki/piki/biki*. This sound change of /*h-p-b*/ is also used with the classifier *-hon/pon/bon*.

	Pieces/lumps	Flat objects	Bound volumes	Small animals
1	*ik-ko*	*ichi-mai*	*is-satsu*	*ip-piki*
2	*ni-ko*	*ni-mai*	*ni-satsu*	*ni-hiki*
3	*san-ko*	*san-mai*	*san-satsu*	*san-biki*
4	*yon-ko*	*yon-mai*	*yon-satsu*	*yon-hiki*
5	*go-ko*	*go-mai*	*go-satsu*	*go-hiki*
6	*rok-ko*	*roku-mai*	*roku-satsu*	*rop-piki*
7	*nana-ko*	*nana-mai*	*nana-satsu*	*nana-hiki*
8	*hachi-ko/ hak-ko*	*hachi-mai*	*has-satsu*	*hap-piki/ hachi-hiki*
9	*kyū-ko*	*kyū-mai*	*kyū-satsu*	*kyū-hiki*
10	*juk-ko*	*jū-mai*	*jus-satsu*	*jup-piki*
	nan-ko	*nan-mai*	*nan-satsu*	*nan-biki*

GRAMMAR NOTE Expressing Quantities in Japanese

There are two kinds of quantity expressions in Japanese. One consists of a specific number and classifier (*san-bon* "three bottles", *hito-tsu* "one item", etc.) and the other is a general quantity expression (*chotto* "a little", etc.). Within a sentence they usually occur right before the predicate (verb, adjective, or noun+*desu*). In Japanese, the amount follows the noun, e.g., "beer three bottles" rather than "three bottles of beer" in English.

Bīru o san-bon kudasai.   Three (bottles of) beer, please.
Mizu o chotto nomimashita.   I drank a little water.

A quantity expression is typically not followed by a particle, except *wa* "at least" or *mo* "so much".

Mainichi, bīru o ip-pon wa nomimasu.   I drink at least one beer every day.
Bīru o go-hai mo nomimashita.   I drank all five beers.

Suppose we want to say "One coffee and two colas, please." Here is how multiple items and numbers are listed in Japanese.

Kōhī o hito-tsu kudasai.	One coffee, please.
Kōra o futa-tsu kudasai.	Two colas, please.
Kōhī o hito-tsu to kōra o futa-tsu kudasai.	One coffee and two colas, please.

There is no limit on how many things can be listed. Of course, if the list is long, you should slow down and make sure that the person you're speaking to is following along.

CULTURAL NOTE Eating Out

Upon entering a restaurant, you will be greeted with *Irasshaimase*. Respond by just nodding and wait to be seated. Many restaurants display replicas of their dishes near their entrance and provide illustrated menus. If you are not sure what to order, ask for recommendations (*osusume*). In many ramen shops and casual restaurants, meal tickets are bought at a vending machine. If you want to avoid certain ingredients at a restaurant or stores, ask X, *haitte imasu ka*. "Is X in it?"

Some restaurants have a *tatami* floor. Remove your shoes before stepping on *tatami* and avoid stepping on the cushions. Wet towels or *oshibori* are provided at most restaurants to clean your hands before eating. Napkins are not provided at traditional restaurants.

It is good manners to pick up your bowl of rice or *miso* soup when eating and hold it in your hand to scoop the rice or soup towards your mouth. It's bad manners to leave grains of rice in your bowl. When eating from shared dishes, use the opposite end of your chopsticks or the dedicated serving chopsticks.

The bill will be placed face down either as you receive the meal or after you have finished eating. It is not common to pay at the table. You are supposed to bring your bill to the cashier when leaving. Paying in cash is most common, although many restaurants also accept credit cards. It is not customary to tip in Japan, but service charges are sometimes added to your bill. Do not forget to say *Gochisō-sama deshita* as you leave.

CULTURAL NOTE Drinking

Different cultures have different attitudes towards alcohol. In Japan there is no equivalent of Open-Container Laws prohibiting carrying and drinking alcohol in certain areas. In general alcohol is more readily accessible and public drinking is largely accepted in Japan. It's rare for restaurants and stores to check the ID of younger customers. Alcoholic beverages can also be bought at vending machines across the country.

After-work social gatherings that involve drinking have an important role in Japanese society. Co-workers often go out together, although this is more common

among men. Entertaining business associates often involves drinking. These social interactions should be used to develop personal bonds rather than to conduct business. On these occasions, make sure you do not start drinking until everybody at the table has a drink and the glasses are raised for *kanpai*. It is customary to pour for each other rather than to pour your own drink, and to keep refilling before glasses become empty. It's polite to lift your glass while being served rather than leaving it on the table to be filled. Oolong tea is a common substitute for those who do not drink alcohol at these occasions.

It is not uncommon to see people obviously drunk at *izakaya* or in public, but this is accepted as long as no one is being bothered. Japanese people draw a clear boundary between what is official and what happens while drinking, and tend to excuse misbehavior while under the influence. However, laws against drinking and driving must be strictly observed.

PATTERN PRACTICE 1

Cue:	*Futa-tsu desu ka.*	Do you mean two (units)?
Response:	*Ie, mit-tsu desu.*	No, I mean three.
Cue:	*Ip-pon desu ka.*	Do you mean one (bottle)?
Response:	*Ie, ni-hon desu.*	No, I mean two.

Repeat the drill using the following information.

1. *Rop-pon desu ka.*
2. *Futa-ri desu ka.*
3. *Itsu-tsu desu ka.*
4. *Tō-desu ka.*
5. *Kyū-mai desu ka.*
6. *Nana-mei-sama desu ka.*
7. *Rok-ko desu ka.*
8. *Ni-jus-satsu desu ka.*
9. *Yat-tsu desu ka.*
10. *Jū-go-nin desu ka.*

PATTERN PRACTICE 2

Cue:	*Bīru desu ka.*
	Beer?
Response:	*Ee, toriaezu bīru o ni-hon kudasai.*
	Yes, two beers to start, please.
Cue:	*Sashimi desu ka.*
	Sashimi?
Response:	*Ee, toriaezu sashimi o futa-tsu kudasai.*
	Yes, two orders of sashimi to start, please.

Repeat the drill with the following information:
1. *Osake desu ka.*
2. *Kōra desu ka.*
3. *Sushi desu ka.*
4. *Nama desu ka.*
5. *Bīru to edamame desu ka.*

EXERCISE 1
Say it in Japanese
1. You've been asked what you are going to order at a restaurant.
    1) Two draft beers, please.
    2) Three bottles of sake to start, please.
    3) One order of **sashimi** and two orders of **tempura**, please.
    4) Four beers, one oolong tea, three orders of sushi, and two orders of **yakitori**, please.
    5) What are today's recommendations?

2. You are discussing some items. Confirm their quantities.
    6) Do you mean five pieces of sushi?
    7) Do you mean three tickets?
    8) Do you mean ten books?
    9) Do you mean four meetings?
    10) Do you mean two American women?

EXERCISE 2
Role Play
1. At a restaurant, ask your group what you are going to order.
2. You've been asked what is good at this restaurant. Recommend curry.
3. You arrived late. Apologize and thank your group for waiting.
4. Drinks are here for everyone. Acknowledge your group's hard work today and suggest a toast.
5. You are done eating. Ask for the check.

DIALOGUE 2 At a Ramen Shop

It's lunchtime. Ms. Sato and Michael are discussing what to eat.

Michael: I'm hungry.
           Onaka ga sukimashita.
           お腹がすきました。

Sato: What would you like?
           Nani ga i'i desu ka.
           何がいいですか。

Michael: How about ramen?
           Rāmen wa dō desu ka.
           ラーメンはどうですか。

Sato: Sounds good! (I'd like that.)
           I'i desu nē.
           いいですねえ。

At a ramen shop

Sato: Look! Here's the ramen. (lit., Here comes ramen.)
           Hora, rāmen ga kimashita yo.
           ほら、ラーメンが来ましたよ。

Michael: Wow, that was fast. Let's start.
           Wā, hayai desu nē. Itadakimasu.
           わあ、早いですねえ。 いただきます。

Michael: It's delicious.
           Oishi'i desu nē.
           おいしいですねえ。

Sato: Aren't you hot?
           Atsuku nai desu ka.
           暑くないですか。

Michael: I'm fine.
           Daijōbu desu.
           大丈夫です。
           Done. Ah, it was good!
           Gochisō-sama. Ā, oishikatta!
           ごちそうさま。ああ、おいしかった!

VOCABULARY

onaka	お腹	stomach
ga	が	particle indicating subject
sukimasu	すきます	get empty
onaka ga sukimasu	お腹がすきます	get hungry
rāmen	ラーメン	ramen
dō	どう	how
i'i	いい	good (not food)
Hora!	ほら!	Look!
Wā!	わあ!	Whoa!
hayai	速い、早い	fast; early
oishi'i	おいしい	delicious; good (food)
atsui	熱い、暑い	hot
daijōbu	大丈夫	okay; fine
oishikatta	おいしかった	was delicious

ADDITIONAL VOCABULARY

ippai	いっぱい	full; many
onaka ga ippai	お腹がいっぱい	stomach is full

COMMON ADJECTIVES

takai	高い	expensive; high
yasui	安い	cheap; inexpensive
ōki'i	大きい	big
chi'isai	小さい	small
furui	古い	old
atarashi'i	新しい	new; fresh
i'i	いい	good; okay
warui	悪い	bad
oishi'i	おいしい	delicious
mazui	まずい	bad tasting
hayai	速い、早い	fast; early
osoi	遅い	slow; late
atsui	暑い、熱い	hot
samui	寒い	cold (atmospheric)
tsumetai	冷たい	cold (to the touch)
omoshiroi	おもしろい	interesting
tsumaranai	つまらない	boring
yasashi'i	やさしい	easy; kind-hearted
muzukasi'i	むずかしい	difficult

chikai	近い	close; near
tōi	遠い	far

Popular Lunches

It's common for co-workers to eat lunch together. Many Japanese bring homemade box lunches (*obentō*) to school and work. At restaurants and company dining halls (*shokudō*), relatively cheap lunches are served quickly. Follow groups of office workers on the street around lunchtime to find the best spots in that area.

(o)bentō	（お）弁当	Bento (box lunch)
teishoku	定食	complete meal on a tray
rāmen	ラーメン	ramen
udon	うどん	udon (noodles)
soba	そば	soba (buckwheat noodles)
onigiri	おにぎり	onigiri (rice ball)
hanbāgā	ハンバーガー	hamburger
pan	パン	bread; pastry
sando	サンド	sandwich
sarada	サラダ	salad
piza	ピザ	pizza

Restaurants

Many restaurants in Japan specialize in only one type of food while others offer a broader range of dishes.

mise	店	shop
resutoran	レストラン	restaurant
kafe	カフェ	café
izakaya	居酒屋	restaurant bar
kissaten	喫茶店	coffee shop
shokudō	食堂	dining hall; diner (small, casual)
famirī resutoran	ファミリーレストラン	family restaurant
sushi-ya	寿司屋	sushi shop
rāmen-ya	ラーメン屋	ramen shop
soba-ya	そば屋	soba-noodle shop

GRAMMAR NOTE Subject of a Sentence and the Particle *ga*

The subject of a sentence, when stated, is usually placed before the object and is marked by particles *wa*, *mo*, *ga* or no particle at all.

Rāmen	*kimashita.*	(The) ramen has come.
Rāmen wa	*kimashita.*	At least the ramen has come.
Rāmen mo	*kimashita.*	(The) ramen has come, too.
Rāmen ga	*kimashita.*	Here is the ramen (new information) or It's the ramen that has come.

There are certain parallels between particles *o* (object) and *ga* (subject). They both place a special focus on the noun or the entire sentence, and are usually used with question words.

Nani ga i'i desu ka.	What is good?
-Rāmen ga i'i desu.	Ramen is good.
Satō-san ga kimasu ka.	Is it Ms. Sato who is coming?
-Ie, Tanaka-san ga kimasu. Satō-san wa kimasen yo.	

No, it's Mr. Tanaka who is coming. Ms. Sato is not coming.

Note that in the answer above *Satō-san* is followed by the particle *wa*, while *Tanaka-san* is followed by the particle *ga*. This is because *Tanaka-san* is the the correct answer to the question and thus is the focus. *Satō-san* has been already mentioned and the particle *wa* here indicates that she is being compared to *Tanaka-san*.

When the entire sentence presents new information the subject takes particle *ga* and the object takes *o*. In the dialogue above, Ms. Sato announces the arrival of ramen using particle *ga* for the subject, ramen. The whole sentence *Rāmen ga kimashita* is presented as new information, rather than just *Rāmen*.

GRAMMAR NOTE Adjective Predicates

All Japanese adjectives end in *-i* (Non Past) and *-katta* (Past). To make the Negative form, change *-i* to *-ku nai* for Non-past and to *-ku nakatta* for Past. To make it formal, add *desu*.

Yasui desu.	It's cheap.
Yasuku nai desu.	It's not cheap.
Yasukatta desu.	It was cheap.
Yasuku nakatta desu.	It was not cheap.

Noun and verb predicates were introduced in Lessons 2 and 3. With the adjective predicates introduced in this lesson you have now seen all three Japanese sentence types. The chart on the next page shows all the basic predicate forms.

Predicate	Non-Past		Past	
	Affirmative	Negative	Affirmative	Negative
Verb	*Wakarimasu.* I understand.	*Wakarimasen.* I don't understand.	*Wakarimashita.* I understood.	*Wakarimasen deshita.* I didn't understand.
Noun	*Nihon desu.* It's Japan.	*Nihon ja nai desu.* It's not Japan.	*Nihon deshita.* It was Japan.	*Nihon ja nakatta desu.* It was not Japan.
Adjective	*Yasui desu.* It's cheap.	*Yasuku nai desu.* It's not cheap.	*Yasukatta desu.* It was cheap.	*Yasuku nakatta desu.* It wasn't cheap.

The adjective *i'i* is an exception and has special forms.

I'i desu.	It's good.
Yoku nai desu.	It's not good.
Yokatta desu.	It was good.
Yoku nakatta desu.	It wasn't good.

Yokatta desu nē is a common response to good news. *Yoku* is one of the most commonly used adverbs and was already introduced in Lesson 3 as in *yoku wakarimashita*. The *-ku* form of adjectives serves as an adverb in general.

Yoku wakarimasu.	I understand it well.
Ōkiku kakimasu.	I'll write it big.
Atarashiku tsukurimasu.	I'll remake it.

The adjectives also modify a noun to make a noun phrase. Unlike noun modifiers, which were discussed in Lesson 2, adjective modifiers do not require *no*. Compare:

Nihon no rāmen	Japanese ramen
oishi'i rāmen	delicious ramen
Nihon no oishi'i rāmen	Japan's delicious ramen

PATTERN PRACTICE 3

Cue: *Ōki'i desu ka.*	Is it big?
Response: *Ie, ōkiku nai desu. Chi'isai desu.*	No, it isn't. It's small.
Cue: *Atsui desu ka.*	Is it hot?
Response: *Ie, atsuku nai desu. Tsumetai desu.*	No, it isn't. It's cold (to touch).

Use the following information and repeat the drills:
1. *Takai desu ka.*
2. *Atarashi'i desu ka.*
3. *Warui desu ka.*
4. *Hayai desu ka.*
5. *Mazui desu ka.*

* Repeat this drill with the following response.
   Mae wa ōkikatta desu kedo, ima wa ōkiku nai desu.
   It was big before, but it is not big now.

PATTERN PRACTICE 4

Cue: *Bīru desu ka.*	Is it beer?
Response: *Hai, bīru o chūmon-shimashita.*	Yes, I ordered beer.
Cue: *Satō-san desu ka.*	Is it Ms. Sato's?
Response: *Hai, Satō-san ga chūmon-shimashita.*	Yes, Ms. Sato ordered it.

Repeat the drill using the following information:
1. *Gakusei desu ka.*
2. *Rāmen desu ka.*
3. *Hanbāgā toka sando desu ka.*
4. *Otoko no hito desu ka.*
5. *Sensei no hiru-gohan desu ka.*

EXERCISE 3
Say it in Japanese
You've been asked about a restaurant.
1. It's expensive.
2. Isn't it expensive?
3. It was small before, but now it is big.
4. Do you mean the ramen shop? I go there often because their ramen is delicious.
5. Do you mean the new ramen shop? I went there yesterday, but it was not very good.

Ask the following questions about the meeting yesterday.
1. Who came?
2. How many people came?
3. What time did they come?
4. How many *obento* did we order? And how many bottles of water?
5. How was the *obento*? Were they good? Were they expensive?

EXERCISE 4
Role Play
1. Tell a co-worker that you are hungry. Suggest that you eat lunch now, although it's a little early.
2. Your group is trying to pick a restaurant. Express your opinion that a family restaurant would be good.
3. Pizza has been delivered to your office. Announce it to your co-workers.
4. Greet a neighbor in the morning. Mention:
    1) it's hot today;
    2) it was cold yesterday.
5. A stranger has just fallen in front of you. React!
6. You've just heard good news. React!

⊙ DIALOGUE 3 Traditional Japanese Cuisine

Michael and Ms. Sato are having dinner at a traditional Japanese restaurant. Food has been served.

Michael: Whoa, it looks good (how appetizing)!
          Wā, oishisō desu nē!
          わあ、おいしそうですねえ！

Sato: It is a traditional Japanese dish.
          Nihon no dentō-teki na ryōri desu.
          日本の伝統的な料理です。

Michael: Really? (I didn't know) Amazing!
          Hē. Sugoi desu nē.
          へえ。すごいですねえ！
          What is this red one?
          Kono akai no wa nan desu ka.
          この赤いのは、何ですか。

Sato: Oh it's a vegetable.
          Ā, sore wa yasai desu.
          ああ、それは野菜です。

Sato: Do you want some more? (lit., How about more?)
          Motto ikaga desu ka.
          もっといかがですか。

Michael: Then, just a little more…
          Ja mō sukoshi dake...
          じゃ、もうすこしだけ。

VOCABULARY

oishi-sō (na)	おいしそう（な）	appetizing; looking delicious
dentō	伝統	tradition
dentō-teki (na)	伝統的（な）	traditional
ryōri	料理	dish; cooking
hē	へえ	really? (I didn't know; I'm intrigued)
sugoi	すごい	amazing; awesome
akai	赤い	red (adjective)
no	の	one (pronoun)
akai no	赤いの	red one
yasai	野菜	vegetable
motto	もっと	more
ikaga	いかが	how (polite)
mō	もう	more

mō hito-tsu	もう一つ	one more
dake	だけ	only; limited to
yūmei (na)	有名 (な)	famous

Snacks

okashi	お菓子	snacks; sweets
suītsu	スイーツ	sweets
pan	パン	bread
kēki	ケーキ	cake
kukkī	クッキー	cookie
chokorēto	チョコレート	chocolate
aisukurīmu	アイスクリーム	ice cream
kudamono	くだもの	fruit
ringo	りんご	apple
mikan	みかん	mandarin orange
ichigo	いちご	strawberry
budō	ぶどう	grapes
banana	バナナ	banana

Colors

aka/akai	赤	red
ao/aoi	青	blue
ki'iro/ki'iroi	黄色	yellow
shiro/shiroi	白	white
kuro/kuroi	黒	black
cha'iro/cha'iroi	茶色	brown
midori	緑	green
murasaki	紫	purple
hai'iro	灰色	gray
kon'iro	紺色	navy, indigo
orenji	オレンジ	orange
pinku	ピンク	pink
nani iro	何色	what color

GRAMMAR NOTE *Na*–Nouns

The words *kirei* "beautiful" and *dentō-teki* "traditional" belong to a smaller group of nouns that are called *na*-nouns. They have adjective-like meanings and form of nouns. They do not have adjective endings such as *-katta-* and *-ku*. As nouns, their negative forms end in *-ja nai desu*. When modifying another noun, they take *na* instead of *no*, unlike regular nouns.

    kirei na Nihongo "beautiful Japanese"
    dentō-teki na okashi "traditional sweets"

To distinguish them from regular nouns, they are marked with *na* added in the dictionaries in this book. Note that all *na*-nouns are intangible, but not all intangibles are *na* nouns.

GRAMMAR NOTE Noun Phrases and the Pronoun *no* = "One"

We have so far discussed four ways of extending a noun into a longer noun phrase as follows.

1. Noun *no* Noun   *watashi no kētai*   my cellphone
2. *Kono* + Noun   *kono kētai*   this cellphone
3. Adjective + Noun   *yasui kētai*   cheap cellphone
4. *Na*-noun + Noun   *kirei na kētai*   beautiful cellphone

More than one modifier can modify a noun and the order of the modifiers is rather free.

    kono watashi no atarashi'i kirei na kētai "this beautiful cheap cellphone of mine"
    watashi no kono kirei na atarashi'i kētai "this beautiful cheap cellphone of mine"

When the main noun is already known, it can be replaced by the pronoun *no* "one" in the following structure.

    Adjective + Noun: *yasui kētai* → *yasui no* "cheap one"
    Na-noun + Noun: *kirei na kētai* → *kirei na no* "beautiful one"

Note what happens when different modifiers are combined.

    kono atarashi'i kētai → *kono atarashi'i no*
    this new cellphone   this new one

    chi'isai kirei na kēki → *kono chi'isai kirei na no*
    beautiful small cake   this small, beautiful one

Note that it is rude to use the pronoun *no* to refer to people.

GRAMMAR NOTE "More" *Motto* vs. *Mō*

Both *mō* and *motto* mean "more" in English, but they combine with different parts of a sentence. *Motto* combines with a predicate—verb, adjective, noun+*desu*—to indicate a greater degree than what has been mentioned.

Motto benkyō-shimasu.	I'll study more.
motto yasui no	cheaper one
Motto kirei desu.	It's prettier.

On the other hand, *mō* combines with a quantity expression to indicate an added amount. Note that in Japanese *mō* "more" precedes the quantity.

mō chotto	a little more
mō hito-tsu	one more

When you offer something, *motto* is more polite, but when you accept an offer, *mō sukoshi* "a little more" is more polite.

Motto nomimasen ka.	Won't you drink more?
-Ja, mō sukoshi itadakimasu.	Well then, I'll take a little more.

GRAMMAR NOTE Colors

Some colors have both an adjective and a noun form, as shown in the list above. Thus it is possible to say both *aka desu* and *akai desu* to mean "It's red". The negative forms are *aka ja nai desu* and *akaku nai desu* respectively. The correct one to use largely depends on the convention. It is probably safe to assume the noun versions indicate classification and the adjective versions indicate characteristics (*aka* for red wines and *ao* for the green traffic light, for example). The color words borrowed from other languages such as *howaito* "white" and *pinku* "pink" are nouns in Japanese.

CULTURAL NOTE Tea

Tea is the most common beverage in Japan. Various types of tea are widely available but green tea is the most common. *Ocha* usually refers to green tea and is to be enjoyed without sugar or milk.

Tea is commonly served to visitors at homes or in offices. It is complimentary at restaurants. Many types of tea, hot or cold, are also sold in plastic bottles and cans at stores and vending machines.

Powdered green tea, *matcha*, is the central element of the refined tea ceremony at which a host serves guests tea in a ritualized manner within the confined space of a tearoom. The emphasis is on etiquette, hospitality, and spirituality.

PATTERN PRACTICE 5

Cue: *Chi'isai pasokon wa ikaga desu ka.*
           How would you like a small laptop?

Response: *Ā, chi'isai no ga i'i desu ne.*
           Oh, a small one would be good.

Cue: *Dentō-teki na ryōri wa ikaga desu ka.*
           How would you like a traditional dish?

Response: *Ā, dentō-teki na no ga i'i desu ne.*
           Oh, a traditional one would be good.

Repeat the above drill using the following information.
1. *Yasai no piza wa ikaga desu ka.*
2. *Yūmei na mise wa ikaga desu ka.*
3. *Ichigo no kēki wa ikaga desu ka.*
4. *Kono kirei na okashi wa ikaga desu ka.*
5. *Amerika no ōki'i kaisha wa ikaga desu ka.*

PATTERN PRACTICE 6

Cue: *Osake, motto ikaga desu ka.*
           How about more sake?

Response: *Osake desu ka. Ja, mō sukoshi dake.*
           Sake? Then, just a little more.

Cue: *Kēki, motto ikaga desu ka.*
           How about more cake?

Response: *Kēki desu ka. Ja, mō sukoshi dake.*
           Cake? Then, just a little more.

Repeat the above drill using the following information.
1. *Ocha, motto ikaga desu ka.*
2. *Gohan, motto ikaga desu ka.*
3. *Okashi, motto ikaga desu ka.*
4. *Mikan, motto ikaga desu ka.*
5. *Kudamono, motto ikaga desu ka.*

EXERCISE 5
Say it in Japanese
You have found something unusual in your dish.
1. What is this red thing (one)?
2. What is this small black thing?
3. Is this white one a vegetable?
4. Is this yellow one a fruit?
5. Is this purple one a grape?

At a store, request the following items.
6. That blue one, please.
7. One more piece of this cake, please.
8. A cheaper one, please.
9. Three green ones and two brown ones, please.
10. More traditional ones, please.

EXERCISE 6
Role Play
1. A dish has been served. Exclaim how appetizing it looks.
2. You've been served an unusual dish. Exclaim how beautiful it is and ask if it is a traditional dish.
3. As a host, urge your guests to eat and drink more. As a guest, be polite and respond.
4. Discuss certain schools, restaurants, and companies. (big/small, old/new, expensive/cheap, famous, beautiful, close/far, difficult/easy, interesting/boring, etc.)
5. A friend got a perfect score on a test. Express that you are completely impressed.

DIALOGUE 4 My Favorite Foods

Sato: What kind of food do you like?
            Donna tabemono ga suki desu ka.
            どんな食べ物が好きですか。

Michael: I like Japanese food.
            Washoku ga suki desu.
            和食が好きです。

Sato: Do you make them often?
            Yoku tsukurimasu ka.
            よく作りますか。

Michael: Well... sometimes.
            Mā, tokidoki.
            まあ、時々。

Sato: Are you okay with chopsticks?
            Ohashi wa daijōbu desu ka.
            お箸は大丈夫ですか。

Michael: Yes.
            Ee.
            ええ。

VOCABULARY

don'na	どんな	what kind
tabemono	食べ物	food
suki(na)	好き	like
Washoku	和食	Japanese food
tsukurimasu	作ります	make
mā	まあ	well; I guess (non-committal)
tokidoki	時々	sometimes
(o)hashi	（お）箸	chopsticks
daijōbu (na)	大丈夫（な）	okay; fine
kaimasu	買います	buy
kirai (na)	きらい（な）	dislike
dame (na)	だめ（な）	no good; broken
Yōshoku	洋食	Western food
Chūka	中華	Chinese food
Furenchi	フレンチ	French food
Itarian	イタリアン	Italian
esunikku	エスニック	ethnic food

For other non-Japanese food, add ***-ryōri*** to the country name, as ***kankoku-ryōri*** "Korean food".

Tableware

supūn	スプーン	spoon
fōku	フォーク	fork
naifu	ナイフ	knife
osara	お皿	plate; dish
chawan	茶碗	rice bowl; tea cup
owan	お椀	small bowl (for soup)
donburi	丼	bowl; bowl of rice with food on top
koppu	コップ	glass; cup
kappu	カップ	cup (tea, coffee)

More Food

niku	肉	meat
sakana	魚	fish
gyū-niku	牛肉	beef
buta-niku	豚肉	pork
tori-niku	鶏肉	chicken
yasai	野菜	vegetable
tamago	卵、玉子	egg
nori	のり	seaweed
ebi	えび	shrimp
sake	鮭	salmon

Condiments

shōyu	しょうゆ	soy sauce
miso	みそ	miso
shio	塩	salt
koshō	こしょう	pepper
satō	砂糖	sugar

GRAMMAR NOTE Double Subject Structures

A Japanese sentence can have more than one subject phrase. This is called a double-subject sentence. Consider the following sentences.

Watashi wa	[*ohashi wa daijōbu desu.*]	I'm fine with chopsticks.
Furansu wa	[*kēki ga oishi'i desu.*]	France has good cake.
Satō-san wa	[*Eigo mo jōzu desu.*]	Ms. Sato is good at English, too.

In each of these sentences, the bracketed portion describes an attribute or some fact about the main subject outside of the bracket. Both of the subject nouns (inside and outside of the brackets) can take the particles *ga*, *wa*, *mo*, or no particle at all, with a shift in meaning (*ga* = new information, *wa* = contrast, *mo* = addition, or no particle = neutral).

Special note should be taken of nouns such as *suki* "like", and *kirai* "dislike", and a group of verbs such as *wakarimasu* "understand" and *dekimasu* "can do", which indicate a state rather than an action in Japanese. Therefore, particle *o* (object-marker) is impossible with these predicates.

Honda-san wa Eigo ga dekimasu.	Ms. Honda can speak English.
Kodomo wa yasai wa kirai desu.	Children do not like vegetables. (They may like other things.)

PATTERN PRACTICE 7

Cue:	*Tabemasu yo.*	I'm going to eat.
Response:	*Nani o tabemasu ka.*	What are you going to eat?
Cue:	*Suki desu.*	I like it.
Response:	*Nani ga suki desu ka.*	What do you like?

Repeat the above exercise using the following information.
1. *Kaimasu.*
2. *Wakarimasu.*
3. *Benkyō-shimasu.*
4. *Jōzu desu.*
5. *Dekimasu.*

PATTERN PRACTICE 8

Cue:	*Sushi, yoku tabemasu nē.*	
	You eat sushi a lot, don't you!	
Response:	*Ee, watashi wa sushi ga suki desu kara.*	
	Yes, because I like sushi.	
Cue:	*Gēmu, yoku shimasu nē.*	
	You play a lot of games, don't you!	
Response:	*Ee, watashi wa gēmu ga suki desu kara.*	
	Yes, because I like games.	

Repeat the above exercise using the following information.
1. *Bīru, yoku nomimasu nē.*
2. *Sanpo, yoku shimasu nē.*
3. *Manga, yoku yomimasu nē.*
4. *Chūka, yoku tsukurimasu nē.*
5. *Obentō, yoku kaimasu nē.*

EXERCISE 7
Say it in Japanese
You've been asked about what kind of food you like.
1. I like Chinese food. And I like Japanese food as well.
2. I like meat. I often eat steak, hamburgers, *yaki-niku*, etc.
3. I like traditional Japanese dishes. However, I like French cuisine more.
4. I like fruit and vegetables. Fish is okay. I don't hate it, but I don't eat it very much.

EXERCISE 8
Role Play
1. Ask a co-worker what kind of 1) food; 2) color; 3) movie she likes.
2. Ask a co-worker if he makes dinner.
3. At a restaurant, ask a waiter for 1) chopsticks; 2) more water; 3) two more forks.
4. At the dinner table, ask someone to pass the salt and pepper.
5. You've been asked how the food was. Give a non-committal (wishy washy) response.

REVIEW QUESTIONS
1. a) How do you count people in Japanese?
    b) How about books, tickets, dogs, meetings, apples, and bottles of drinks?
2. Where in a Japanese sentence do quantity expressions usually occur?
3. What is the difference between the following?
    1) *Sato-san o mimashita.*
    2) *Sato-san ga mimashita.*
4. What is the difference among the following?
    1) *Piza kimashita.*   3) *Piza mo kimashita.*
    2) *Piza wa kimashita.*   4) *Piza ga kimashita.*
5. a) What endings do Japanese adjectives have? b) What is the difference?
6. How is the adjective *i'i* different from other adjectives?
7. a) What are *na*-nouns?   b) How are they different from regular nouns?
8. Describe four ways to extend a noun into a longer noun phrase.
9. a) How do you say the following in Japanese?
    1) American company
    2) big company
    3) famous company
    b) How can you avoid repeating "company" in these phrases?
10. What is the difference between *mō* and *motto*?
11. Describe the double-subject sentence structure.
12. What kinds of predicate occur in a double-subject sentence?

Um, where would the elevator be?
Anō… erebētā wa dochira deshō ka.

Elevator? It's over there. It's right near the stairs.
Erebētā desu ka. Achira ni gozaimasu. Kaidan no sugu soba desu.

Sorry. Can you say it slowly one more time?
Sumimasen. Mō ichi-do yukkuri, onegai-shimasu.

Excuse me. Fourth floor, please.
Sumimasen. Yon-kai, onegai-shimasu.

LESSON 5

Where is it?

When in Rome, do as Romans do (Lit., When enter the village, obey the village)
郷に入っては郷に従え ***Gou ni itte wa gou ni shitagae***

🔘 DIALOGUE 1 Going Shopping

Mei is about to go shopping (***kaimono***) with students of the International Club. She
is in charge of locking the room.

Mei: Where is everyone?
 Minna wa doko desu ka.
 みんなはどこですか。

Yuki: They are in the lobby.
 Robī ni imasu.
 ロビーにいます。

Mei: Huh? Where is the key?
 Are? Kagi, doko desu ka.
 あれ? かぎ、どこですか.

Yuki: Isn't it on the desk?
 Tsukue no ue ni arimasen ka.
 机の上にありませんか。

Mei: Oh, here it is! Good!
 A, arimashita! Yokatta!
 あ、ありました。よかった。

VOCABULARY

*minna**	みんな	everyone
doko	どこ	where
robī	ロビー	lobby
ni	に	at; in
imasu	います	be; exist (animate)
Are?	あれ?	Huh? (That's strange)
kagi	かぎ	key; lock
tsukue	机	desk
ue	上	top
arimasu	あります	is there; exist (inanimate)
arimasen	ありません	is not there
arimashita	ありました	was there

ADDITIONAL VOCABULARY

minasan	みなさん	everyone (polite)
koko	ここ	here
soko	そこ	there near you
asoko	あそこ	over there

Location Words

ue	上	the top; above
shita	下	under; below
mae	前	front; ahead
ushiro	後ろ	back; behind
naka	中	inside
soto	外	outside
migi	右	right
hidari	左	left
aida	間	between
tonari	隣	neighboring; next to
yoko	横	side
temae	手前	this side
saki	先	ahead
mukō	向こう	the other side; over there
soba	そば	near: in the vicinity

Furniture and Appliances

tēburu	テーブル	table
tsukue	机	desk
isu	いす	chair
sofā	ソファー	sofa
beddo	ベッド	bed
kyabinetto	キャビネット	cabinet
hondana	本棚	bookshelf
hikidashi	引き出し	drawer
hako	箱	box
purintā	プリンター	printer
kopī	コピー	photocopier (photo copying machine)
reizōko	冷蔵庫	refrigerator
sentaku-ki	洗濯機	washer
sōji-ki	掃除機	vacuum cleaner
eakon	エアコン	air conditioner

GRAMMAR NOTE Particle *ni* indicating Location

In Lesson 2, it was explained that particle *ni* indicates the time when something happens. In this lesson two more uses of the particle are introduced: the location of where someone/something is currently at, and the location where an action ends (goal).

With the verbs *imasu* or *arimasu* and their variations, the particle *ni* indicates where something/someone is located.

Nihon ni imasu.   He is in Japan. (person/animal)
Nihon ni arimasu.   It is in Japan. (thing)

With motion verbs such as *ikimasu* "go" and *kimasu* "come" and other verbs, the particle *ni* indicates the location the action is directed towards.

Amerika ni ikimasu.   I'll go to America.
Satō-san ni mēru-shimasu.   I'll email Ms. Sato.
Kaisha ni denwa shimasu.   I'll call my office.
Amerika ni kaerimasu.   I'll go back to the US.

Recall that *wa* and *mo* replace the particle *ga* for the subject or particle *o* for the object respectively. However, *wa* and *mo* are added to other particles (*de*, *ni*, *kara*, *made*, etc.)

Amerika ni mo arimasu.   They are in America, too.
Amerika ni wa ikimasen.   I will not be going to America.
                            (lit., As for America, I will not go.)

GRAMMAR NOTE *Arimasu, Imasu* = "There is", "Have", "Exists"

Both *X arimasu* and *X imasu* mean "there is X", "X exists", or "I have X". The difference is that *arimasu* is used for inanimate objects, plants, ideas, and events, while *imasu* is used for living things, such as people and animals. Even bacteria and ghosts are *imasu*. Live fish in the ocean are *imasu* while dead fish sold in a market are *arimasu*. Mechanical factory robots are *arimasu* while humanoid robots with artificial intelligence are more likely *imasu*. Now you get the idea.

There are two negative forms for *arimasu*: *arimasen* and *nai desu*. The latter is less formal. For the negative forms of noun and adjective predicates, *arimasen* and *arimasen deshita* can substituted for *nai desu* and *nakatta desu* respectively. These alternatives sound a little more elegant.

Sushi ja nai desu.→ Sushi ja arimasen.   It's not sushi.
Sushi ja nakatta desu.→ Sushi ja arimasen deshita.   It wasn't sushi.
Takaku nai desu.→ Takaku arimasen.   It's not expensive.
Takaku nakatta desu.→ Takaku arimasen deshita.   It wasn't expensive.

The chart below shows all the forms including these alternatives.

	Present/Future Tense		Past Tense	
	Affirmative	Negative	Affirmative	Negative
Verb predicate	*Arimasu.* It is there.	*Nai desu.* It is not there (casual). *Arimasen.* It is not there.	*Arimashita.* It was there.	*Nakatta desu.* It was not there (casual). *Arimasen deshita.* It was not there.
Noun predicate	*Sushi desu.* It is sushi.	*Sushi ja nai desu.* It is not sushi (casual). *Sushi ja arimasen.* It is not sushi.	*Sushi deshita.* It was sushi.	*Sushin ja nakatta desu.* It was not sushi (casual). *Sushin ja arimasen deshita.* It was not sushi.
Adjective Predicate	*Takai desu.* It is expensive.	*Takaku nai desu.* It is not expensive (casual). *Takaku arimasen.* It is not expensive.	*Takakatta desu.* It was expensive.	*Takaku nakatta desu.* It was not expensive (casual). *Takaku arimasen deshita.* It was not expensive.

An important warning is in order. Do not confuse the following sentences.
  Kagi ja arimasen/nai desu.   It's not a key. (Identity)
  Kaigi wa arimasen/nai desu.   There is no key. (Existence)

Also note that as seen earlier, X *desu* can replace any predicate that is understood from the context. Thus, it commonly replaces *ni arimasu/imasu.*
  Kagi wa doko ni arimasu ka.   Where is the key?
  Tsukue no ue desu yo.   It's on the desk.

GRAMMAR NOTE Location Words

The location words above are all nouns and take the structure of X *no* Y when combined with another noun. Recall that in X *no* Y, Y is the main noun. Compare:

mae no biru   the building in front

biru no mae   the front of the building; in front of the building

These location words, unlike other nouns, can combine with degree expressions.

sukoshi migi   a little to the right

motto mae   more to the front

mō shukoshi saki   a little further ahead

There are three *ko-so-a-do* sets for locations: *koko* "here", *kocchi* "this side; this direction", and *kochira* "this area; this direction". The *kochira* set is often used as more polite equivalents of the *koko* series.

	Here (near me)	There (near you)	Over there	Where
location	*koko*	*soko*	*asoko*	*doko*
direction	*kocchi*	*socchi*	*acchi*	*docchi*
general area/direction	*kochira*	*sochira*	*achira*	*dochira*

PATTERN PRACTICE 1

Cue: *Ue ni arimasu ka.*   Is it on top?

Response: *Ie, shita ni arimasu yo.*   No, it's underneath.

Cue: *Resutoran no mae ni arimasu ka.*

               Is it in front of the restaurant?

Response: *Ie, resutoran no ushiro ni arimasu yo.*

               No, it's at the back of the restaurant.

Repeat the drill using the following information:

1. *Migi ni arimasu ka.*
2. *Naka ni arimasu ka.*
3. *Kaisha no ushiro ni arimasu ka.*
4. *Tsukue no hidari ni arimasu ka.*
5. *Daigaku no soto ni arimasu ka.*

PATTERN PRACTICE 2

Cue: *Satō-san wa kaisha desu ka.*   Is Ms. Sato in the office?
Response: *Hai, kaisha ni imasu.*   Yes, she is in the office.
Cue: *Konpyūtā wa tonari desu ka.*
                   Is the computer in the (room) next door?
Response: *Hai, tonari ni arimasu.*   Yes, it is in the (room) next door.

Repeat the drill with the following information.
1. *Kaisha wa Taiwan desu ka.*
2. *Minna wa mukō desu ka.*
3. *Tomodachi wa ushiro desu ka.*
4. *Sensei no hon wa asoko desu ka.*
5. *Minna no obentō wa hako no naka desu ka.*

EXERCISE 1
Say it in Japanese
You've been asked where someone is.
1. She is beside Ms. Sato.
2. She is between Ms. Sato and Mr. Tanaka.
3. She was in the back before, but now she is not there.
4. She is in the coffee shop on the left.
5. She is in front of the coffee shop.

You've been asked where the key is.
1. Isn't it in the box?
2. Isn't it in the box on the desk?
3. Isn't it under the box on the desk?
4. Isn't it in the drawer of that desk over there?
5. Isn't it next to the TV?

EXERCISE 2
Role Play
1. Ask a tour guide where everyone is.
2. You misplaced your cellphone. Ask a co-worker if she has seen it.
3. You've heard the name of a Japanese city. Find out where in Japan it is located.
4. Discuss with a co-worker what pieces of furniture and appliances you have and how they are arranged in your room.
5. You see a stranger sitting next to a *senpai*. Ask a co-worker who that is.

DIALOGUE 2 Driving in Town

On a business trip Ms. Sato drives while Michael checks the GPS.

Sato: Where might the parking lot be?
Chūsha-jō wa dono hen deshō ka.
駐車場はどの辺でしょうか。

Michael: You (should) turn right at the next intersection.
Tsugi no kōsaten de migi ni magarimasu.
次の交差点で右に曲がります。

They approach the parking structure.

Sato: Here we are, right?
Koko desu ne?
ここですね？

Michael: Hey, watch out! This is the exit, right? The entrance is on the opposite side.
A abunai! Koko wa deguchi deshō. Iriguchi wa hantai-gawa desu yo.
あ、危ない！ここは出口でしょう。入り口は反対側ですよ。

VOCABULARY

chūsha-jō	駐車場	parking lot
hen	辺	area
tsugi	次	next
kōsaten	交差点	intersection
de	で	at
magarimasu	曲がります	make turn
abunai	危ない	dangerous
deguchi	出口	exit
iriguchi	入り口	entrance
hantai	反対	opposite
-gawa	側	side
hantai-gawa	反対側	opposite side

ADDITIONAL VOCABULARY

kuruma	車	car
unten-shimasu	運転します	drive (verb)
tomemasu	止めます	park (verb)
norimasu	乗ります	get on (a vehicle)
watarimasu	渡ります	cross

Gī-pī-esu,	GPS	GPS
Kā-nabi (car navigation)	カーナビ	
chizu	地図	map
eria mappu	エリアマップ	area map

Buildings and Structures in Town

michi	道	street; road
biru (modern),	ビル、	building
tatemono	建物	
kōban	交番	police box
an'nai-jo	案内所	information booth
taishikan	大使館	embassy
ryōjikan	領事館	consulate
ie	家	house
apāto	アパート	apartment
manshon	マンション	condominium
ryō	寮	dormitory
depāto	デパート	department store
sūpā	スーパー	supermarket
mōru	モール	shopping mall
konbini	コンビニ	convenience store
eki	駅	station
eki-biru	駅ビル	station building
ginkō	銀行	bank
byōin	病院	hospital
kōen	公園	park
gakkō	学校	school
toshokan	図書館	library
eigakan	映画館	movie theater
sābisu eria	サービスエリア	service area
gasorin sutando	ガソリンスタンド	gas station
singō	信号	traffic light
kado	角	corner
hashi	橋	bridge
ōdan-hodō	横断歩道	pedestrian crossing
hodō-kyō	歩道橋	pedestrian bridge

GRAMMAR NOTE X *deshō* to Indicate Probability

Deshō is a tentative form of *desu* and indicates probability or the likelihood of something happening. It replaces *desu* and can occur after an adjective or a noun.

Oishi'i deshō.　　　It's probably tasty.

Nihon-jin deshō.　　She's probably a Japanese.

When the particle *ka* is added to *deshō*, it becomes even less sure. For this reason, *deshō ka* sounds more polite than *desu ka* in asking questions. Note the falling intonation on *ka*.

Doko deshō ka. Where might it be?

When *deshō* is used with a question intonation, it indicates that the speaker feels something is self-evident and the other person would certainly agree. In the dialogue, Michael thinks it's unmistakably clear that it is an exit and alerts Ms. Sato to it by saying **Deguchi deshō?** You can also use **deshō?** alone to this effect when the topic is clear.

Ā, oishi'i desu! Oh, it's delicious!

-Deshō? Isn't it? (I knew you would say so.)

GRAMMAR NOTE Particle *de* Indicating Location of Activity

A place noun followed by particle *de* indicates the location where some activity takes place. Depending on the context, it can be translated as "in", "at", or "on" in English.

Kōsaten de magarimasu. We'll turn at the intersection.

Amerika de benkyō-shimashita. I studied in America.

Note that both *ni* and *de* can follow a location noun but there is a clear difference between them. The particle *ni* indicates the location of existence or the point towards which an action is directed. On the other hand, the particle *de* indicates a broader area where an action occurs.

Kōsaten de migi ni magarimasu.

I'll turn right at the intersection.

When an activity such as a meeting is held somewhere, the location is marked by the particle *de* rather than *ni* because it is an activity. Compare the following.

Kaigi wa kaisha de arimasu.

The meeting is (held) in the company.

Konpyūtā wa kaisha ni arimasu.

The computer is (located) in the company.

The particles *wa* and *mo* can be added to particle *de* to indicate contrast or addition.

Nihon de wa ohashi o tsukaimasu. In Japan, we use chopsticks.

Chūgoku de mo ohashi o tsukaimasu. In China, they use chopsticks, too.

CULTURAL NOTE *Konbini* "Convenience Store"

Convenience stores are everywhere in Japan and truly convenient. You can find a large range of hot and cold meals, snacks, alcoholic and non-alcoholic beverages, and other goods for sale 24 hours a day seven days a week. Convenience stores

are known for the high quality of their food. They also offer services such as ATM access, copying, faxing, digital photo developing, ticket reservations, bill pay, and delivery drop-off/pick-up. Many convenience stores also offer a small eat-in area, a clean restroom, and Wi-Fi service free of charge. However, make sure you buy a little something as a courtesy to the store, when you use Wi-Fi or the toilet.

Some convenience stores do not accept credit cards unless your purchase exceeds a certain amount. However, they accept digital train fare passes such as "Suica" and "PASMO". These digital cards can be purchased from vending machines and pre-loaded and re-loaded as needed.

PATTERN PRACTICE 3

Cue:	*Ikimasu ka.*	Will you go?
Response:	*Hai, asoko ni ikimasu.*	Yes, I'll go there.
Cue:	*Magarimasu ka.*	Will you (make a) turn?
Response:	*Hai, asoko de magarimasu.*	Yes, I'll (make a) turn there.

Repeat the drill using the following information:
1. *Kaimasu ka.*
2. *Arimasu ka.*
3. *Tabemasu ka.*
4. *Imasu ka.*
5. *Benkyō-shimasu ka.*

PATTERN PRACTICE 4

Cue:	*Are wa iriguchi desu ka.*	Is that an entrance?
Response:	*Yoku wakarimasen kedo, iriguchi deshō.*	
	I'm not sure, but it probably is.	
Cue:	*Are wa depāto desu ka.*	Is that a department store?
Response:	*Yoku wakarimasen kedo, depāto deshō.*	
	I'm not sure, but it probably is.	

Repeat the drill using the following information:
1. *Are wa chūsha-jō desu ka.*
2. *Are wa kōen desu ka.*
3. *Are wa gakkō desu ka.*
4. *Are wa taishikan desu ka.*
5. *Are wa eki desu ka.*

EXERCISE 3
Say it in Japanese
You've been asked where something is located. Answer in Japanese.
1. Station? It's a little further ahead.
2. The entrance to the mall? It's on the other side.
3. A map? It's probably at the entrance of this building.
4. A park? It's probably behind the library.
5. A convenience store? It's in front of that brown building, right? (You should know it.)

You've been asked how to get to a destination.
6. You take this street.
7. You turn left at the next corner.
8. You cross the bridge. Then you go to the right.
9. You park behind the building. The entrance is on the right.
10. You turn left at the next traffic light. You'll see it right there. (*Sugu wakarimasu.*)

EXERCISE 4
Role Play
1. Stop a stranger and politely ask if the following are in this area:
   1) a gas station;
   2) ATM;
   3) hospital;
   4) police box;
   5) information booth
2. A stranger has mistaken an exit for an entrance. Warn him that it is the exit. The entrance is over there.
3. You've been asked about a restaurant. Mention that you are not sure, but it is probably:
   1) expensive;
   2) not expensive;
   3) a sushi shop;
   4) not a sushi shop.
4. A pedestrian is not aware of an approaching car. Warn him.
5. Using a map, explain how to get to a destination.

🔘 DIALOGUE 3 In the Department Store

Mei wants to go to the fourth floor but cannot find the elevator. She asks a shop clerk for help.

Mei: Um, where would the elevator be?
Anō... Erebētā wa dochira deshō ka.
あのう、エレベーターは、どちらでしょうか。

Clerk: Elevator? It's over there. It's right near the stairs.
Erebētā desu ka. Achira ni gozaimasu. Kaidan no sugu soba desu.
エレベーターですか。あちらにございます。階段のすぐそばです。

Mei: Sorry. Can you say (that) slowly one more time?
Sumimasen. Mō ichi-do yukkuri, onegai-shimasu.
すみません。もう一度ゆっくりお願いします。

In the elevator...

Mei: Excuse me. Fourth floor, please.
Sumimasen. Yon-kai, onegai-shimasu.
すみません。四階、お願いします。

VOCABULARY

erebētā	エレベーター	elevator
gozaimasu	ございます	exist

*Gozaimasu is a polite version of *arimasu*, which is typically used by service people.

kaidan	階段	staircase
sugu	すぐ	soon
soba	そば	nearby
ichi-do	一度	one time
mō ichi-do	もう一度	one more time
yukkuri	ゆっくり	slowly; in a relaxed manner

*Yukkuri-shimasu means "relax and enjoy the time". *Dōzo go-yukkuri* means "Please take your time and enjoy", which you may often hear from service people.

yon-kai	四階	4th floor; four floors

ADDITIONAL VOCABULARY

esukarētā	エスカレーター	escalator
toire	トイレ	toilet
chika	地下	basement
sābisu kauntā	サービスカウンター	service counter

Department Store Items

kutsu	靴	shoes
kasa	傘	umbrella
kaban	かばん	bag
handobaggu	ハンドバッグ	handbag
fuku	服	clothes
kimono	着物	kimono
nekutai	ネクタイ	necktie
keshō-hin	化粧品	cosmetics
omocha	おもちゃ	toy
kagu	家具	furniture
megane	めがね	glasses, spectacles
tokei	時計	watch; clock
bunbōgu	文房具	stationery
akusesarī	アクセサリー	accessories

GRAMMAR NOTE **More Classifiers** *-kai, -do/-kai*

The classifier for floors of a building is *-kai/-gai* 階 and the classifiers for counting the number of times are *-do* and *-kai* 回 (recall *Mō ichi-do onegai-shimasu.* "One more time, please.") Note the difference between these two questions:

Nan-kai arimasu ka. "How many floors are there?"
Nan-kai ni arimasu ka. "On which floor is it?"

	floors	times/occasions	
1	*ik-kai*	*ichi-do*	*ik-kai*
2	*ni-kai*	*ni-do*	*ni-kai*
3	*san-kai/san-gai*	*san-do*	*san-kai*
4	*yon-kai*	*yon-do*	*yon-kai*
5	*go-kai*	*go-do*	*go-kai*
6	*rok-kai*	*roku-do*	*rok-kai*
7	*nana-kai*	*nana-do*	*nana-kai*
8	*hachi-kai/hak-kai*	*hachi-do*	*hachi-kai/hak-kai*
9	*kyū-kai*	*kyū-do*	*kyū-kai*
10	*juk-kai/jikkai*	*jū-do*	*juk-kai/jikkai*
11	*nan-kai*	*nan-do*	*nan-kai*

CULTURAL NOTE *Depa-chika* "The Basement of a Department Store"

Japanese department stores (*depāto*) provide a one-stop shopping experience offering a wide range of high quality goods from well-known brands. Prices are generally higher, but customer service is unparalleled.

Depa-chika refers to the basement floor of a department store and is a gourmet heaven of fine-quality foods, fresh foods, ready-to-eat dishes, sweets, delicacies and beverages from around Japan and the world, all of which are enticingly displayed. It caters to all shoppers, providing them with take-away lunches or dinners, souvenirs and gifts, or dishes to celebrate special occasions. Most department stores open around 10 a.m. and stay open until 8. Late in the day, stores slash prices to move perishable items. Naturally *depa-chika* is most crowded around that time.

PATTERN PRACTICE 5

Cue: *Erebētā wa dochira deshō ka.*
              Where might the elevator be?
Response: *Erebētā desu ka. Iriguchi no sugu soba desu.*
              Elevator? It's right near the entrance.
Cue: *Kaidan wa dochira deshō ka.*
              Where might the stairs be?
Response: *Kaidan desu ka. Iriguchi no sugu soba desu.*
              Stairs? They are right near the entrance.

Repeat the drill using the following information.
1. *Esukarētā wa dochira deshō ka.*
2. *Toire wa dochira deshō ka.*
3. *Sābisu kauntā wa dochira deshō ka.*
4. *Shokudō wa dochira deshō ka.*
5. *Eki wa dochira deshō ka.*

PATTERN PRACTICE 6

Cue: *Kasa to kaban wa ik-kai desu ka.*
              Are umbrellas and bags on the 1st floor?
Response: *Kasa wa ik-kai desu kedo, kaban wa ni-kai desu.*
              Umbrellas are on the 1st floor, but bags are on the 2nd floor.
Cue: *Megane to omocha wa rok-kai desu ka.*
              Are glasses and toys on the 6th floor?
Response: *Megane wa rok-kai desu kedo, omocha wa nana-kai desu.*
              Glasses are on the 6th floors, but toys are on the 7th floors.

Repeat the drill using the following information.
1. *Kutsu to kasa wa ni-kai desu ka.*
2. *Handobaggu to kasa wa yon-kai desu ka.*
3. *Tokei to megane wa go-kai desu ka.*
4. *Omocha to kagu wa hachi-kai desu ka.*
5. *Kimono to fuku wa san-gai desu ka.*

EXERCISE 5
Say it in Japanese
Politely ask the following at the information desk in a department store.
1. Where is the customer service counter?
2. Where are the bags, handbags, etc.?
3. On what floor is the women's clothing located?
4. At what time do you close today? (Until what time is it today?)
5. Are there maps in English?

EXERCISE 6
Role Play
1. You didn't get the directions someone has just provided you. Politely request that she repeat it slowly one more time.
2. The elevator door has just opened. Ask if it is going:
    1) up;
    2) down;
    3) to the tenth floor.
3. Suggest that you take (go by means of)
    1) an elevator;
    2) escalator;
    3) stairs.
4. You've been asked if this is your first time in Japan. Mention that you came here twice before.
5. Using a floor map of the following to ask and answer where you can find the goods you are looking for.
    1) a department store;
    2) a supermarket;
    3) a convenience store

⊙ DIALOGUE 4 Taking a Break in a Café

Michael and Ms. Sato have been out on business all day. They decide to take a break at a nearby café.

Michael: Exhausted, aren't we?
           Tsukaremashita ne.
           疲れましたね。
Sato: Let's just take a break.
           Chotto kyūkei-shimashō.
           ちょっと休憩しましょう。

As they enter the café, they look for a place to sit.

Michael: Where shall we sit?
           Doko ni suwarimashō ka.
           どこにすわりましょうか。
Sato: You'd like near the window, right?
           Mado no soba ga i'i deshō.
           窓のそばがいいでしょう。
Michael: Right.
           Sō desu ne.
           そうですね。

VOCABULARY

tsukaremasu	疲れます	become tired
kyūkei	休憩	(short) break
kyūkei-shimasu	休憩します	take a break
kyūkei-shimashō	休憩しましょう	Let's take a break
suwarimasu	座ります	sit
mado	窓	window

ADDITIONAL VOCABULARY

doa	ドア	door
seki	席	seat
benchi	ベンチ	bench

GRAMMAR NOTE Verb–*mashō* = "Let's Do Something"

V-*mashō* can replace V-*masu* and means "let's do X" or "why don't I do X". It is used to make a suggestion or offer to do something.

Yasumimashō.	Let's take a break.
Yasumimashō ka.	Shall we take a break?

Note that the question form **-*mashō ka*** typically has a falling intonation. It is more polite than **-*mashō*** alone because the addressee can say no to the question. Verbs such as **arimasu**, **dekimasu**, and **wakarimasu** do not occur in the **-*mashō*** form because they all indicate something beyond one's control.

As for the doer of the action in this pattern, the speaker is always included, but the addressee might not be included, depending on the context.

Watashi ga shimashō.	Why don't I do it?

Now, how do you respond to a suggestion or an offer made to you?
* When you're responding to a suggestion:

To agree	*-Sō shimashō.*	Let's do that.
To disagree	*-Iya, chotto….*	No, just….

* When someone has offered to do something for you:

To accept it	*-Hai, onegai-shimasu.*	Yes, please.
To turn it down	*-Ie, daijōbu desu.*	No thank you (I'm fine.)

Warning: Make sure you do not confuse *deshō* "probably" and V-*mashō*.

PATTERN PRACTICE 7

Cue:	*Yasumimasen ka.*
	Why don't we take a break?
Response:	*Sō desu ne. Yasumimashō.*
	Right. Let's take a break.
Cue:	*Koko ni suwarimasen ka.*
	Why don't we sit here?
Response	*Sō desu ne. Koko ni suwarimashō.*
	Right. Let's sit here.

Repeat the drill using the following information.
1. *Depāto de kaimasen ka.*
2. *Kuruma ni norimasen ka.*
3. *Hashi o watarimasen ka.*
4. *Chūsha-jō ni tomemasen ka.*
5. *Erebētā de ikimasen ka.*

PATTERN PRACTICE 8

Cue: ***Kasa o kaimashō.***
              Let's buy an umbrella.
Response: ***Doko de kaimashō ka.***
              Where shall we buy it?
Cue: ***Ohirugohan o tabemashō.***
              Let's have lunch.
Response: ***Doko de tabemashō ka.***
              Where shall we have it?

Repeat the drill using the following information.
1. ***Chotto yasumimashō.***
2. ***Chizu o mimashō.***
3. ***Michi o watarimashō.***
4. ***Kōhī o nomimashō.***
5. ***Yukkuri hanashimashō.***

EXERCISE 7
Say it in Japanese
You are discussing weekend plans. Suggest the following.
1. Let's watch Star Wars one more time.
2. Let's shop at a department store.
3. Let's do our Japanese homework, then let's eat dinner at the new restaurant.
4. Why don't we make a reservation for the table near the window? Why don't I call now?
5. Let's have an organizational meeting at an ***izakaya***. Why don't I email ***Senpai***?

EXERCISE 8
Role Play
1. Your group has been working hard. Acknowledge this and suggest that everyone take a break.
2. You and a friend are picking seats on a tour bus. Suggest that you sit:
   1) more front;
   2) further back;
   3) near the door;
   4) on the right side.
3. At a restaurant, ask your group what food and drinks you should order.
4. Your boss cannot attend a meeting. Volunteer to go in her place.

5. A co-worker wants to practice English. Offer to talk:
    1) in English;
    2) more slowly.

REVIEW QUESTIONS

1. What is the difference between *arimasu*, *imasu*, and *gozaimasu*?
2. a) What does *deshō* mean?
   b) What about when it has a rising intonation?
3. a) What does verb-*mashō* mean?
   b) Who is always included as a doer of the action?
4. What particle is most appropriate in the following blanks?
    1) *Satō-san wa Amerika____imasu.*
    2) *Yon-kai made erebētā ___ikimashō.*
    3) *Mainichi gakkō ___ikimasu.*
    4) *Koko ___suwarimashō.*
    5) *Soto ___hanashimashō ka.*
5. a) How are floors counted or named?
   b) How about the number of times?

LESSON 6
Leisure Activities and Hobbies

Liking shows where your talent lies (What you like, you'll do well)
好きこそものの上手なれ ***Suki koso mono no jōzu nare***

🔘 DIALOGUE 1 Invitation to Kabuki

Yuki and Mei have been friends for a couple of months, and are now comfortable talking with each other casually. He asks Mei about her plans for the next day.

Yuki: Will you be busy tomorrow?
     Ashita isogashi'i?
     あした忙しい？

Mei: Not particularly.
     U'un, betsu ni.
     ううん、別に。

Yuki: Are you interested in things like Kabuki?
     Kabuki toka kyōmi aru?
     歌舞伎とか、興味ある？

Mei: Yes. It's a (part of) traditional Japanese culture, isn't it?
     Un, Nihon no dentō-bunka deshō.
     うん。日本の伝統文化でしょう。

Yūki: Then will you go?
     Ja, iku?
     じゃ、行く？

Mei: Okay.
     Okkē.
     オッケー。

After the show

Yuki: How was it? Was it interesting?
     Dō datta? Omoshirokatta?
     どうだった？おもしろかった？

Mei: Yes, it was the best.
     Un, saikō datta.
     うん、最高だった。

VOCABULARY

isogashi'i	忙しい	busy
betsu ni	別に	not particularly, not really
Kabuki	歌舞伎	Kabuki
kyōmi	興味	interest; curiosity
aru	ある	exist (plain form of *arimasu*)
bunka	文化	culture
dentō-bunka	伝統文化	traditional culture
Okkē	オッケー	OK
dō	どう	how
datta	だった	was (informal form of *deshita*)
omoshiroi	おもしろい	interesting
omoshirokatta	おもしろかった	was interesting
saikō	最高	best

ADDITIONAL VOCABULARY

tsumaranai	つまらない	boring
tanoshi'i	楽しい	enjoyable; fun
ima-ichi	いまいち	not quite; not quite satisfactory
sankyū	サンキュー	Thank you
baibai	バイバイ	bye

Traditional Cultural Activities
Performing Arts

Kabuki	歌舞伎	all-men Kabuki theater
Nō	能	Noh theater
Bunraku	文楽	puppetry theater

Martial Arts

Kendō	剣道	Japanese fencing
Kyūdō	弓道	Japanese archery
Jūdō	柔道	Judo
Aikidō	合気道	Aikido
Karate	空手	Karate
Sumō	相撲	Japanese wrestling

Aesthetic Arts

Sa-dō	茶道	tea ceremony
Ka-dō	華道	Japanese flower arrangement
Sho-dō	書道	Japanese calligraphy

GRAMMAR NOTE Speech Styles

Japanese people speak in different speech styles depending on the relationship between the speaker and addressee, the setting where the conversation occurs, the topic of the conversation, and other elements. The styles are not binary or clearly divided, but rather span a spectrum ranging from very careful to very casual.

Different linguistic features collectively contribute to an overall impression of how casual or careful the speech is.

Features	Careful Style	Casual Style
Predicate form	Formal	Informal
Words and expressions	Polite	Plain or colloquial
Contractions, abbreviations, Inversions, etc.	Less	More
Pronunciation	More enunciated	
Pitch, pace	Higher pitch, slower	Lower pitch, faster
Body language	Stiff	Relaxed

We started this book with the careful style because it is socially less risky. This is the style typically observed between people who have just met, between strangers, and in business situations. On the other hand, casual speech style is used in informal settings when the speaker is conversing with people close to him such as a friend, family member, child, or himself. Speech styles indicate the social and psychological distance between speakers. However, the distance can change even during the course of a conversation between the same pair of speakers. Each shift carries some linguistic and social meaning. Mature speakers will switch styles appropriately in a full range of linguistic arenas.

In this chapter, we introduce the most prominent feature of casual speech, the Informal forms of predicates.

GRAMMAR NOTE Informal Forms of Predicates

All Japanese sentences contain a predicate in either Formal or Informal form. The choice is binary. *Masu, desu,* and their negative and past forms are all Formal forms. Dictionaries do not list words in these forms. They list the Informal forms. How do we make Informal forms from the Formal forms?

• For Adjective predicates, drop *desu.*

Takai desu.	→ *Takai.*	It's expensive.
Takaku nai desu.	→ *Takaku nai.*	It's not expensive.
Takakatta desu.	→ *Takakatta.*	It was expensive.
Takaku nakatta desu.	→ *Takaku nakatta.*	It was not expensive.

• For Noun predicates, replace *desu* with *da* and *deshita* with *datta.* However, *da* in the sentence final position is often dropped.

Nihon-go desu.	→ *Nihon-go.*	It's Japanese.
Nihon-go ja nai desu.	→ *Nihon-go ja nai.*	It's not Japanese.
Nihon-go deshita.	→ *Nihon-go datta.*	It was Japanese.
Nihon-go ja nakatta desu	→ *Nihon-go ja nakatta.*	It was not Japanese.

• For verb predicates, you need to know the Informal form of each verb. There are conjugation rules for verbs in different groups. Japanese verbs are divided into the four groups: 1) *U*-verbs 2) *Ru*-verbs 3) Irregular verbs and 4) Special Polite verbs.

U-Verbs

This is the largest verb group. To make the plain form of a verb in this group, replace *-imasu* with *-u.* (Or drop *-masu* and change *i* to *u.*) A verb stem is the portion of the verb before *-masu.* The stem of the verbs in this group all end in *-i.*

Stem	Meaning	Informal Form
wakar-i	understand	→ *wakar-u*
ka-i	buy	→ *ka-u*
kak-i	write	→ *kak-u*
nom-i	drink	→ *nom-u*
oyog-i	swim	→ *oyog-u*
hanash-i	talk	→ *hanas-u*

Ru-Verbs

To make the plain form of the verbs in this group, replace *-masu* with *-ru.* In other words, you add *-ru* to the stem. The stem of the verbs in this group ends in *-e* or *-i.*

Stem	Meaning	Informal Form
tabe	eat	→ *tabe-ru*
mi	look	→ *mi-ru*

Note that the *-masu* ending indicates that the verb is a **Ru**-verb but the *-imasu* ending can indicate either a **U**-verb or a **Ru**-verb. You need to check the word's other forms to determine which group it belongs to. Also note that verbs with the *-eru* or *-iru* ending can be either **U** or **Ru**-verbs while verbs that have other endings are **U**-verbs (except for the few irregular verbs below). *Iru*, for example, can be either in **U**-verb or **Ru**-verb depending on where the cut is. Examine the following:

imasu	exist	→	*i-ru*
irimasu	need	→	*ir-u*
kaemasu	change	→	*kae-ru*
kaerimasu	go home	→	*kaer-u*

Irregular Verbs

There are only four irregular verbs in Japanese.

Formal form	Meaning		Informal Form
kimasu	come	→	*kuru*
shimasu	do	→	*suru*
arimasu	be	→	*aru*
ikimasu	go	→	*iku*

The reason why **arimasu** and **ikimasu** are in this group and not **U**-verbs will be explained later when we discuss the negative and past forms.

Special Polite Verbs

This group has only five verbs.

Formal form	Meaning		Informal Form
irasshaimasu	be; go; come	→	*irasshar-u*
gozaimasu	be	→	*gozar-u*
kudasaimasu	give (to me)	→	*kudasar-u*
nasaimasu	do	→	*nasar-u*
osshaimasu	say	→	*osshar-u*

The reasons why these are separated from **U**-verbs is because the /r/ before *-u* drops in the formal form before **masu**.

CULTURAL NOTE *Dō* 道 —a Spiritual Path to Mastery

Dō in *Yūki-dō* (Japanese fencing), *sa-dō* (Japanese tea ceremony) and other traditional arts literally means "the way" or "path", and carries an ethical and aesthetic connotation, strongly influenced by Zen philosophy. People study these disciplines (sometimes, more than one, since all paths lead to the same end) to acquire skill and also to achieve greater self-revelation, enlightenment, and character development.

There is a systematized practice (***keiko*** 稽古) and process leading to mastery. Fundamentals are learned through repetitive and choreographed practice of prescribed forms (***kata*** 型). Mastering the ***kata*** leads to an exploration of one's own practice style and an eventual parting with traditional wisdom. The repetitive and choreographed aspect of the practice and the emphasis on ethics and mind and body unity, rather than competition, differentiates Japanese martial arts from sports.

There are schools and training places (***dojo*** 道場) that teach these disciplines. Master teachers offer private lessons as well. In Japanese middle and high schools, many of these disciplines are taught as part of the curriculum and as after school club activities. Clubs provide opportunities for students to enjoy their hobbies, improve particular skills, and discipline themselves in the process. Clubs also teach students how to behave within the ***senpai-kōhai*** relationship.

PATTERN PRACTICE 1

Cue: ***Arimasu ka.***   Do you have it?
Response: ***Un, aru yo.***   Yes, I do.
Cue: ***Ikimasu ka.***   Do you go?
Response: ***Un, iku yo.***   Yes, I do.

Repeat this drill with the following information.
1. *Tabemasu ka.*
2. *Nomimasu ka.*
3. *Shimasu ka.*
4. *Kimasu ka.*
5. *Kaimasu ka.*
6. *Wakarimasu ka.*
7. *Hanashimasu ka.*
8. *Yomimasu ka.*
9. *Nemasu ka.*
10. *Kikimasu ka.*

PATTERN PRACTICE 2

Cue: ***Omoshirokatta desu nē.***   It was interesting, wasn't it?
Response: ***Un, omoshirokatta kedo…***   Yes, it was, but…
Cue: ***Saikō deshita nē.***   It was the best, wasn't it?
Response: ***Un, saikō datta kedo…***   Yes, it was, but…

Repeat this drill with the following information:
1. *Kirei deshita nē.*
2. *Tsumaranakatta desu nē.*
3. *Oishisō deshita nē.*
4. *Dame deshita nē.*
5. *Tanoshikatta desu nē.*

EXERCISE 1
Say it in Japanese
Ask a friend the following questions.
1. Are you busy tomorrow?
2. Do you work on Saturday?
3. Are you interested in Judo, Karate, etc.?
4. What do you do on Sunday?
5. Do you like Japanese traditional culture?

EXERCISE 2
Role Play
1. Ask a friend if he is interested in things like
    1) tea ceremony;
    2) Sumo;
    3) traditional sports.
2. Ask a friend if he is going to:
    1) go to the meeting;
    2) watch Sumo on TV;
    3) use this laptop;
    4) come again tomorrow;
    5) study more.
3. A friend has just taken an exam. Ask how it was.
4. Recommend some tourist attractions in your country to a friend. Explain why.
5. Find out what aspect of traditional culture of Japan a friend is interested in.

DIALOGUE 2 Vacations

Yuki: What are your plans for summer vacation?
        Natsu-yasumi wa dō suru no?
        夏休みはどうするの？

Mei: I'll be traveling with a friend.
        Tomodachi to ryokō-suru no.
        友だちと旅行するの。

Yuki: Where to?
        Doko ni?
        どこに？

Mei: Okinawa.
        Okinawa.
        沖縄。
        I can't wait to swim in the ocean.
        Hayaku umi de oyogitai nā!
        早く海で泳ぎたいなあ！

VOCABULARY

natsu	夏	summer
natsu-yasumi	夏休み	summer vacation
dō suru	どうする	what to do
no	の	it's the case
Okinawa	沖縄	Okinawa
hayaku	早く	quickly; soon
umi	海	ocean; sea
oyogu	泳ぐ	swim
oyogitai	泳ぎたい	want to swim
nā	なあ	casual version of *nē*

ADDITIONAL VOCABULARY

haru	春	spring
aki	秋	autumn
fuyu	冬	winter
kisetsu	季節	season
yama	山	mountain; hill
asobu	遊ぶ	play
noboru	登る	climb
hairu	入る	go in; take (a bath)
odoru	踊る	dance
utau	歌う	sing

Leisure Activities

kaigai ryokō	海外旅行	trip abroad
inaka	田舎	countryside; hometown
onsen	温泉	hot spring
yama ni noboru	山に登る	climb a mountain
haikingu-suru	ハイキングする	hike
Fuji-san	富士山	Mt. Fuji
(o)tera	お寺	Buddhist temple
jinja	神社	Shinto shrine
kyōkai	教会	Christian church
(o)shiro	お城	castle
(o)matsuri	お祭り	festival
bijutsu-kan	美術館	museum

Islands	Cities	
Honshū	*Tōkyō*	*Fukuoka*
Kyūshū	*Kyōto*	*Sapporo*
Hokkaidō	*Ōsaka*	*Hiroshima*
Shikoku	*Nagoya*	*Kobe*
Okinawa	*Yokohama*	*Nara*

GRAMMAR NOTE V–*tai* Form = "Want to Do"

Verb-*tai* means " I want to do X". To make the *tai* form of a verb, add -*tai* to the verb stem (the portion before -*masu*). *Desu* can be added for the Formal form.

Tabe(masu)	→ *Tabetai* or *Tabetai desu.*	I want to eat it.
Nomi(masu)	→ *Nomitai* or *Nomitai desu.*	I want to drink it.

Note that the V-*tai* form is no longer a verb. It's an adjective. All of its forms follow the adjective patterns.

	Affirmative	Negative	
Non-past	*tabetai*	*Tabetaku nai.* (casual)	I don't want to eat it.
		Tabetaku arimasen.	I do not want to eat it.
Past	*tabetakatta*	*Tabetaku nakatta.* (casual)	I didn't want to eat it.
		Tabetaku arimasen deshita.	I did not want to eat it.

X-tai is typically used to express the speaker's desire ("I want to …") and to ask the addressee's desire ("Do you want to…?") but not a third person's desire ("He wants to …."). Also note that with the -*tai* form, the object of the verb can be marked either by the particle *ga* or *o*.

Nani o tabetai?	What do you want to eat?
Nani ga tabetai?	What do you want to eat?

Be careful not to use the *-tai* form when inviting or suggesting someone to do something. Use negative questions, instead.

    Tabemasen ka.   Wouldn't you like to have some? (Invitation)

    Tabetai desu ka.   Do you want to eat it? (Question)

GRAMMAR NOTE Predicate + *no* to Explain Situation

In the dialogue, Yuki asks what Mei's vacation plans are and Mei answers that she plans to travel with friends. Both of these sentences end with ***no***. The ***no*** added at the end of a sentence refers to the circumstance, or how things are. It provides an explanation or background information regarding the situation, similar to how we would say "So...", or "It's that...". In the dialogue, Yuki is aware that the summer holidays are approaching and assumes that Mei has plans. Thus he uses ***no*** to ask what her plans are, effectively saying, "So, what are your plans for the summer vacation?" Without ***no***, the question would sound general, and indicate no connection between the question and his assumption about the vacation.

No can be added to an adjective, noun, or verb predicate. Note that for a noun predicate, you need to insert ***na*** before ***no***. To make a Formal form, change ***no*** to ***n desu***. The ***no*** or ***n desu*** can be added to the Negative forms and Past forms as well.

    Adjective: ***Takai no.***   ***Takai n desu.***   It's that it's expensive.

    Verb: ***Kaeru no.***   ***Kaeru n desu.***   It's that I'm going home.

    Noun: ***Yasumi na no.***   ***Yasumi na n desu.***   It's that it's a break.

The /Sentence + ***no*** (***n desu***)/ pattern is VERY common in Japanese, and not using this pattern where it is expected may make the speaker seem insensitve or unaware of the circumstances.

How is the /***n desu***/ pattern different from ***kara*** "because"? A ***kara*** sentence specifically provides THE reason for something. On the other hand the /***n desu***/ pattern just draws attention to the background of the situation, and is softer and more indirect.

GRAMMAR NOTE Particle *to* Indicating Accompaniment

We learned earlier that the particle *to* connects nouns.

    ringo to mikan   apples and oranges

In this chapter, we introduce the particle *to* indicating with whom an action is performed. It connects the preceding noun to the verb.

    Tomodachi to Okinawa ni ikimasu.   I'm going to Okinawa with a friend.

    Sensei to hanashimashita.   I talked with a teacher.

Now how do you say, "I ate with chopsticks" in Japanese? This "with" does not refer to who you ate with but rather the means by which you ate. So, *Ohashi de tabemashita* is the correct answer.

CULTURAL NOTE **Religions in Japan**

Shinto (*Shintō* 神道), Buddhism (*Bukkyō* 仏教) and Christianity (*Kirisuto-kyō* キリスト教) are the three major religions in Japan with Shinto being the largest, practiced by nearly 80% of the population. However, religion in Japan usually refers to organized faiths and doctrines, and only a small percentage of people identify themselves as members of such organized religions. Most Japanese on the other hand participate in rituals and customs derived from Shinto and Buddhist traditions. They tend to consider these cultural traditions rather than religion.

Many Japanese households display both Shinto and Buddhist altars. The birth of a new baby is celebrated with a visit to a Shinto shrine. Wedding ceremonies are often performed by Shinto priests, but Christian-style wedding ceremonies are also popular these days. Funerals and memorial anniversaries for deceased family members are usually performed according to Buddhist traditions. This syncretism—blending of religions—is often described as "Born Shinto, Marry Christian, Die Buddhist".

Most festivals (*matsuri* 祭り) are associated with local Shinto shrines and follow local traditions. The two most significant holidays in Japan are New Year's Day, when people visit Shinto shrines (*jinja* 神社), and *Obon*, when people visit Buddhist temples (*otera* お寺) and honor the spirit of family ancestors.

Generally speaking, shrines can be identified by the entrance gate (*tori'i* 鳥居), often painted red. As you enter through the gate, you will find a water fountain where you wash your hands and rinse your mouth using water scooped with a bamboo ladle. Approach the altar, ring the bell with the rope, throw a coin into the offering box before the altar, clap three times, then clasp your hands together to pray. At a temple, take off your shoes before entering the main building and kneel on the *tatami*-floor before the altar and pray. Refrain from clapping while inside.

PATTERN PRACTICE 3

Cue:	*Ikitai?*	Do you want to go?
Response:	*U'un, ikitaku nai.*	No, I don't want to.
Cue:	*Nomitai?*	Do you want to drink?
Response:	*U'un, nomitaku nai.*	No, I don't want to.

Repeat this drill with the following:
1. *Tabetai?*
2. *Mitai?*
3. *Hatarakitai?*
4. *Kaitai?*
5. *Benkyō-shitai?*

PATTERN PRACTICE 4

Cue: *Umi de oyogu no?*
              So, you going to swim in the ocean, right?
Response: *Un, hayaku umi de oyogitai nā.*
              Yes, I can't wait.
Cue: *Okinawa ni iku no?*
              So, you are going to Okinawa, right?
Response: *Un, hayaku Okinawa ni ikitai nā.*
              Yes, I cannot wait.

Repeat the drill with the following information:
1. *Ryokō-suru no?*
2. *Sumaho kau no?*
3. *Bīru nomu no?*
4. *Kabuki miru no?*
5. *Fuji-san ni noboru no?*

EXERCISE 3
Say it In Japanese
You've been asked why you are going to Kyoto.
1. It's that it's a spring vacation.
2. It's that I love Kyoto.
3. It's that I have a friend there.
4. It's that I want to see shrines, temples, etc.
5. It's that I am interested in the traditional culture.

You are discussing your upcoming vacation. Express your excitement.
6. I can't wait to climb Mt. Fuji.
7. I can't wait to watch Kabuki.
8. I can't wait to go to Hokkaido with my friends.
9. I can't wait to take a hot spring bath.
10. I can't wait to play in Osaka and Kobe.

EXERCISE 4
Role Play
1. Ask a friend what his plans are for the winter vacation.
2. You are discussing vacations. Ask a friend where she wants to go and why.
3. A co-worker recommends that you visit Kyushu. Ask him what is interesting there.
4. You see a friend carrying a suitcase. Ask her if that means she is going to:
   1) travel;
   2) go back to China;
   3) take a trip abroad.
5. You are lost. Stop a stranger; let her know that you want to go to the castle (that's why you stopped her); and see if she knows where it is.

🄳 DIALOGUE 3 Going Sightseeing

Mei greets her neighbor outside her apartment.

Mei: It's a beautiful day, isn't it?
I'i otenki desu nē.
いいお天気ですねえ。

Yamamoto: Oh. Are you going out?
Ara. Odekake?
あら。お出かけ？

Mei: Yes, I'm sightseeing today.
E'e, kyō wa kankō desu.
ええ、今日は観光です。

Yamamoto: Oh, is that right? Have fun.
Ā, sō. Itte rasshai.
ああ、そう。行ってらっしゃい。

Mei and Yuki are checking bus tours to take.

Mei: How much is this tour?
Kono tsuā, ikura?
このツアー、いくら？

Yuki: It costs 5,980 yen per person.
Hitori go-sen kyū-hyaku hachi-jū-en.
一人5980円。

Mei: About how many dollars is that?
Sore wa nan-doru gurai?
それは何ドルぐらい？

Yuki: Let's see…approximately 55 dollars.
Etto, yaku go-jū-go-doru.
えっと、約55ドル。

Mei goes to the ticket counter.

Mei: Two adults (tickets) for Tour #15, please.
Jū-go-ban no tsuā, otona ni-mei onegai-shimasu.
15番のツアー、大人二名、お願いします。

Clerk: Certainly. That will be 11,960 yen.
Kashikomarimashita. De wa, ichi-man sen kyū-hyaku roku-jū-en ni narimasu.
かしこまりました。では、11,960円になります。

VOCABULARY

dekakeru	出かける	go out
kankō	観光	sightseeing
tsuā	ツアー	tour
ikura	いくら	how much
-en	円	yen
sen	千	thousand
go-sen	五千	five thousand
kyū-hyaku	九百	nine hundred
doru	ドル	dollar
nan doru	何ドル	how many dollars
-gurai	ぐらい	about
yaku	約	approximately
-ban	番	number; #
jū-go-ban	１５番	number 15
otona	大人	adult
de wa	では	then (formal version of *ja*)
ichi-man	一万	ten thousand
naru	なる	become; amount to
X ni naru	Xになる	it is X; it amounts to X

ADDITIONAL VOCABULARY

ame	雨	rain
yuki	雪	snow
atsui	暑い	hot
samui	寒い	cold
atatakai	暖かい	warm
suzushi'i	涼しい	cool
kodomo	子供	child
shinia	シニア	senior citizen
gaku-wari	学割	student discount
doru	ドル	dollar
tada	ただ	free of charge (colloquial)
muryō	無料	free of charge

Tokyo Tourist Spots

Tokyo Skytree	Ginza	Roppongi Hills	Asakusa	Meiji Jingu
Tokyo Tower	Akihabara	Harajuku	Sensō-ji	Ueno Park
Shinjuku	Shibuya	Hachiko		

Numbers (1 – 50,000)

1 *ichi*	11 *jū-ichi*	21 *nijū-ichi*	31 *sanjū-ichi*
2 *ni*	12 *jū-ni*	22 *nijū-ni*	32 *sanjū-ni*
3 *san*	13 *jū-san*	23 *nijū-san*	33 *sanjū-san*
4 *shi/yo/yon*	14 *jū-shi/yon*	24 *nijū-shi/yon*	34 *sanjū-shi/yon*
5 *go*	15 *jū-go*	25 *nijū-go*	35 *sanjū-go*
6 *roku*	16 *jū-roku*	26 *nijū-roku*	36 *sanjū-roku*
7 *shichi/nana*	17 *jū-shichi/ nana*	27 *nijū-shichi/ nana*	37 *sanjū-shichi/ nana*
8 *hachi*	18 *jū-hachi*	28 *nijū-hachi*	38 *sanjū-hachi*
9 *kyū/ku*	19 *jū-kyū/ku*	29 *nijū-kyū/ku*	39 *sanjū-kyū/ku*
10 *jū*	20 *nijū*	30 *sanjū*	40 *yonjū*

41 *yonjū-ichi*	51 *gojū-ichi*	61 *rokujū-ichi*	71 *nanajū-ichi*
42 *yonjū-ni*	52 *gojū-ni*	62 *rokujū-ni*	72 *nanajū-ni*
43 *yonjū-san*	53 *gojū-san*	63 *rokujū-san*	73 *nanajū-san*
44 *yonjū-shi/yon*	54 *gojū-shi/yon*	64 *rokujū-shi/yon*	74 *nanajū-shi/yon*
45 *yonjū-go*	55 *gojū-go*	65 *rokujū-go*	75 *nanajū-go*
46 *yonjū-roku*	56 *gojū-roku*	66 *rokujū-roku*	76 *nanajū-roku*
47 *yonjū-shichi/ nana*	57 *gojū-shichi/ nana*	67 *rokujū-shichi/ nana*	77 *nanajū-shichi/ nana*
48 *yonjū-hachi*	58 *gojū-hachi*	68 *rokujū-hachi*	78 *nanajū-hachi*
49 *yonjū-kyū/ku*	59 *gojūkyū/-ku*	69 *rokujūkyū/-ku*	79 *nanajū-kyū/ku*
50 *gojū*	60 *rokujū*	70 *nanajū*	80 *hachijū*

81 *hachijū-ichi*	91 *kyūjū-ichi*	100 *hyaku*	1,000 *sen*
82 *hachijū-ni*	92 *kyūjū-ni*	200 *ni-hyaku*	2,000 *ni-sen*
83 *hachijū-san*	93 *kyūjū-san*	300 *san-byaku*	3,000 *san-zen*
84 *hachijū-shi/yon*	94 *kyūjū-shi/yon*	400 *yon-hyaku*	4,000 *yon-sen*
85 *hachijū-go*	95 *kyūjū-go*	500 *go-hyaku*	5,000 *go-sen*
86 *hachijū-roku*	96 *kyūjū-roku*	600 *rop-pyaku*	6,000 *roku-sen*
87 *hachijū-shichi/ nana*	97 *kyūjū-shichi/ nana*	700 *nana-hyaku*	7,000 *nana-sen*
88 *hachijū-hachi*	98 *kyūjū-hachi*	800 *hap-pyaku*	8,000 *has-sen*
89 *hachijū-kyū/ku*	99 *kyūjūkyū/-ku*	900 *kyū-hyaku*	9,000 *kyū-sen*
90 *kyūjū*			

10,000 *ichi-man*	60,000 *roku-man*	how many 100's?	*nan-byaku*
20,000 *ni-man*	70,000 *nana-man*	how many 1,000's?	*nan-zen*
30,000 *san-man*	80,000 *hachi-man*	how many 10,000's?	*nan-man*
40,000 *yon-man*	90,000 *kyū-man*		
50,000 *go-man*	0 *rei/zero*		

GRAMMAR NOTE **Numbers Above 100**

In English numbers are grouped by thousands, millions, billions, and thus you see a comma after every three places to the left of the decimal—1,000,000,000. In Japanese, numbers are counted in groups of four places and traditionally a comma was inserted every four places—10,0000,0000. Ten thousand in Japanese has a special name *man*, and succeeding groups of four places, have the names *-oku* "one hundred million", and *-chō* "one trillion".

Note that you need to say *ichi* only for the last place in each four-place group. So, 10, 100 and 1000 do not require *ichi*.

1 *ichi*	10,000 *ichi-man*
10 *jū*	100,000 *jū-man*
100 *hyaku*	1,000,000 *hyaku-man*
1,000 *sen*	10,000,000 *sen-man*

¥1111,1111 is *sen hyaku jū ichi man sen hyaku jū ichi en*.

Also note the following sound changes.

For 100s (*hyaku*)	$h \rightarrow b$	300 *sanbyaku*
		?00 *nanbyaku* (how many hundreds?)
	$h \rightarrow pp$	600 *roppyaku*; 800 *happyaku*
For 1000s (*sen*)	$s \rightarrow z$	3000 *sanzen*
		?000 *nanzen* (how many thousands?)
	$s \rightarrow ss$	8000 *hassen*

The classifier *-en* is used for Japanese currency and *-doru* for US currency. *-ban* is used for numbers in order (first, second, etc.) As shown in the chart below, before *-en* the number four is *yo*, and the numbers seven and nine before *-en*, *doru* and *-ban* are *nana*, and *kyū*.

	-en	*-doru*	*-ban*
1.	*ichi-en*	*ichi-doru*	*ichi-ban*
2.	*ni-en*	*ni-doru*	*ni-ban*
3.	*san-en*	*san-doru*	*san-ban*
4.	*yo-en*	*yon-doru*	*yon-ban*
5.	*go-en*	*go-doru*	*go-ban*
6.	*roku-en*	*roku-doru*	*roku-ban*
7.	*nana-en*	*nana-doru*	*nana-ban*
8.	*hachi-en*	*hachi-doru*	*hachi-ban*
9.	*kyū-en*	*kyū-doru*	*kyū-ban*
10.	*jū-en*	*jū-doru*	*jū-ban*
	nan-en	*nan-doru*	*nan-ban*

The classifier *-ban* is also used for ranking (first place, second place, etc.) *Ichi-ban* is also used as an adverb to mean "most" or "best". The pitch accent changes for the adverbial use (*iCHIban → iCHIBAN*)

Ichi-ban suki   favorite; what you like the most
Ichi-ban atarashi'i   newest

GRAMMAR NOTE **Approximation**

Recall that *goro* combines with time classifiers to indicate approximate point in time. *Ichi-ji goro* means "around one o'clock". On the other hand, *gurai* and *yaku* both indicate an approximate quantity. *Gurai* follows quantity expressions while *yaku* precedes them.

Ichi-man-en gurai desu.   It's about ten thousand yen.
Yaku ichi-man-en desu.   It's about ten thousand yen.

You may even hear *yaku ichi-man-en gurai*. It may seem redundant to have the approximation expressed twice in the same phrase, but this is common. *Dore gurai* and *dono gurai* both ask "how long/how much" and *ikura gurai* asks "how much money".

Approximation, or making things vague, is preferred over being exact and considered more polite in many situations in Japan, possibly since an approximation allows for wiggle room. However, if a store clerk asks you how many items you want, using the phrase "about five of these", you will most likely get exactly five of that item.

PATTERN PRACTICE 5

Cue: *Hyaku-en desu ka.*   Is it 100 yen?
Response: *Ie, sen-en desu.*   No, it's 1,000 yen.
Cue: *Sen go-hyaku-en desu ka.*   Is it 1,500 yen?
Response: *Ie, ichi-man go-sen-en desu.*   No, it's 15,000 yen.

Repeat this drill with the following information:
1. *Yon-man-en desu ka.*
2. *Hap-pyaku-en desu ka.*
3. *San-zen-en desu ka.*
4. *San-byaku go-jū-en desu ka.*
5. *Nana-hyaku-man-en desu ka.*

PATTERN PRACTICE 6

Cue:　　　　*Go-jū-doru gurai desu ka.*　　Is it about $50?
Response:　*E'e, yaku go-jū-doru desu.*　　Yes, it's approximately $50.
Cue:　　　　*San-bon gurai desu ka.*　　Is it about three (bottles)?
Response:　*E'e, yaku san-bon desu.*　　Yes, it's approximately three (bottles).

Repeat the drill with the following information:
1. *Jū-nin gurai desu ka.*
2. *Hyak-ko gurai desu ka.*
3. *Mit-tsu gurai desu ka.*
4. *Ichi-man-en gurai desu ka.*
5. *Yon-jū go-man-doru gurai desu ka.*

EXERCISE 5
Say it in Japanese
You bumped into a neighbor on your way to work. Greet her with the following phrases.
1. It's a beautiful day, isn't it? Are you taking a walk?
2. It's cold today, isn't it? Are you going out?
3. It's raining today again, isn't it? It's cold, isn't it?
4. It was hot yesterday, but it's cool today, isn't it? See you later.
5. Do you suppose it is going to snow today? I can't wait to see snow!

EXERCISE 6
Role Play
1. At the ticket counter, ask how much the tour #10 is for:
    1) one adult;
    2) two adults and one child;
    3) a student and a senior citizen.
2. At a bank, ask a teller what the dollar to yen exchange rate is today (how many yen a dollar is equivalent to).
3. At an information desk, mention that you want to do sightseeing in this area and ask what places would be good to visit.
4. You are checking the budget for a trip. Ask a travel agent approximately how much this trip will amount to.
5. Discuss with a friend:
    1) what the best Japanese food is;
    2) what the most interesting video game is;
    3) who the coolest person is;
    4) when he is busiest at work/school.

⊙ DIALOGUE 4 At a *Nomi-kai* (After-work drinking)

Ms. Suzuki, the project chief, invites everyone to go out for drinks after work.

Suzuki: Why don't we go drink after this?
           Kono ato nomi ni ikanai?
           この後、飲みに行かない？

Sato: I'm busy today…
           Kyō wa chotto yotei ga…
           今日はちょっと予定が．．．

Michael: I'll go.
           Boku, ikimasu.
           僕、行きます。

At an *Izaka-ya*

Suzuki: What are your hobbies?
           Shumi wa nani?
           趣味は何？

Michael: It's sports. Skiing, soccer, etc.
           Supōtsu desu. Sukī toka sakkā toka.
           スポーツです。スキーとかサッカーとか。
           How about you?
           Suzuki-san wa?
           鈴木さんは？

Suzuki: My work is my hobby, so…
           Watashi wa shigoto ga shumi da kara.
           私は仕事が趣味だから。

Michael: C'mon! (You're) kidding, right?
           Matā! Jōdan deshō.
           またあ！冗談でしょう。

VOCABULARY

ato	後	later; after
kono ato	この後	after this
ni	に	for the purpose of X
nomi ni	飲みに	for the purpose of drinking
iku	行く	go
ikanai	行かない	not go
yotei	予定	plan
shumi	趣味	hobby
supōtsu	スポーツ	sports
sukī	スキー	ski
sakkā	サッカー	soccer

| *matā* | またあ | Again?; C'mon! (You always do this to me.) |
| *jōdan* | 冗談 | joke; kidding |

ADDITIONAL VOCABULARY

| *uso* | うそ | lie |
| *iu* | 言う | say; tell |

Hobbies

karaoke	カラオケ	karaoke
dokusho	読書	reading
ryokō	旅行	travel
ryōri	料理	cooking
ongaku	音楽	music
eiga	映画	movies
Netto	ネット	Internet
gēmu	ゲーム	(video) games
e	絵	painting; drawing
manga	マンガ	comic
anime	アニメ	animation
Shōgi	将棋	Japanese chess
Igo; Go	囲碁；碁	game of Go
shashin	写真	photography
uta	唄；歌	singing
gādeningu	ガーデニング	gardening
Pachinko	パチンコ	Japanese pinball

Sports and Physical Activities

yoga	ヨガ	yoga
dansu	ダンス	dance
basuke(tto bōru)	バスケットボール	basketball
yakyū	野球	baseball

GRAMMAR NOTE [Purpose] *Ni Iku* "Go to Do X"

Earlier we saw that the /X *ni iku*/ means "go to X" and X stands for the goal of the movement. Therefore, X is usually a location. When X is NOT a location, this pattern usually means "go to do X" and X indicates the purpose for going. The purpose X is presented by two kinds of items: action nouns and verb stems (the portion before *masu*).

- Action nouns: *benkyō* "study", *renshū* "practice", *kaimono* "shopping"
  Tokyo ni kaimono ni ikimasu.   I'll go to Tokyo for shopping.
  Toshokan ni benkyō ni ikimashita.   I went to the library to study.

- Verb stems
  Kōhī o kai ni ikimasu.   I'll go to buy coffee.
  Nani o shi ni iku n desu ka.   What are you going there to do?

GRAMMAR NOTE Informal Negative Forms of Verbs

Each verb group has different conjugation rules to make the Informal Negative forms.

U–Verbs

In order to make the negative form of a verb in this group, change the final *u* of the affirmative form to *anai*.

nomimasu	→ *nomu*	→ *nomanai*	not drink

If there is no consonant before *u* as in *kau* "buy", drop *u* and add *wanai*.

kaimasu	→ *kau*	→ *kawanai*	not buy
tsukaimasu	→ *tsukau*	→ *tsukawanai*	not use

Ru–Verbs

For the verbs in this group, replace *ru* with *nai*.

tabemasu	→ *taberu*	→ *tabenai*	not eat

Irregular Verbs

The members of this group have the following negative forms.

kimasu	→ *kuru*	→ *konai*	not come
shimasu	→ *suru*	→ *shinai*	not do
arimasu	→ *aru*	→ *nai*	not exist
ikimasu	→ *iku*	→ *ikanai*	not go

Special Polite Verbs

The stem of the verbs in this group actually end in *r*, although it disappears in the *masu* form. This is why these five verbs are separated from *U*-verbs.

irasshaimasu	→ *irasshari*	→ *irassharu*	there is
gozaimasu	→ *gozari*	→ *gozaru*	there is
kudasaimasu	→ *kudasari*	→ *kudasaru*	please give me
nasaimasu	→ *nasari*	→ *nasaru*	please do
ossahaimasu	→ *osshari*	→ *ossharu*	please say

To make the negative form, follow the rule for *U*-verbs: change *u* to *anai*.

irasshaimasu	→ *irassharu*	→ *irassharanai*	there is not
gozaimasu	→ *gozaru*	→ *gozaranai*	there is not
kudasaimasu	→ *kudasaru*	→ *kudasaranai*	please do not give me
nasaimasu	→ *nasaru*	→ *nasaranai*	please do not do
ossahaimasu	→ *ossharu*	→ *ossaharanai*	please do not say

Remember that adjectives and nouns have two alternative Formal negative forms. Similarly, *desu* can follow the Informal negative verb form to form the alternative Formal negative forms.

Adjective:	*Takaku nai desu.*	*Takaku arimasen.*	It is not expensive.
Noun:	*Nihon ja nai desu.*	*Nihon ja arimasen.*	It is not Japanese.
Verb:	*Tabenai desu.*	*Tabemasen.*	I won't eat.

Both forms are formal, but the form on the left is a little more casual than the one on the right. For individual verb forms, check the verb conjugation chart in Lesson 7.

CULTURAL NOTE **After Work Parties**

Many Japanese offices have parties for their employees such as year-end parties (**bōnen-kai** 忘年会), New Year parties (**shinnen-kai** 新年会), welcome parties for new hires (**kangei-kai** 歓迎会), and farewell parties for retirees and transferees (**sōbetsu-kai** 送別会). In addition, it is common in Japan for co-workers to dine and drink together after work. These drinking parties (**nomi-kai** 飲み会) can be an important and useful way to get to know your co-workers and enhance relationships. When bosses (**jōshi** 上司) and senior team members (**senpai** 先輩) invite subordinates (**buka** 部下) or junior members (**kōhai** 後輩), attendance can be an unspoken requirement. If you do not want to attend, it is important to defuse your negative response (**Kyō wa chotto** "Today is a little..." works well in such cases). It used to be uncommon for female employees to be invited to or be welcomed at these parties, but as the number of working women increased, now women often have parties of their own, a girls' night out type of party (**joshi-kai** 女子会).

Office drinking parties were more common during the era of high economic growth in Japan and when lifetime employment (**shūshin-koyō** 終身雇用) was the standard. The employment system and corporate culture have now become more westernized, and career changing is no longer uncommon. As Japanese now seek a good balance between work and private life (**wāku-raifu baransu** ワークライフバランス), the younger generation tend to spend less time with their co-workers and focus more on self-improvement, hobbies and their family. Recently, private mixer parties resembling group blind dates (**gōkon** 合コン) are becoming popular among young people, from university students to working singles. These are typically organized by friends or co-workers.

Who pays for these parties? When a boss invites the team, she is expected to pay for all or at least a substantial portion. Do not forget to thank her by saying **Gochisō-sama deshita**. In other cases, splitting bills (**warikan** 割り勘) among attendees is common. In some cases, set fees (**kai-hi** 会費) are collected beforehand. Be prepared to bar-hop as the party rarely ends after one stop (**niji-kai** 二次会 "after-party", **sanji-kai** 三次会 "after-after-party").

PATTERN PRACTICE 7

Cue:	*Osake, nomitai nā.*	I want to drink sake.
Response:	*Nomi ni ikanai?*	Why don't we go and drink?
Cue:	*Sushi tabetai nā.*	I want to eat sushi.
Response:	*Tabe ni ikanai?*	Why don't we go and eat?

Repeat the drill with the following information:
1. *Omatsuri mitai nā.*
2. *Obentō kaitai nā.*
3. *Umi de oyogitai nā.*
4. *Shibuya de asobitai nā.*
5. *Sukī shitai nā.*

PATTERN PRACTICE 8

Cue:	*Wakaru?*	Do you understand?
Response:	*U'un, wakaranai.*	No, I don't.
Cue:	*Dekiru?*	Can you do?
Response:	*U'un, dekinai.*	No, I can't.

Practice the drill again with the following information:
1. *Yomu?*
2. *Kaku?*
3. *Miru?*
4. *Kau?*
5. *Suru?*
6. *Kuru?*
7. *Kaeru?*
8. *Asobu?*
9. *Noboru?*
10. *Iru?* (Need?)

EXERCISE 7
Say it in Japanese
A friend has asked you why you came to Japan for. Explain.
1. I've come to Japan to study Japanese.
2. I've come to Japan to work.
3. I've come to Japan to see the summer festivals.
4. I've come to Japan for vacation (*asobi*).
5. I've come to Japan to do shopping.

Invite a friend to do the following activities.
6. Why don't we check/look at the map?
7. Why don't we go eat ramen?
8. Why don't we ask the service counter one more time?

9. Why don't we park behind that brown building?
10. Will you practice English with me?

EXERCISE 8
Role Play
1. Your group has been working hard. Suggest that you go for a drink afterwards.
2. It's 12:00. Invite a friend to go eat lunch.
3. At a reception, you meet another guest. Ask about her company, hometown, college, major, favorite food, favorite music, and hobbies.
4. You've been asked to go to karaoke with everyone. Politely turn down the invitation, explaining that:
    1) you have a previous engagement (plan) today;
    2) you are not good at singing.
5. Discuss what leisure activities:
    1) you like and do often;
    2) you want to do but don't do very much;
    3) you don't do at all.

REVIEW QUESTIONS
1. a) How do you make the Informal Affirmative forms of noun predicate, adjective predicate, and verb predicates?
    b) What about Informal Negative forms?
2. a) What are the irregular verbs in Japanese?
    b) List all four.
3. In order to say "I want to do X" in Japanese, you attach *-tai* to the verb stem.
    a) What is the verb stem?
    b) What is the other pattern introduced in this chapter that uses the verb stem?
4. What is the difference between *Wakaranai* and *Wakaranai no*?
5. a) What is the difference between *Nihon no* and *Nihon na no*?
    b) What does /*no*/ refer to in each?
6. a) How do you count numbers above 100 in Japanese?
    b) How do you say 10,000 in Japanese?
    c) What sound changes occur with hundreds?
    d) What sound changes occur with thousands?
7. What does the particle /*to*/ indicate in each of the following?
    1) *Furansu to Igirisu ni iku.*
    2) *Tomodachi to Igirisu ni iku.*
8. What does the particle /*ni*/ indicate in each of the following?
    1) *Kai ni iku.*
    2) *Depāto ni iku.*

LESSON 7
Getting Around

Home is where you make it. (lit., Wherever you live, it's the capital.)
住めば都 **Sumeba miyako**

DIALOGUE 1 Commuting

Sato: Is your home far from the station?
Otaku wa eki kara tōi n desu ka.
お宅は駅から遠いんですか。

Michael: No, it's about a ten-minute walk.
Ie, aruite jup-pun gurai desu.
いえ、歩いて十分ぐらいです。

Sato: How long does it take to get to the office?
Kaisha made dono gurai kakaru n desu ka.
会社までどのぐらいかかるんですか。

Michael: It's about one hour by train.
Densha de ichi-jikan gurai desu.
電車で一時間ぐらいです。

Sato: That's tough, isn't it?
Sore wa taihen desu nē.
それは大変ですねえ。

VOCABULARY

otaku	お宅	(your) home (polite)
eki	駅	station
tōi	遠い	far
aruku	歩く	walk
aruite	歩いて	(by) walking
dono gurai	どのぐらい	how long
kakaru	かかる	take; cost
densha	電車	train
-jikan	時間	hour
ichi-jikan	一時間	one hour
taihen(na)	大変	difficult; very much; tough

ADDITIONAL VOCABULARY

uchi	家; 内	(my) home; inside
chikai	近い	close; nearby
raku(na)	楽	easy; comfortable
toho	徒歩	(by) foot
tsūkin	通勤	commute to work
tsūgaku	通学	commute to school

Transportation

kuruma	車	car
basu	バス	bus
takusī	タクシー	taxi
densha	電車	train
chikatetsu	地下鉄	subway
Shinkansen	新幹線	bullet train
hikōki	飛行機	plane
fune	船	boat; ship
JR	ジェイアール	Japan Railway
shitetsu	私鉄	private railroad
monorēru	モノレール	monorail
rimujin	リムジン	limousine
jitensha	自転車	bicycle
baiku	バイク	motorcycle

GRAMMAR NOTE Counting Hours

You saw the classifier *-ji* for telling time in Lesson 3, as in *ichi-ji* "one o'clock" and *ichi-ji han* "1:30". This classifier refers to a specific time. On the other hand, the classifier *-jikan* counts hours, e.g., *ichi-jikan* "one hour" and *ichi-jikan han* "one and a half hours". The classifiers *-ji* and *jikan* both attach to Chinese numbers. The question word for "how many hours" is *nan-jikan*, while the question word for "what time" is *nan-ji*. Note that for the numbers four, seven, and nine, the alternative of *yo*, *shichi*, and *ku* are used with these classifiers. Also note that *jikan* alone means time in general.

> *Jikan ga arimasen.*   There is no time.
> *Jikan ga kakarimasu.*   It takes time.

There are three expressions for approximation: *-goro* for an approximate point in time and *-gurai* and *yaku-* are for an approximate length of time or amount of things. Therefore, *-jikan* is used with *-gurai* or *yaku* while *-ji* is used with *-goro*.

> *sanji-goro*   around 3:00
> *san-jikan gurai*   about three hours
> *yaku san-jikan*   about three hours

CULTURAL NOTE **Taking Trains**

Japan's rail system is one of the most extensive in the world. It takes you almost anywhere in the country—on time! In big cities, many train and subway lines intertwine to make a complex network. Larger stations have multiple entrances/ exits and transfers located blocks apart. All of the exits are named or numbered. Travel guides tell you which exit to take for local spots. You can follow the signs in most stations to the correct exit.

Determining your train fare from the fare maps and buying tickets at the ticket vending machines can be confusing. But you can bypass this altogether by purchasing a SUICA or PASMO Card. Just hold your card to the reader at the fare gates upon entry and exit and the correct fare will be deducted from your balance.

Using a smartphone while walking (*aruki-sumaho* 歩きスマホ) is particularly dangerous on the station platforms. Avoid this by all means. When the train arrives, do not stand in front of the door. Stand to one side to allow passengers to exit the car. Most passengers on Japanese trains are either reading, sleeping, or using smartphones. When having a conversation, keep your voice down. Talking on phones inside trains is prohibited. Keep your phone on silent mode or "manner mode" (*manā-mōdo* マナーモード). Do not eat or drink on the trains (except for *Shinkansen* or inter-regional travel trains). Try to minimize the space you occupy by keeping your belongings on your lap or close to your chest. Do not stretch your legs. Avoid the "Silver Seats" (*shirubā shīto* シルバーシート), which are designated for the handicapped and the elderly. Last but not least, there are no trash cans in most stations or on the streets, but should be more common in department stores or subway station restrooms. Wherever possible, recycle your cans and bottles—the bins should be beside the vending machines.

PATTERN PRACTICE 1

Cue: ***Densha de daigaku ni ikimasu.***
              I'll take the train to the university.
Response: ***Daigaku made densha de dono gurai kakaru n desu ka.***
              How long does it take to go to (the) university by train?
Cue   ***Aruite konbini ni ikimasu.***
              I'll walk to the convenience store.
Response: ***Konbini made aruite dono gurai kakaru n desu ka.***
              How long does it take to walk to the convenience store?

Repeat the drill using the following:
1. ***Hikōki de Kyūshū ni ikimasu.***
2. ***Jitensha de kōen ni ikimasu.***
3. ***Fune de Okinawa ni ikimasu.***
4. ***Kuruma de Fuji-san ni ikimasu.***
5. ***Chikatetsu de Ginza ni ikimasu.***

PATTERN PRACTICE 2

Cue:	*Ichi-jikan desu ka.*	Is it one hour?
Response:	*Hai, ichi-jikan gurai desu.*	Yes, it's about one hour.
Cue:	*Ichi-ji desu ka.*	Is it one o'clock?
Response:	*Hai, ichi-ji goro desu.*	Yes, it's about one o'clock.

Repeat the drill using the following information:
1. *Jū-ji desu ka.*
2. *Hachi-jikan desu ka.*
3. *Ni-jikan han desu ka.*
4. *Go-ji jūp-pun desu ka.*
5. *Roku-ji han desu ka.*

EXERCISE 1
Say It in Japanese
Ask a co-worker how long it takes:
1. by bicycle from your home to college.
2. from the station to your company.
3. from here to the subway station.
4. from Tokyo to Kyoto by bullet train.
5. to walk from the first floor to the top floor (*ichi-ban ue*).

EXERCISE 2
Role Play
1. Ask the following persons where their homes are. Comment on how far or close they are.
   1) a friend;
   2) a co-worker;
   3) a boss where her home is.
2. Ask a friend how she commutes to school/work. Ask how long it takes.
3. A co-worker confided in you about a stressful situation. Empathize with him/her.
4. Ask a co-worker
   1) how long he has been in this company;
   2) how long he was in America.
5. Google how long it takes to fly to different places in Japan and the world, and share the information with a friend.

🔘 DIALOGUE 2 Meeting at Hachiko, the Dog Statue

Yuki: Why don't we meet at six at Hachiko?
   Hachi-kō de roku-ji ni awanai.
   ハチ公で六時に会わない。

Mei: Got it.
   Wakatta.
   わかった。

Yuki arrives late.

Yuki: Sorry for being late.
   Osoku natte, gomen.
   遅くなってごめん。

Mei: What happened?
   Dō shita no.
   どうしたの。

Yuki: There was an accident. Did you wait (long)?
   Jiko ga atta n da. Matta.
   事故があったんだ。待った。

Mei: No, I just arrived too.
   U'un, watashi mo sakki tsuita no.
   ううん、私もさっき着いたの。

Yuki: Really?
   Hontō.
   本当。

Mei: Yes. (It's that) I took the wrong train.
   Un. Densha o machigaeta no.
   うん、電車を間違えたの。

VOCABULARY

au	会う	meet
awanai	会わない	do not meet
Hachi-kō	ハチ公	Hachiko, the loyal dog statue outside Shibuya station—a popular meeting spot.
wakatta	わかった	understood
osoku naru	遅くなる	become late
natte	遅くなって	become (*te*-form)
gomen	ごめん	sorry (casual)
shita	した	did
Dō shita?	どうした？	What happened?
jiko	事故	accident

atta	あった	there was
matsu	待つ	wait
matta	待った	waited
sakki	さっき	just now; a little while ago
tsuku	着く	arrive
tsuita	着いた	arrived
hontō	本当	true; truth
machigaeru	まちがえる	make (an) error
machigaeta	まちがえた	made (an) error

ADDITIONAL VOCABULARY

Kita-guchi	北口	North exit/entrance
Minami-guchi	南口	South exit/entrance
Higashi-guchi	東口	East exit/entrance
Nishi-guchi	西口	West exit/entrance

Changing Verbs to the Informal Forms

U-Verbs				
1.	*kaimasu*	*kau*	*katta*	buy
2.	*aimasu*	*au*	*atta*	meet
3.	*tsukaimasu*	*tsukau*	*tsukatta*	use
4.	*tetsudaimasu*	*tetsudau*	*tetsudatta*	help
5.	*wakarimasu*	*wakaru*	*wakatta*	understand
6.	*norimasu*	*noru*	*notta*	get on
7.	*tsukurimasu*	*tsukuru*	*tsukutta*	make
8.	*kaerimasu*	*kaeru*	*kaetta*	go back
9.	*hashirimasu*	*hashiru*	*hashitta*	run
10.	*irimasu*	*iru*	*itta*	need
11.	*kakimasu*	*kaku*	*kaita*	write
12.	*okurimasu*	*okuru*	*okutta*	send
13.	*kikimasu*	*kiku*	*ki'ita*	listen
14.	*arukimasu*	*aruku*	*aruita*	walk
15.	*tsukimasu*	*tsuku*	*tsuita*	arrive
16.	*nomimasu*	*nomu*	*nonda*	drink
17.	*yomimasu*	*yomu*	*yonda*	read
18.	*yasumimasu*	*yasumu*	*yasunda*	rest
19.	*asobimasu*	*asobu*	*asonda*	play
20.	*isogimasu*	*isogu*	*isoida*	hurry
21.	*hanashimasu*	*hanasu*	*hanashita*	talk

Ru–Verbs			
22.	*tabemasu*	*taberu*	*tabeta*	eat
23.	*mimasu*	*miru*	*mita*	look
24.	*imasu*	*iru*	*ita*	exist (animate)
25.	*dekimasu*	*dekiru*	*dekita*	can do
26.	*demasu*	*deru*	*deta*	leave, go out
27.	*orimasu*	*oriru*	*orita*	get off
28.	*dekakemasu*	*dekakeru*	*dekaketa*	go out
29.	*norikaemasu*	*norikaeru*	*norikaeta*	transfer

Irregular Verbs			
30.	*shimasu*	*suru*	*shita*	do
31.	*kimasu*	*kuru*	*kita*	come
32.	*ikimasu*	*iku*	*itta*	go
33.	*arimasu*	*aru*	*atta*	exist

Special Polite Verbs			
34.	*irasshaimasu*	*irassharu*	*irasshatta*	exist (animate)
35.	*gozaimasu*	*gozaru*	*gozatta*	exist (inanimate)
36.	*kudasaimasu*	*kudasaru*	*kudasatta*	give to me
37.	*nasaimasu*	*nasaru*	*nasatta*	do
38.	*osshaimasu*	*ossharu*	*osshatta*	say

GRAMMAR NOTE Informal Past forms of Verbs

Each verb group has different rules governing the formation of Informal Past forms.

U-Verbs: Five different rules depending on the final verb consonant.

-(w)u	→	*tta*	*kau*	→ *katta*
-tsu	→	*tta*	*matsu*	→ *matta*
-ru	→	*tta*	*wakaru*	→ *wakatta*
-mu	→	*nda*	*nomu*	→ *nonda*
-nu	→	*nda*	*shinu*	→ *shinda*
-bu	→	*nda*	*asobu*	→ *asonda*
-ku	→	*ita*	*kaku*	→ *kaita*
-gu	→	*ida*	*isogu*	→ *isoida*
-su	→	*shita*	*hanasu*	→ *hanashita*

Ru-Verbs:
-*ru* → *ta*   *taberu* → *tabeta*

Irregular Verbs:
kuru → *kita*   *suru* → *shita*   *iku* → *itta*   *aru* → *atta*

Special Polite Verbs:
ru → *tta*   *irassharu* → *irasshatta*   *ossharu* → *osshatta*

To make the negative past form, change *nai* → *nakatta*
nomu → *nomanai*   → *namanakatta*
taberu → *tabenai*   → *tabenakatta*

GRAMMAR NOTE Combining Sentences: *Te*–Form of Predicates

When we discussed earlier how to combine two nouns using the particle *to*, a warning was given not to use this particle to combine anything else. Now we will learn how to combine sentences. To combine two sentences into one, change the predicate of the first sentence to the *te*-form.

>   *Osoku natta. Gomen.*   I'm late. I'm sorry.
> → *Osoku natte, gomen.*   I'm sorry for being late.

How do we make a *te*-form? There are different rules depending on the type of predicate (verb, adjective, or noun predicate.) For an adjective predicate, add -*te* to the adjective -*ku* form.

>   *takai* → *takakute*   expensive and…
>   *Takakute oishi'i desu.*   It's expensive and delicious.

For a noun predicate, add *de* (the *te*-form of *desu/da*) to the noun.

>   *rāmen da* → *rāmen de*   It's ramen and…
>   *Hirugohan wa rāmen de bangohan wa sushi desu.*
>   (We'll have) ramen for lunch and sushi for dinner.

For a verb, switch the vowel *a* of the Informal Past form to *e* (*ta*→*te*; *da*→*de*).

>   *U*-verb: *nomu* → *nonda* → *nonde*   drinking and…
>   *Ru*-Verb: *taberu* → *tabeta* → *tabete*   eating and…
>   *Tabete, kaerimasu.*   I'll eat and go home.

When the *te*-forms is combined with *i'i desu* "it's okay", the entire sentence typically means "it's fine if/given that…" or "It's good that …".

Kaette i'i desu. It's okay if you go home.

Rāmen de i'i desu. Ramen is fine (although it may not be my first choice.)

Kirei de i'i desu nē. It's nice and beautiful. (I'm happy with it.)

Yasukute yokatta desu. I'm happy that it turned out to be cheap.

Note the difference in meaning between the following.

Densha ga i'i desu. Train is good. (I'd like to take a train.)

Densha de i'i desu. I'm fine with (taking) a train.

CULTURAL NOTE **Apology First**

In Japan causing trouble or inconvenience (*meiwaku* 迷惑) to others (*Hito ni meiwaku o kakeru* 人に迷惑をかける) is considered irresponsible and should be avoided as much as possible. Japanese children are repeatedly taught this from an early age at home and at school. Signs in many public places remind people of this standard of behavior. Naturally, an apology is expected for not meeting this norm in all types of social interactions in Japan. This concept is closely related to the perception of humility as a virtue.

An apology is commonly expected in Japan in the following situations: 1) at the beginning of making a public speech; 2) leaving someone's home or office; 3) on behalf of others in your group such as your family members or co-workers; 4) when greeting someone you previously met in case you inadvertently committed a rudeness at that time; 5) and also for any slight inconveniences. The offended person will usually acknowledge your apology and smilingly deny any trouble was caused. This exchange is very common in the "apology first" culture of Japan and is almost a ceremonial ritual for maintaining harmony.

There are equally many—about 20 or so—ways of expressing apology ranging in formality and depth. Consider your relationship with the offended and how severe the offence was to choose the right expression. The most common—and safest— is **Sumimasen** and add **dōmo** or **taihen** to express that you are very sorry. **Gomen**, on the other hand, is casual and is typically used between friends and family. Children and females would more likely use the gentler version **Gomen nasai**. The formal **Mōshiwake arimasen** and its more polite version **mōshiwake gozaimasen** (lit., I have no excuse) are typically used by service staff. Remember to change the phrases to the past or Non-past forms depending on when the incident occurred.

There are three things to consider when apologizing. First, remember that how you say something is more important than what you say. Synchronize your facial expression, tone of voice, and body language with what you are saying. When apologizing, remember to bow—the deeper the bow, the more sincerity you are

expressing. The stiffer the body and the finger tips, the more formal. However, too deep a bow can be interpreted as conveying sarcasm. So, observe how Japanese people bow in different situations and follow accordingly.

Second, when you express what you are apologizing for, use the *te*-form, which indicates a chronological order but not necessarily a direct causal relation. e.g., **Okurete sumimasen** "I'm sorry for being late." Do not use **kara**, which indicates the causal relation and sounds less sincere.

Third, you cannot use these expressions exactly like "I'm sorry" in English. In emotion-laden situations like a co-worker losing a family member, Japanese people usually exchange certain ritual expressions. NEVER say **sumimasen**, unless you were responsible for the death.

PATTERN PRACTICE 3

Cue: *Wakarimashita ka.*   Did you understand?
Response: *Un wakatta.*   Yes, I did.
Cue: *Machimashita ka.*   Did you wait?
Response: *Un matta.*   Yes, I did.

Repeat this drill with the following information:
1. *Arimashita ka.*   6. *Hanashimashita ka.*
2. *Machigaemashita ka.*   7. *Asobimashita ka.*
3. *Kaimashita ka.*   8. *Kaerimashita ka.*
4. *Nomimashita ka.*   9. *Ikimashita ka.*
5. *Kakimashita ka.*   10. *Aimashita ka.*
* Repeat this drill with the response " No, I didn't."

PATTERN PRACTICE 4

Cue: *Osoku narimashita ne.*   You were late, weren't you?
Response: *Osoku natte, sumimasen.*   I'm sorry for being late.
Cue: *Tōi desu ne.*   It's far, isn't it?
Response: *Tōkute sumimasen.*   I'm sorry that it's far.

Repeat this drill with the following information:
1. *Machigaemashita ne.*
2. *Isogashi'i desu ne.*
3. *Eigo desu ne.*
4. *Yasumimashita ne.*
5. *Imaichi desu ne.*

EXERCISE 3
Say It in Japanese
A friend asks you why you are late. Explain and apologise. Next, he asks what you did over the weekend.
1. There was an accident.
2. I was mistaken about the time (I misinterpreted the time).
3. I took a wrong exit.
4. It snowed and the *Shinkansen* was delayed (became late).
5. It's that I bumped into (met) an old friend.
6. I watched TV and slept.
7. I saw (met) a friend, did some shopping, and had dinner.
8. I was busy and didn't have time.
9. It rained and was cold, so I stayed home.
10. It was a beautiful day, so I biked to the park and studied outside.

EXERCISE 4
Role Play
1. Suggest to to meet a friend at the West exit of the station at 11:00 on Saturday.
2. You've just heard a friend scream. Respond. She has mentioned something unbelievable. Check if it is true.
3. Apologize to a boss for the following. Repeat the scenario but to a friend.
   1) being late;
   2) making mistakes.
4. You are making plans for a business trip. Using a *Shinkansen* schedule, discuss the destinations to visit and arrival times with co-workers.
5. Discuss with a friend the following:
   1) what you did last weekend;
   2) what you wanted to do but didn't, and why.

🔘 DIALOGUE 3 Taking a Taxi

A taxi stops for Michael, who is planning to travel to Kyoto for a short getaway and needs to take the 10 A.M. Shinkansen.

Michael: Please go to Tokyo Station.
　　　　 Tōkyō-eki made itte kudasai.
　　　　 東京駅まで行ってください。

Driver: Are you taking the Shinkansen?
　　　　 Shinkansen desu ka.
　　　　 新幹線ですか。

Michael: Yes. Can you please hurry a bit? I want to take the 10 o'clock Shinkansen.
　　　　 E'e. Chotto isoide itadakemasen ka. Jū-ji no shinkansen ni noritai kara.
　　　　 ええ。ちょっと急いでいただけませんか。十時の新幹線に乗りたいから。

Michael sees traffic congestion near the station.

Michael: Please stop here. I'll get off and walk. So…
　　　　 Koko de tomete kudasai. Orite arukimasu kara.
　　　　 ここで止めてください。降りて歩きますから。
　　　　 I'd like to pay with my (credit) card, please.
　　　　 Kādo de onegai-shimasu.
　　　　 カードでお願いします。

VOCABULARY

Tōkyō-eki	東京駅	Tokyo Station
Shinkansen	新幹線	bullet train
isogu	急ぐ	hurry
isoide	急いで	hurry (*te*-form)
…itadakemasen ka.	…いただけませんか。	Could I have…?
tomeru	とめる	stop (something)
oriru	降りる	get off
kādo	カード	credit card

ADDITIONAL VOCABULARY

unten-shu	運転手	driver
hashiru	走る	run
genkin	現金	cash
…kudasaimasen ka.	…くださいませんか。	Could you please …?

| *okane* | お金 | money |
| *harau* | 払う | pay |

GRAMMAR NOTE Making Requests

You may recall that to request things you can say "X (*o*) *kudasaī*" or "X (*o*) *onegai-shimasu*". You can make it even more polite by saying "X (*o*) *kudasaimasen ka*" or "X (*o*) *itadakemasen ka*." Request for coffee in the following four ways:

Kōhī o kudasai.
Kōhī o onegai-shimasu.
Kōhī o kudasaimasen ka.
Kōhī o itadakemasen ka.

When requesting an action, use the *te*-form of the verb alone (casual) or the *te*-form with *kudasai*, *itadakemasen ka*, or *kudasaimasen ka*. Do NOT use *onegai-shimasu* with the *te*-form. Make the request casual by using the *te*-form alone. Ask someone to wait for you in the following four ways:

Chotto matte.
Chotto matte kudasai.
Chotto matte kudasaimasen ka.
Chotto matte itadakemasen ka.

These are the most common request patterns in Japanese, but there are many more—dozens, perhaps. It's important to choose the right request pattern for each situation. The choice is made based on the relationship between the speakers, the nature of the request, the setting, etc. For example, *chotto matte* is most common when speaking with friends while *chotto matte itadakemasen ka* is appropriate when you are communicating with business associates.

PATTERN PRACTICE 5

Cue:	*Isogimashō ka.*	Shall I hurry?
Response:	*Hai, isoide kudasai.*	Yes, please hurry.
Cue:	*Tomemashō ka.*	Shall I stop (the car)?
Response:	*Hai, tomete kudasai.*	Yes, please stop.

Repeat this drill with the following information:
1. *Tsukurimashō ka.*
2. *Machimashō ka.*
3. *Yomimashō ka.*
4. *Kikimashō ka.*
5. *Benkyō-shimashō ka.*
* Repeat this drill replacing *kudasai* with *kudasaimasen ka* or *itadakemasen ka*.

PATTERN PRACTICE 6

Cue:	*Koko de orite kudasai.*	Please get off here.
Response:	*Wakarimashita. Koko de orimashō.*	Okay. I'll get off here.
Cue:	*Chotto isoide kudasai.*	Please hurry a bit.
Response:	*Wakarimashita. Chotto isogimashō.*	Okay. I'll hurry a bit.

Repeat this drill with the following information:
1. *Tōkyō-eki made itte kudasai.*
2. *Takushī ni notte kudasai.*
3. *Ryūgakusei ni atte kudasai.*
4. *Jup-pun gurai yasunde kudasai.*
5. *Senpai ni mēru-shite kudasai.*

EXERCISE 5
Say It in Japanese
In a taxi, ask the driver to do the following.
1. Please go to Ginza.
2. Please hurry because I have a bus tour at 10:30.
3. Please slow down (go slower) because it's dangerous.
4. Please turn left at the traffic light and stop there.
5. Please let me pay with a card because I don't have cash.

EXERCISE 6
Role Play
1. Suggest that you and a co-worker take a taxi to the station.
2. You wrote something in Japanese. Ask the following people to take a look at it.
   1) a boss;
   2) a friend
3. You are running late. Suggest to a co-worker that you
   1) hurry;
   2) run;
   3) walk faster.
4. You want to visit Tokyo Skytree (*Tōkyō Sukai tsurī*). Ask a friend where you should get off the subway.
5. Describe how you commute from home to work/school. Link sentences in chronological order using *-te* forms.

🔘 DIALOGUE 4 Going to the Airport

Michael: I'd like to go to Haneda Airport, but how do I get there?
Haneda-kūkō e ikitai n desu kedo, dō yatte iku n desu ka.
羽田空港へ行きたいんですけど、どうやって行くんですか。

Sato: Oh, the monorail is the most convenient way.
Ā, monorēru ga ichi-ban benri desu yo.
ああ、モノレールが一番便利ですよ。

Go to Hamamatsu-cho by JR and transfer to the monorail.
JR de Hamamatsu-chō made itte, monorēru ni norikaete kudasai.
JRで浜松町まで行って、モノレールに乗り換えてください。

Michael: How do I buy tickets?
Kippu wa dō suru n desu ka.
切符はどうするんですか。

Sato: Just use your IC card. The IC cards are better than tickets.
IC kādo wo tsukatte kudasai. Kippu yori IC kādo no hō ga i'i desu yo.
ICカードを使ってください。切符よりICカードの方がいいで
すよ。

VOCABULARY

kūkō	空港	airport
Haneda Kūkō	羽田空港	Haneda Airport
yaru	やる	do (casual)
yatte	やって	do (*te*-form)
dō yatte	どうやって	how; how to do something
monorēru	モノレール	monorail
benri (na)	便利	convenient; handy
JR	JR	Japan Rail
Hamamatsu-chō	浜松町	Hamamatsu-cho (a station in Tokyo)
itte	行って	go (*te*-form)
norikaeru	乗り換える	transfer
norikaete	乗り換えて	transfer (*te*-form)
kippu	切符	ticket
yori	より	than
IC kādo	ICカード	IC card
X no hō	Xの方	X (the alternative)
X no hō ga i'i	Xの方がいい	X is better

ADDITIONAL VOCABULARY

fuben (na)	不便	inconvenient
Pasumo	PASMO	PASMO (IC card for private railroad)
Narita kūkō	成田空港	Narita Airport
kō	こう	in this way; like this
sō	そう	in that way; like that
ā	ああ	in that way; like that

GRAMMAR NOTE **Comparing Two or More Items**

When comparing X and Y, the question word *dochira* or *docchi* "which alternative of the two" is commonly used. In answering the question, the particle *-yori* "rather than" and *-hō* "the alternative of Y out of the two" are commonly used, but if the item X is clear from the context, you can omit it.

X to Y to, dochira (no hō) ga i'i desu ka.	Which is better, X or Y?
X ga i'i desu.	X is better.
Y yori X no hō ga i'i desu.	X is better than Y.

When comparing three items or more, you can specify the items compared by saying "*X no naka de* "among X (the group)", or list each member of the group like *X to Y to Z no naka de* "among X, Y, and Z". The question word is *dore*, *dare*, *doko*, etc., depending on the items being compared, and the word *ichi-ban* indicates the superlative.

Kono naka de dore ga ichi-ban i'i desu ka.
Among these, which is the best?
X to Y to Z no naka de dore ga ichi-ban i'i desu ka.
Which is the best among X, Y, and Z?
X ga ichiban i'i desu.
X is the best.

GRAMMAR NOTE *Dō* **"How"**

Dō literally means "how" and it is part of the *ko-so-a-do* set with *kō*, *sō*, *a'a* and *dō*.

Onamae wa dō kaku n desu ka.	How do you write your name?
– Kō kaku n desu.	You write it this way.

There are several expressions that include *dō*, whose meanings are hard to guess directly from the original meaning of *dō*. Let's review them.

Dō mo.	Thank you.
Dō shita no.	What's wrong?
Dō yatte.	How
Dō shite	Why
Dō suru?	How to solve it?

PATTERN PRACTICE 7

Cue: *Takushī ga hayai desu ne.*
               A taxi is fast, right?

Response: *Ie, takusī yori densha no hō ga hayai desu yo.*
               No, a train is faster than a taxi.

Cue: *Fune ga benri desu ne.*
               A boat is convenient, right?

Response: *Ie, fune yori densha no hō ga benri desu yo.*
               No, a train is more convenient than a boat.

Repeat the drill with the following information.
1. *Chikatetsu ga suki desu ne.*
2. *Basu ga yasui desu ne.*
3. *Kuruma ga raku desu ne.*
4. *Hikōki ga omoshiroi desu ne.*
5. *Basu ga suzushi'i desu ne.*

PATTERN PRACTICE 8

Cue: *Hamamatsu-chō made ikimasu ne.*
               We are going to Hamamatsu-cho, right?

Response: *E'e, Hamamatsu-chō made itte, norikaete kudasai.*
               Right. Please go to Hamamatsu-cho and then transfer.

Cue: *Tsugi no eki de orimasu ne.*
               We are getting off at the next station, right?

Response: *E'e, tsugi no eki de orite, norikaete kudasai.*
               Right. Please get off at the next station, and transfer.

Repeat the drill with the following information.
1. *Nishi-guchi ni ikimasu ne.*
2. *Kippu o kaimasu ne.*
3. *Kyōto ni tsukimasu ne.*
4. *Chikatetsu o orimasu ne.*
5. *IC kādo o tsukaimasu ne.*

EXERCISE 7
Say it in Japanese
Tell a co-worker what you want to do and ask how to do it.
1. I'd like to go to *Hachi-kō*, but how do I do that?
2. I'd like to buy tickets, but how do I do that?
3. I'd like to transfer to the subway, but how do I do that?
4. I'd like to commute to work in *Hamamatsu-chō*, but how do I do that?
5. I'd like to use the Internet here, but how do I do that?

A friend has asked you to compare two items.
6. IC cards are easier (*raku*) than tickets.
7. Haneda Airport is closer than Narita Airport.
8. A plane is probably faster than the Shinkansen.
9. The West exit is more convenient than the East exit.
10. (Taking) a train is better than (driving) a car, but (taking) the monorail is the best.

EXERCISE 8
Role Play
1. Ask a friend how to eat a dish you have never seen before.
2. Ask your co-worker whether taking a plane or the Shinkansen to Osaka is better.
3. Ask a friend what she wants to do most in America.
4. Ask a co-worker whether he likes traditional Japanese food or Western food more.
5. Discuss your favorite (*ichi-ban suki na*) food, sports, movie, color, game, etc.

REVIEW QUESTIONS
1. a) What is the difference between *ichi-ji* and *ichi-jikan*?
   b) How do you express approximation with each of them?
2. How do you make the Informal Past forms of verbs?
3. How do you make the *te*-forms of verb, adjective and noun predicates?
4. How do you ask which is better, X or Y and what is the best among X, Y, and Z?
5. How do you answer the questions in (4)?
6. a) How do you make a polite request for things?
   b) For actions?
   c) Casually?
7. English "and" has several equivalents in Japanese. How do you say the following in Japanese?
   1) trains and subways
   2) Trains are fast and cheap.
   3) Trains are clean and convenient.
   4) We'll go to Ginza and shop.

8. On the basis of the conjugation rules explained so far, fill out the blanks in the following chart. This tests your ability to change the forms of unknown verbs correctly.

Formal Non-past Affirmative	Informal Non-Past Affirmative	Informal Non-past Negative	Informal Past Affirmative
tomemasu			
	sumu		
	niru	*ninai*	
hiraku		*kawaranai*	

LESSON 8
Family and Personal History

Life is full of ups and downs (Lit: If you fall seven times, get up eight.)
七転び八起き *Nana-korobi ya-oki*

🔘 DIALOGUE 1 Birthday

Michael: When is your birthday?
   Tanjōbi wa itsu desu ka.
   誕生日はいつですか。
Sato: April 7th.
   Shi-gatsu nano-ka desu.
   四月七日です。
Michael: It's exactly (during) the cherry blossom viewing season, isn't it?
   Chōdo hanami no shīzun desu ne.
   ちょうど花見のシーズンですね。

Michael's office celebrates Ms. Sato's birthday during its Hanami party.
Michael: Happy birthday! How old are you now?
   Tanjōbi, omedetō. Nan-sai ni natta no?
   誕生日おめでとう。何歳になったの。
Sato: Already 27.
   Mō ni-jū nana yo.
   もう27よ。
Michael: You mean only 27, right?
   Mada ni-jū nana darō.
   まだ27だろう。

VOCABULARY

tanjōbi	誕生日	birthday
-gatsu	月	naming classifier for months

* To count the number of months, use the classifier *-kagetsu*.

Shigatsu	四月	April
-ka/-nichi	日	classifier for days of the month
nano-ka	七日	the seventh; seven days
hana	花	flower
hanami	花見	cherry blossom viewing

shīzun	シーズン	season
Omedetō!	おめでとう！	Congratulations!

* To make it more polite, add *gozaimasu*. おめでとうございます。

-sai	オ／歳	classifier for human age
nan-sai	何オ／何歳	how many years old
naru	なる	become
X ni naru	Xになる	became X
mō	もう	already; no longer
mada	まだ	still; not yet
darō	だろう	probably (informal version of *deshō*)

Trees and flowers

ki	木	tree
hana	花	flower
kusa	草	grass; weed
sakura	桜	cherry
ume	梅	plum
matsu	松	pine
take	竹	bamboo
bara	バラ	rose
kiku	菊	chrysanthemum

GRAMMAR NOTE Counting Days

The classifier for both naming and counting days is: *ka* or *nichi*. When naming the days of the month, you only go up to the 31st, but when counting days, you can go a lot higher. So, *go-jū nichi* can only mean "fifty days" while *tōka* can mean "the tenth of the month" or "ten days". Here is the chart for all the days of the month.

Sun *Nichi*	Mon *Getsu*	Tue *Ka*	Wed *Sui*	Thu *Moku*	Fri *Kin*	Sat *Do*
1 *tsuitachi*	2 *futsu-ka*	3 *mik-ka*	4 *yok-ka*	5 *itsu-ka*	6 *mui-ka*	7 *nano-ka*
8 *yō-ka*	9 *kokono-ka*	10 *tō-ka*	11 *jū-ichi-nichi*	12 *jū-ni-nichi*	13 *jū-san-nichi*	14 *jū-yok-ka*
15 *jū-go-nichi*	16 *jū-roku-nichi*	17 *jū-shichi-nichi*	18 *jū-hachi-nichi*	19 *jū-ku-nichi*	20 *hatsu-ka*	21 *ni-jū-ichi-nichi*
22 *ni-jū-ni-nichi*	23 *ni-jū-san-nichi*	24 *ni-jū-yok-ka*	25 *ni-jū-go-nichi*	26 *ni-jū-roku-nichi*	27 *ni-jū-shichi-nichi*	28 *ni-jū-hachi-nichi*

29 *ni-jū-ku-* *nichi*	30 *san-jū-* *nichi*	31 *san-jū-* *ichi-nichi*				

Please note the following:

- the first day of the month is **tsuitachi** (naming) while one day is **ichi-nichi** (counting).
- The Japanese number series with the classifier **-ka** is used up through ten, and then the Chinese number series with **-nichi** is used for the rest.
- two exceptions: **hatsuka** "the 20th" or "20 days" and combinations ending with four such as **jū-yok-ka** and **ni-jū-yok-ka**.
- **Nan-nichi** asks "what date?" or "how many days?" Please distinguish between "what day of the month" by using **nan-nichi** and "what day of the week" by using **nan-yōbi**.

The classifier for counting weeks is **-shūkan**. It is combined with the Chinese numbers. There is no naming classifier for weeks. Note the sound change (**s** → **ss**) with one, eight and ten and the choice of alternatives for four, seven, and nine.

1	*is-shūkan*	4	*yon-shūkan*
7	*nana-shūkan*	8	*has-chūkan*
9	*kyū-shūkan*	10	*jus-shūkan*

The naming classifier for months is **-gatsu**, and when naming dates, the month precedes the day. The counting classifier is **-kagetsu**. Both are combined with the Chinese numbers. Note the sound change /ka/ → /kka/ with one, six, eight, and ten.

Naming Months

Ichi-gatsu	一月	January
Ni-gatsu	二月	February
San-gatsu	三月	March
Shi-gatsu	四月	April
Go-gatsu	五月	May
Roku-gatsu	六月	June
Shichi-gatsu	七月	July
Hachi-gatsu	八月	August
Ku-gatsu	九月	September
Jū-gatsu	十月	October
Jūichi-gatsu	十一月	November
Jūni-gatsu	十二月	December
nan-gatsu	何月	what month

Counting Months

ik-kagetsu	一ヶ月	one month
ni-kagetsu	二ヶ月	two months
san-kagetsu	三ヶ月	three months
yon-kagetsu	四ヶ月	four months
go-kagetsu	五ヶ月	five months
rok-kagetsu	六ヶ月	six months
nana-kagetsu	七ヶ月	seven months
hachi-kagetsu	八ヶ月	eight months
kyū-kagetsu	九ヶ月	nine months
juk-kagetsu	十ヶ月	ten months
jūik-kagetsu	十一ヶ月	eleven months
jūni-kagetsu	十二ヶ月	twelve months
nan-kagetsu	何ヶ月	how many months

The classifier for naming and counting years is *-nen*, but *-nenkan* is often used for counting to avoid confusion. The question word is ***nan-nen*** "what year/how many years" or ***nan-nenkan*** "how many years?" So, 17 ***nen*** can mean either 17 years or the year 2017/***Heisei*** 29 depending on the context. When naming dates, the year and the month precede the day. So, for example, September 20, 2017 is ***ni-sen jū-nana-nen ku-gatsu hatsu-ka*** in Japanese or 2017/9/20.

The existence or non-existence of the particle *ni* tells you if it's the naming expression or counting expression as well as the kind of approximation expression used with it, ***goro*** or ***gurai***. Compare the following:

Jū-go-nen ni ikimashita.	I went there in 2015.
Jū-go-nen ikimashita.	I went there for 15 years.
Jū-go-nen-goro ikimashita.	I went there around 2015.
Jū-go-nen-gurai ikimashita.	I went there for about 15 years.

GRAMMAR NOTE Counting Human Age

The classifier *-sai* is used to count the age of people and animals while *-nen* is used to count the age of inanimate things. Note the sound change of /sai/→ /ssai/ with the numbers one, eight, and ten. Use the classifier *-tsu* to count people's ages. *Hatachi* "twenty years old" is the special form of this series. The age of babies less than one year old is counted by days, weeks and months. To ask how old someone is you can use one of the following.

Nan-sai desu ka.
(Toshi wa) ikutsu desu ka.
(Otoshi wa) oikutsu desu ka. (Polite)

Japanese society is very age-conscious, probably more so than other cultures. Age often determines the hierarchy in interpersonal relationships. Even being a year

older gives one seniority over another and affects the conversation. Therefore, age is an important part of personal identity and is commonly asked if not already known. Remember that when you ask any personal questions including age, first say *shitsurei desu kedo* "It's rude of me to ask this, but…" and go on.

GRAMMAR NOTE *Mō* and *Mada*

Recall the expression *Mada mada desu* as a response to a compliment on your language skills. This is a humble response saying "not yet, not yet" and implies that you still have a long way to go before becoming skillful at the language.

Mada is often translated as "still" in an affirmative sentence, and "(not) yet" in a negative sentence. Its basic meaning is that there is no significant change in the situation. When the context is clear, you can just say *mada* on its own.

Wakarimashita ka.	Did you understand it?
Ie, mada wakarimasen.	No, I still don't get it.
Satō-san, kaerimashita ka.	Has Ms. Sato gone home?
Ie, mada desu.	No, not yet.

Mō, on the other hand, indicates that there is a change in the situation, and is often translated as "already" in an affirmative sentence, and "(not) any longer" in a negative sentence.

Hirugohan, tabemasen ka.	Won't you eat lunch?
Mō tabemashita.	I've already eaten.
Sushi, mada arimasu ka.	Is there still some sushi?
Ie, mō arimasen.	No, there is no more.

Do not confuse this *mō* with the other *mo* meaning "more". Note the contrast of the rising and falling intonation.

Mo-U hito-tsu arimasu.	We have one more. (with a rising intonation)
MO-u hito-tsu arimasu.	We already have one. (with a falling intonation)

Mō and *mada* carry a clear implication regarding a prior situation. Compare the following.

Yasui desu.	It's cheap. (No indication of how it was before)
Mada yasui desu.	It's still cheap. (It was also cheap before.)
Mō yasui desu.	It's cheap now. (It was not cheap before.)

Also note how *mō* and *mada* express different perspectives, like seeing a glass half full or half empty. Consider the exchange between Michael and Sato.

Mō 27-sai desu.	I'm already 27 years old. (I'm old.)
Mada 27-sai desu.	You are still 27 years old. (You are only 27, you're still young.)

GRAMMAR NOTE Noun *ni naru*, Adjective–*ku naru* "become X"

The verb *naru* means "become", and expresses a change. It combines with a noun or an adjective that indicates the post-change state. When paired with a noun, the particle *ni* indicating a "goal" is required. When used with an adjective, the adjective needs to be in the *-ku* form.

With a noun: *Ame ni narimashita.*	It's raining now. (It has become rainy!)
With an adjective: *Yasuku narimashita.*	It is cheaper now.

It can combine with the negative forms of all the predicate types as follows.

Verb: *Wakaranaku narimashita.*	You've lost me now (I don't get it anymore).
Adjective: *Yasuku naku narimashita.*	It's no longer cheap.
Noun: *Kodomo ja naku narimashita.*	He is no longer a child.

Now compare the following:

Yasuku narimasen deshita.	It's not cheaper now. (It didn't become cheap. There was no change)
Yasuku naku narimashita.	It's no longer cheap. (It was cheap before.)

GRAMMAR NOTE *Darō* "Probably"

Darō is the informal form of *deshō* "probably", although some female speakers will use *deshō* instead even in a casual conversation. Both *deshō* and *darō* follow the informal form of the predicates.

Formal	Informal	
Takai deshō.	*Takai darō.*	It's probably expensive.
Ame deshō.	*Ame darō.*	It will probably rain.
Kuru deshō.	*Kuru darō.*	She will probably come.

Like *deshō*, when *darō* is used alone with a rising intonation, it means "Isn't it?" or "Didn't I tell you so?"

CULTURAL NOTE *Hanami* **"Flower–Viewing Picnic"**

Cherry blossoms (*sakura* 桜) are said to be the country's most popular flowers, and can be found everywhere in Japan. The trees blossom at different times throughout Japan from late March to mid-April. April is the beginning of the fiscal and school year in Japan, and it coincides with the cherry blossom season, thus the flowers are celebrated as the symbol of a new beginning and schools and public buildings have cherry trees outside. However, their blooming period is short, usually lasting about a week or two. Their transient nature is often associated with mortality and the fleeting nature of beauty. Cherry blossoms appear in the design of many traditional goods and products—and limited-edition items during this time—such as the kimono, stationery, and tableware as well as in art and literature.

Hanami "flower-viewing" (花見) is a centuries-old Japanese custom. In the old days, aristocrats wrote poems under the trees while taking the time to view the flowers, but nowadays people picnic under the trees with families, friends, and co-workers. It is often observed that people are more into eating and drinking, taking pictures and sharing them to their social media platforms, than appreciating the flowers, just as the old saying of *Hana yori Dango* 花より団子 (Rice cake over flowers—practicality over aesthetics) describes. Many parks are filled with such parties all day and well into the night. Go early to reserve a good spot in popular *hanami* locations like the Shinjuku Gyoen and Ueno Park.

Every year, the Japanese Meteorological Agency tracks the "cherry blossom front" (*sakura zensen* 桜前線) as it moves northward along with the warmer weather. They provide daily updates as part of the weather forecast. People—not just locals but also international travelers—follow these closely and plan flower viewing parties (and their travels) to coincide with when the blossoms are at their peak.

CULTURAL NOTE **Japanese Calendar and Birthday Celebrations**
There are two systems of naming years in Japan. In addition to the western calendar
(*seireki* 西暦), Japan uses its own calendar (*gengō* 元号, *wareki* 和暦). The latter
is often used in official documents. The Japanese year designations are based on
the year of the reign of the emperors. When one emperor dies and a new emperor
ascends to the throne, a new period or era starts. The first year of a period is called
gan-nen (元年). The years are named and counted with the Chinese numbers plus
-nen. It's highly recommended to know your birthday according to the Japanese
calendar. Dates by the Japanese calendar will be used in official documents in
Japan and are quite common in everyday conversation. Having this—and key
measurements such as shoe size, height and weight that have been converted to
the Japanese sizing system—will be useful when going to Japan. The most recent
periods include:

Meiji	明治	1868-1912
Taisho	大正	1912-1926
Showa	昭和	1926-1989
Heisei	平成	1989-April 2019
Reiwa	令和	*May 1, 2019-present

A note on celebrating birthdays in Japan. Traditionally everyone's chronological
age increases by one on the first day of the year regardless of one's actual date of
birth. This system is called *kazoe-doshi* (数え年). In this system—which gradually
faded due to the influence of western culture—a newborn baby is one-year old
immediately and turns two on the next New Year's day. As a result, celebrating
individual birthdays was not common. Birthdays are generally celebrated privately
among family and friends, but rarely at the workplace. The emperor's birthday is
an exception and is declared as a national holiday.

Milestone ages include the seventh night (*oshichiya* お七夜), third, fifth, and
seventh birthdays (*shichi-go-san* 七五三), 20th (*hatachi* 二十歳), 60th (*kanreki*
還暦), 77th (*kiju* 喜寿), 88th (*beiju* 米寿), and 99th (*hakuji* 白寿). Every
milestone is celebrated with different rituals.

NATIONAL HOLIDAYS

Date	English name	Official name	
January 1	New Year's Day	元日	*Ganjitsu*
2nd Monday of January	Coming of Age Day	成人の日	*Seijin no hi*

---

* Prince Naruhito offically ascended to the throne on May 1, 2019 when Emperor Akihito
  abdicated because of ill-health.

February 11	National Foundation Day	建国記念 の日	*Kenkoku kinen no hi*
February 23	The Emperor's Birthday	天皇誕生日	*Tennō tanjōbi*
March 20 or 21	Vernal Equinox Day	春分の日	*Shunbun no hi*
April 29	Shōwa Day	昭和の日	*Shōwa no hi*
May 3	Constitution Memorial Day	憲法記念日	*Kenpō kinenbi*
May 4	Greenery Day	みどりの日	*Midori no hi*
May 5	Children's Day	子供の日	*Kodomo no hi*
3rd Monday of July	Marine Day	海の日	*Umi no hi*
August 11	Mountain Day	山の日	*Yama no hi*
3rd Monday of September	Respect for the Aged Day	敬老の日	*Keirō no hi*
September 23 or 24	Autumnal Equinox Day	秋分の日	*Shūbun no hi*
2nd Monday of October	Health-Sports Day	体育の日	*Tai'iku no hi*
November 3	Culture Day	文化の日	*Bunka no hi*
November 23	Labor Thanksgiving Day	勤労感謝 の日	*Kinrō kansha no hi*

Source: http://en.wikipedia.org/wiki/Japanese_calendar

PATTERN PRACTICE 1

Cue: *Nano-ka desu ka.*
              Is it the 7th?
Response: *Ie, yō-ka desu.*
              No, it's the 8th.
Cue: *Jū-go-nichi desu ka.*
              Is it the 15th?
Response: *Ie, jū-roku-nichi desu.*
              No, it's the 16th.

Repeat the drill with the following:
1. *Mik-ka desu ka.*
2. *Jū-ku-nichi desu ka.*
3. *Kokono-ka desu ka.*
4. *Jū-san-nichi desu ka.*
5. *Sanjū-ichi nichi desu ka.*

PATTERN PRACTICE 2

Cue: ***Ni-jū nana-sai desu ka.***
            Are you 27 years old?
Response: ***E'e, ni-jū-nana-sai ni narimashita.***
            Yes, I have become (just turned) 27.
Cue: ***Takai desu ka.***
            Is it expensive?
Response: ***E'e, takaku narimashita.***
            Yes, it has become expensive.

Repeat the drill with the following:
1. ***Go-sen-en desu ka.***
2. ***Muzukashi'i desu ka.***
3. ***Samui desu ka.***
4. ***Yuki desu ka.***
5. ***Omoshiroku nai desu ka.***

EXERCISE 1
Say it in Japanese
A co-worker is checking the dates of events. Let him know.
1. It is Friday, the 13th.
2. It is February 14th.
3. It was September 11th, 2000.
4. It was July 4th, but it has been changed to the 5th.
5. It was December 25, but since it is Christmas, it has been delayed one week.
   (***Is-shū-kan osoku narimashita.***)

EXERCISE 2
Role Play
1. Ask a friend when her birthday is.
2. It's a friend's birthday. Congratulate her and ask her how old she is. Repeat the
   exercise congratulating a boss instead.
3. Ask a friend if he has had lunch yet.
4. Discuss the changes that have happened lately to the following:
   1) prices of things;
   2) weather;
   3) food at a particular restaurant;
   4) your work schedule.
5. Check the year and date of major historical events.

🔘 DIALOGUE 2 Personal History

Mei is talking to a professor at an event for international students.

Professor: Where are you from?

Go-shusshin wa?

ご出身は？

Mei: I was born in Shanghai and moved to the US when I was in middle school.

Shanhai de umareta n desu kedo, chūgaku no toki Amerika ni hikkoshita n desu.

上海で生まれたんですけど、中学の時アメリカに引っ越したんです。

Professor: Is that so? When did you come to Japan?

Ā, sō desu ka. Nihon ni wa itsu kita n desu ka.

ああ、そうですか。日本にはいつ来たんですか。

Mei: It was September last year, so it will be a year (now). It (the year) went by so fast!

Kyonen no ku-gatsu desu kara, ichi-nen ni narimasu. Atto iu ma deshita.

去年の九月ですから、一年になります。あっという間でした。

Professor: How do you like it in Japan? (Lit., How is life in Japan?)

Nihon no seikatsu wa dō desu ka.

日本の生活は、どうですか。

Mei: I'm enjoying it. At first, I didn't understand the language and it was hard.

Tanoshi'i desu. Hajime wa kotoba ga wakaranakute, komari mashita kedo.

楽しいです。はじめは言葉がわからなくて、困りましたけど。

Professor: Have you gotten accustomed to it by now?

Mō naremashita ka.

もう慣れましたか。

Mei: Yes, pretty much.

Hai, daitai.

はい、だいたい。

VOCABULARY

go-shusshin	ご出身	where one is from (Polite)
Shanhai	上海	Shanghai
umareru	生まれる	be born
chūgaku	中学	middle school
toki	時	time when

hikkosu	引っ越す	move (residence)
kyonen	去年	last year
-nen	年	classifier for years
ichi-nen	一年	one year
atto-iu-ma	あっという間	a blink of time; the time it takes to say "ah"
seikatsu	生活	living; every day life
seikatsu-suru	生活する	daily life
tanoshi'i	楽しい	fun; enjoyable
hajime	はじめ	beginning; at first
kotoba	言葉	language
wakaranai	わからない	not understand
wakaranakute	わからなくて	*te*-form of *wakaranai*
komaru	困る	lit., no understanding, have trouble; have difficulty
nareru	慣れる	get used to
daitai	だいたい	for the most part; generally speaking

ADDITIONAL VOCABULARY

sodatsu	育つ	grow up
nyūgaku-suru	入学する	enter school
sotsugyō-suru	卒業する	graduate
hairu	入る	enter
deru	出る	leave; emerge
owari	終わり	ending
shō-gakkō	小学校	elementary school
kōkō	高校	high school
daigaku-in	大学院	graduate school
kotoshi	ことし	this year
rainen	来年	next year
ototoshi	おととし	year before the last
sarainen	再来年	year after the next

GRAMMAR NOTE **More on the *Te*-Form**

We have seen how changing the first sentence's predicate into its *te*-form can combine two sentences.

Verb: ***Okinawa ni itte, asobimasu.***   I'll go to Okinawa and play.

Adjective: ***Kore, atarashikute, oishi'i desu.***   This is fresh and delicious.

Noun: ***Kyō wa ame de, samui desu.***   It's raining and (it's) cold today.

Let's look at what happens if the predicate in the first part of the sentence is in its negative form. All the negative forms are adjectives regardless of whether they

are originally a verb or a noun predicate. Therefore, the negative forms follow the adjective pattern, namely changing /-*nai*/ to /-*nakute*/.

Wakaranai → Wakaranakute komatta.
I didn't understand and had a hard time.
Eigo ja nai → Eigo ja nakute, Nihon-go desu.
It's not English; it's Japanese.
Takaku nai → Takaku nakute, yokatta desu.
I'm glad it wasn't expensive. (It wasn't expensive and I'm glad.)

Also note that the -*tai* form of verbs are adjectives as well, and the -*te* form follows the adjective pattern, namely changing -*tai* to -*takute* and -*taku nai* to -*taku nakute*.

Tabetai → Sushi ga tabetakute, chūmon-shita.
I wanted to eat sushi and so I ordered it.
Shitaku nai → Benkyō-shitaku nakute, terebi o mita.
I didn't want to study and so I watched TV.

GRAMMAR NOTE Relative Time Words

Time expressions such as *san-ji* "3 o'clock" and *mik-ka* "the 3rd" indicate specific points in time. In contrast, expressions such as *kyō* "today" and *ima* "now" refer to relative times defined by their relationship to the timing of a statement. These relative time words usually do not require the time particle *ni*. Compare:

Ashita shimasu.   I'll do it tomorrow.
Do-yōbi ni shimasu.   I'll do it on Saturday.

The chart below lists the most common relative time expressions. Please note the regular elements such as *mai* "every X", *sensen* "X before last", *sen* "last X", *kon* "this X", *rai* "next X", *sarai* "X after next".

Relative Time Words

hi day	*ototoi* day before yesterday	*kinō* yesterday	*kyō* today	*ashita/* *asu* tomorrow	*asatte* day after tomorrow	*mai-nichi* every day
asa morning	*ototoi no* *asa* morning of the day before yesterday	*kinō* *no asa* yesterday morning	*kesa* this morning	*ashita no* *asa* tomorrow morning	*asatte no* *asa* morning of the day after tomorrow	*mai-asa* every morning

ban/ yoru evening	*ototoi no ban/yoru* evening of the day before yesterday	*yūbe* yesterday evening	*konban* this evening	*ashita no ban/yoru* tomorrow evening	*asatte no ban/yoru* evening of the day after tomorrow	*mai-ban/ maiyo* every evening
shū week	*sensen-shū* week before last	*sen-shū* last week	*konshū* this week	*rai-shū* next week	*sarai-shū* week after next	*mai-shū* every week
tsuki month	*sensen- getsu* month before last	*sen-getsu* last month	*kongetsu* this month	*rai-getsu* next month	*sarai-getsu* month after next	*mai-tsuki/ getsu* every month
toshi year	*ototoshi* year before last	*kyonen* last year	*kotoshi* this year	*rai-nen* next year	*sarai-nen* year after next	*mai-toshi* every year
gakki academic term		*sen-gakki* last term	*kon- gakki* this term	*rai-gakki* next term		*mai-gakki* every term

PATTERN PRACTICE 3

Cue: *Amerika ni hikkoshimashita.*   I moved to America.
Response: *Itsu hikkoshita n desu ka.*   When did you move?
Cue: *Kodomo ga umaremashita.*   I had a child.
Response: *Itsu umareta n desu ka.*   When did you have a child?

Repeat the drill with the following:
1. *Daigaku ni nyūgaku-shimashita.*
2. *Hatachi ni narimashita.*
3. *Kōkō o sotsugyō-shimashita.*
4. *Nihon no bunka o benkyō-shimashita.*
5. *Amerika ni ryūgaku-shimashita.*

PATTERN PRACTICE 4

Cue: *Wakaranakatta no?*
                So, you didn't understand?
Response: *Un, wakaranakute, taihen datta.*
                Right. I didn't and I had a hard time.
Cue: *Yasashiku nakatta no?*
                So, it wasn't easy?
Response: *Un, yasashiku nakute taihen datta.*
                Right. It wasn't and I had a hard time.

Repeat the drill with the following:
1. *Benri ja nakatta no?*
2. *Eigo ja nakatta no?*
3. *Chikaku nakatta no?*
4. *Benkyō-shinakatta no?*
5. *Dekinakatta no?*

EXERCISE 3
Say it in Japanese
A co-worker has asked how you like living in Japan.
1. I enjoy it (I'm having fun.)
2. It's hard because I'm not used to it.
3. It was hard before, but has become a little easier.
4. I didn't know much about the Japanese culture and traditions before, but now I appreciate them very much (I like them now).
5. I didn't understand Japanese very well before and I had a lot of problems, but I'm okay for the most part now.

At a reception, you've been asked about your personal history.
6. I was born and grew up in Taiwan. I went from elementary school to high school there, but I went to college in America.
7. I moved from Shanghai to America when I was 12. It was hard because I didn't understand English very well.
8. I entered college in 2010, majored in Economics, studied in England for a year, and graduated from college in 2014. Now I'm a first year graduate student.
9. I came to Japan last summer, so it has been about six months. (The time) has gone by so fast!
10. I wasn't used to the Japanese culture and it was hard at first, but now I'm having fun.

EXERCISE 4
Role Play

1. Ask a co-worker the following:
   1) where she was born;
   2) where she grew up;
   3) where she went to school.
2. Ask a friend what she did or will do during the summer vacation
   1) last year;
   2) the year before;
   3) next year.
3. A co-worker has just returned from working in the US office for a year. Ask her how she liked living in the US.
4. Ask a new employee how working in this office has been for him.
5. Discuss a movie, a class, or an event you recently watched or attended with friends:
   1) How well did you understand the movie;
   2) How (difficult or easy) did you find the language used,
   3) How was it at the beginning?
   4) How about at the end?

🔘 DIALOGUE 3 Family

As the conversation continues, the professor asks Mei about her family.

Professor: Is your family doing well?
Go-kazoku wa ogenki desu ka.
ご家族は、お元気ですか。

Mei: Yes. My parents live in America, but we often talk on Skype.
Hai. Ryōshin wa Amerika ni sunde iru n desu kedo, yoku Sukaipu de hanashimasu.
はい。両親はアメリカに住んでいるんですけど、よくスカイプで話します。

Professor: How about (your) siblings?
Gokyōdai wa?
ご兄弟は？

Mei: Actually I'm an only child.
Jitsu wa hitori-kko na n desu.
実は一人っ子なんです。

Professor: Then, will you get a job in America?
Ja, Amerika de shūshoku desu ka.
じゃ、アメリカで就職ですか。

Mei: I don't know yet.
Mada wakarimasen.
まだわかりません。

VOCABULARY

kazoku	家族	family (Plain)
gokazoku	ご家族	family (Formal)
(o)genki (na)	（お）元気（な）	healthy; well; energetic
sumu	住む	live; take up residence
sunde iru	住んでいる	live; reside
Sukaipu	スカイプ	Skype
(go)kyōdai	ご兄弟	brothers; siblings
jitsu wa	実は	actually; the truth is
hitori-kko	一人っ子	only child
shūshoku-suru	就職する	find employment; get employed

Family Terms

Formal term	Plain term	
go-kazoku	*kazoku*	family
go-ryōshin	*ryōshin*	both parents
okā-san	*haha; mama; ofukuro*	mother

Formal term	Plain term	
otō-san	*chichi; papa; oyaji*	father
obā-san	*sobo*	grandmother
ojī-san	*sofu*	grandfather
go-kyōdai	*kyōdai*	brothers; siblings
onē-san	*ane*	older sister
onī-san	*ani*	older brother
imōto-san	*imōto*	younger sister
otōto-san	*otōto*	younger brother
oku-san	*kanai; tsuma*	wife
goshujin; dan'na-san	*shujin; otto*	husband
musume-san; ojō-san	*musume*	daughter
musuko-san; boc-chan	*musuko*	son
oko-san	*ko; kodomo*	child
oba-san	*oba*	aunt
oji-san	*oji*	uncle
o-mago-san	*mago*	grandchild
o-itoko-san	*itoko*	cousin
meigo-san	*mei*	niece
oigo-san	*oi*	nephew

For in-laws, **giri** is added, e.g., **giri no haha** "mother-in-law".

Occupations and Job Titles

isha	medical doctor; physician
bengoshi	attorney; lawyer
kyōshi	teacher (in a school)
hon yakuka	translator
tsūyaku	(language) interpretation; interpreter
ten-in	store clerk
eki-in	train station attendant
ginkō-in	banker
kōmu-in	civil servant
jimu-in	office clerk
bijinesuman	businessman
konsarutanto	consultant
jānarisuto	journalist
enjinia	engineer
wētoresu	waitress
keiei	management
keieisha	business owner; entrepreneur
shachō	company president
buchō	division chief
kachō	section chief

kakarichō	subsection chief
manējā	manager
hisho	secretary
kaisha-in	company employee
sararīman	white collar worker

GRAMMAR NOTE Family Terms

For each family term in Japanese, there is at least one plain form—to refer to your own family and used in legal documents—and one formal form—to refer to other people's family. Thus **uchi no chichi** means "my father" and *otaku no otō-san* "your father".

While one refers to her mother as **uchi no haha** when talking to people outside of her family, she uses *okā-san* when directly addressing her mother or talking to another member of her family about her. Within the family, generally speaking, the younger members call the older members by the formal family terms, while the older members call the younger members by their given names.

Another characteristic of Japanese family terms is that each family member can be referred to and addressed by the family term that is from the viewpoint of the youngest member. It's therefore not uncommon for a husband and wife to call each other *okā-san* "mom" and *otō-san* "dad", or for a parent to call the older son as *onī-chan* "big brother" and the youngest son as **boku** "me".

Sometimes, strangers and non-family members are addressed by the family terms that typically represent the age groups. **Obā-san** "grandma" and **Ojī-san** "grandpa" are often used to address seniors, and *onē-san* "big sister" and *onī-san* "big brother" to address young people. Strangers often call a woman accompanying a little child *okā-san* "mom". Avoid calling any woman **Oba-san** "auntie", which implies a middle-aged, not so attractive woman. Instead, you can use hesitation noises like **anō** or refer to the person as **ano hito** ("that person").

PATTERN PRACTICE 5

Cue:	*Uchi no kazoku desu.*	This is my family.
Response:	*Ā, gokazoku desu ka.*	Oh, it's your family?
Cue:	*Uchi no haha desu.*	This is my mother.
Response:	*Ā, okā-san desu ka.*	Oh, she's your mother?

Repeat the exercise using the following:
1. *Uchi no ryōshin desu.*
2. *Uchi no musuko desu.*
3. *Uchi no sofu desu.*
4. *Uchi no kanai desu.*
5. *Uchi no ane desu.*

PATTERN PRACTICE 6

Cue: ***Onī-san ogenki desu ka.***   Is your brother doing well?
Response: ***Ani desu ka. Hai, genki desu.***   My brother? Yes, he is.
Cue: ***Obā-san ogenki desu ka.***   Is your grandma doing well?
Response: ***Sobo desu ka. Hai genki desu.***   My grandma? Yes, she is.

Repeat the drill with the following information:
1. ***Otō-san ogenki desu ka.***
2. ***Ojō-san ogenki desu ka.***
3. ***Oko-san ogenki desu ka.***
4. ***Go-kyōdai ogenki desu ka.***
5. ***Oku-san ogenki desu ka.***

EXERCISE 5
Say it in Japanese
You are talking about family with a friend.
1. How many people are in your family?
2. Where do they live?
3. Do you have siblings?
4. Are your grandparents doing well?
5. How old are your parents?
6. There are six people in my family; my parents, older brother and two little sisters.
7. Everyone lives in America, but my older sister will move to France next year.
8. My grandma lives with my parents.
9. My little brother will graduate from high school next spring.
10. My grandpa is already 90 years old, but is still very healthy.

EXERCISE 6
Role Play
1. Practice introducing the following family members to Ms. Sato:
    1) mother;
    2) big sister;
    3) daughter;
    4) wife and children.
2. Ask Ms. Sato where her family lives. Are they doing well? Does she talk to them frequently?
3. You've been asked about your future plans. Mention that you want to find a job in Japan.
4. Ask a friend what kind of company she wants to work for (be employed by).
5. Show a family picture to a friend and explain who's who in the picture.

🔘 DIALOGUE 4 Marriage

Michael noticed Ms. Suzuki wearing a wedding ring.

Michael: So, are you married, Ms. Suzuki?
Suzuki-san, kekkon-shite iru n desu ka.
鈴木さん、結婚しているんですか。

Suzuki: Yes, I got married in 2010.
Un, ni-sen jū-nen ni kekkon-shita no.
うん、2010年に結婚したの。

Michael: I didn't know. Do you have any children?
Shirimasen deshita. Oko-san wa?
知りませんでした。お子さんは？

Suzuki: I want children, but it hasn't happened yet.
Hoshi'i kedo ne. Mada na no.
欲しいけどね。まだなの。
Are you dating anyone?
Maikeru-kun wa dareka to kōsai-shite iru no?
マイケル君は誰かと交際しているの？

Michael: No, I'm looking for a girlfriend (lit., now girlfriend wanted).
Ie, ima koibito-boshū-chū desu.
いえ、今、恋人募集中です。

Suzuki: Really? Good luck. (lit., Do your best.)
Ā sō. Ganbatte ne.
ああ、そう。がんばってね。

Michael: Thanks. (lit., I'll try my best.)
Hai, ganbarimasu.
はい、がんばります。

VOCABULARY

kekkon	結婚	marriage
kekkon-suru	結婚する	get married
kekkon-shite iru	結婚している	be married
siru	知る	find out
shitte iru	知っている	know
hoshi'i	ほしい	want
-kun	君	suffix for name of male or subordinate, casual alternative of *-san*, more polite than name alone
dareka	誰か	someone
kōsai	交際	dating; socializing
kōsai-suru	交際する	date; socialize

koibito	恋人	girl/boyfriend
boshū	募集	recruiting
boshū-suru	募集する	recruit; take applications
-chū	中	in progress; in the middle of

* ***Chū*** attaches to action nouns such as ***boshū*** "hiring", ***benkyō*** "study", ***kaimono*** "shopping", etc., and means someone/something is in the middle of the action.

| ***boshū-chū*** | 募集中 | now hiring; wanted |

* This is usually about jobs, but also used for prospective partners.

| ***ganbaru*** | がんばる | try hard; persevere |

*Ganbatte kudasai means "Best wishes" or "Good luck!" ***Ganbarimashō*** means "Let's hang in there" or "Let's do our best!" These are very common expressions of encouragement when facing a challenge. You respond to them by saying ***Ganbarimasu!***

ADDITIONAL VOCABULARY

-chan	ちゃん	affectionate suffix for child's name
aka-chan	赤ちゃん	baby
rikon-suru	離婚する	get divorced
kon'yaku-suru	婚約する	get engaged
dokushin	独身	unmarried; single
wakareru	別れる	split; break up
byōki	病気	sick; disease

*The polite version is *gobyōki*. While *genki/ogenki* is a *na*-noun, *byōki/gobyōki* is a regular noun, e.g., *genki na hito* "healthy person"; *byōki no hito* "sick person".

nakunaru	亡くなる	decease(d)
shinu	死ぬ	die

*Nakunaru is more indirect and appropriate to describe someone's passing. *Shinu* is direct and usually avoided for people.

GRAMMAR NOTE Verb *te*-form + *iru* = Progressive Form

The pattern verb -*te* form + *iru* has two basic meanings: Progressive or Resultative.

1. Progressive: On-going process (similar to the progressive form in English)

Ima, tabete iru.	I'm eating now.
Mainichi renshū-shite iru.	I'm practicing every day.
Sato-san to kōsai-shite iru.	I'm dating Ms. Sato.

In this usage, the action is repeated or continuous over a period of time, and may or may not be happening right at the moment. This pattern implies there is a beginning and ending point, and therefore refers to a current and temporary action as opposed to a permanent and general characteristic. Compare the following.

Yasai o yoku tabemasu.	I eat a lot of vegetables (as a general habit).
Yasai o yoku tabete imasu.	I'm eating a lot of vegetables (these days).

2. Resultative: a state resulting from an action or a past experience

Kekkon-shite imasu.	I'm married.
Kuruma ni notte imasu.	He is in the car.
Daigaku o sotsugyō-shite imasu.	I have graduated from college.

These sentences do not normally mean that you are in the middle of an action. They all indicate the state resulted from the action.

The *te-iru* pattern can be either progressive and resultative and the correct interpretation depends on the context. Study the following example.

Kōhī o nonde imasu.

Progressive: I am drinking coffee right now; I'm drinking coffee these days.
Resultative: I have had coffee (so I'm not sleepy).

However, certain verbs in the *te-iru* form are normally interpreted as resultative only. These are called "instantaneous verbs" and refer to actions that change the status instantaneously and do not persist. These include *kekkon-suru* "marry" and *shiru* "find out". These instantaneous verbs in the *-te-iru* form usually indicate the resultative state. Compare the following pairs.

Kekkon-shimasu.	I will get married. (instantaneous action)
Kekkon-shite imasu.	I'm married. (resulted state)
Shirimashita.	I found out about it. (instantaneous action)
Shitte imasu.	I know it. (resulted state)

So, watch out for the difference in the meaning between the following.

Kekkon-shimasen.	I will not get married.
Kekkon-shite imasen.	I'm not married.

Also, verbs of motion such as *kuru*, *iku*, and *kaeru* in the *te-iru* form normally refer to a state. Compare the following.

Musuko wa daigaku ni ikimasu.
My son will go to college.
Musuko wa daigaku ni itte imasu.
My son has gone to college (and he is there now) or
My son goes to college. (He is currently a college student.)

Itte imasu does not mean someone is on his way to some place. Similarly, *kite imasu* means someone has come here (and is here) or someone comes here regularly over a period of time. Compare the two responses.

Honda-san wa imasu ka.	Is Mr. Honda here?
Hai, kite imasu.	Yes, he is here (he has arrived already).
Ima kimasu.	He'll come soon (but is not here yet).

Note that in casual speech, *i* of *iru* or *imasu* often drops. Thus you have the following.

Nani shite (i)ru no?	What are you doing?
Mēru mite (i)masu.	I'm looking at e-mails.

GRAMMAR NOTE *Shitte iru* = **Know**

The verb *shiru* (*U*-verb) is an instantaneous verb meaning "find out; get to know". Its *te-iru* form means a state of having found out something and having knowledge of something, namely "know". Although the affirmative is in the *te-iru* form, the negative "I do not know" is NOT in the *te-iru* form.

Ano hito shitte imasu ka.	Do you know that person?
Formal: *I'ie, shirimasen.*	I don't know.
Informal: *U'un, shiranai.*	I don't know.

Kore, shitte imashitaka.	Did you know this?
Formal: *I'ie, shirimasen deshita.*	No, I didn't know.
Informal: *U'un, shiranakatta.*	No, I didn't know.

Itsu shirimashita ka.	When did you find out?
Formal: *Kinō shirimashita.*	I found out yesterday.
Informal: *Kinō shitta.*	I found out yesterday.

The polite form (Honorific), which you use to describe the action of someone above you, is *gozonji*, a noun.

Gozonji desu ka.	Do you know?
Sensei wa gozonji ja nai desu.	The teacher does not know.

GRAMMAR NOTE X *ga hoshi'i* = **Want X**

Hoshi'i is translated as "is desired" or "(I) want". It is an adjective and takes the particle *ga* (*wa* or *mo* with the due shift of meaning) for what is wanted, and can make a double subject sentence.

I'i shigoto ga hoshi'i desu nē.	I want a good job.
Kore mo hoshikunai desu ka.	Don't you want this, too?
Watashi wa kodomo wa hoshikunai kedo…	I do not want children, but…

Like the *-tai* form of verbs, *hoshi'i* normally expresses the speaker's "wants" in a statement and the addressee's in a question. When expressing the third person's desire, *hoshi'i* is usually followed by *n desu* or *no* referring to the situation.

Nani ga hoshi'i?	What do you want?
Ano hito wa nani ga hoshi'i n desu ka.	What does that person want?

When combined with a verb *-te* form, *hoshi'i* expresses a desire for someone else to do an action.

Ganbatte hoshi'i desu nē.	I want him to do his best.
Haha ni hayaku genki ni natte hoshi'i.	I want my mother to get well soon.

Contrast this with the verb *-tai* form, which expresses a desire for one's own action.

Ganbaritai desu nē.	I want to do my best.
Hayaku genki ni naritai.	I want to get well soon.

PATTERN PRACTICE 7

Cue:	*Mō tabeta?*	Have you already eaten?
Response:	*Ima tabete (i)ru.*	I'm eating right now.
Cue:	*Mō mita?*	Have you already looked at it?
Response:	*Ima mite (i)ru.*	I'm looking at it right now.

Repeat the drill with the following:
1. *Mō kaita?*
2. *Mō hanashita?*
3. *Mō tsukutta?*
4. *Mō mēru-shita?*
5. *Mō yonda?*

PATTERN PRACTICE 8

Cue:	*Kekkon-suru n desu ka.*	Are you going to get married?
Response:	*Mō kekkon-shite imasu.*	I'm already married.
Cue:	*Mei-san to kōsai-suru n desu ka.*	Are you going to go out with (date) Mei?
Response:	*Mō kōsai-shite imasu.*	I'm already going out with her.

Repeat the drill with the following:
1. *Gakusei o boshū-suru n desu ka.*
2. *Kono apāto ni sumu n desu ka.*
3. *Goshujin ga kuru n desu ka.*
4. *Daigaku ni iku n desu ka.*
5. *Sumaho ga yasuku naru n desu ka.*

EXERCISE 7
Say it in Japanese
On the phone, a friend has asked you what you are doing.
1. I'm working.
2. I'm eating dinner with my older sister. It's her birthday, so...
3. I was studying, but I'm taking a break right now.
4. I was watching a baseball game on TV, but it became boring, and...
5. I haven't eaten lunch yet. Would you like to go have lunch?

You and your co-workers are discussing a project.
6. I want Ms. Sato to look at this schedule, but...
7. I want to make the PowerPoint presentation, but is it okay?
8. I want someone to make copies of this document, but...
9. I want Michael to try harder (*motto ganbatte*), but...
10. I want to know the deadline, but do you know?

EXERCISE 8
Role Play
1. A friend got a new job. Congratulate her and wish her good luck.
2. Ask a co-worker the following:
    1) if he is dating;
    2) if he is married;
    3) when he got married,
    4) if he has any children;
    5) how many children he has and how old they are.
3. You see a stranger in your office. Ask a co-worker if she knows that person.
4. At a career center, confirm the following:
    1) this company is hiring (taking applications from) interns;
    2) this school is hiring an English teacher.
5. Ask a friend what she wants for her birthday. As a child, what did she want for Christmas?

REVIEW QUESTIONS
1. How do you count and name days, months, and years in Japanese?
2. a) Describe two ways to count human age in Japanese.
    b) What are the two ways to say 20 years old?
3. What are the basic meanings of *mō* and *mada*?
4. a) How do you say "It has become beautiful" and "It has become expensive" in Japanese?
    b) How do you explain the difference in their patterns?
5. In relative time expressions, what do "*rai-*" and "*sen-*" mean?
6. a) For each family term in Japanese, there is at least one plain form and one formal form. How are they used?
    b) How are family terms used for non-family members?
7. a) What are the two basic meanings of /-*te* form of a verb + *iru*/?
    b) How do you translate the following:
        1) *tabete iru*;
        2) *sunde iru*;
        3) *kite iru*?
8. a) How do you say "I know Ms. Sato?" in Japanese?
    b) How about "I don't know Ms. Sato"?
9. How are *hoshi'i* and the *-tai* form of verbs different?

LESSON 9

Opinions and Feelings

Fancy may kill or cure. (Worry is the cause of illness.)
病は気から　*Yamai wa ki kara*

DIALOGUE 1 A Good Idea

Michael makes a proposal at a meeting.

Michael: What do you think of this?
 Kore, dō omoimasu ka.
 これ、どう思いますか。

Suzuki: I think it's a good idea.
 I'i aidea da to omou.
 いいアイデアだと思う。

Sato: I think so, too.
 Watashi mo sō omoimasu.
 私もそう思います。

Coming out of the meeting, Michael shares his feelings with Ms. Sato.

Michael: I did it! Actually I was nervous. Now I feel relieved.
 Yatta! Jitsu wa, dokidoki shite ita n desu. Hotto shimashita.
 やった！実はドキドキしていたんです。ほっとしました。

VOCABULARY

omou	思う	think
aidea	アイデア	idea
to	と	particle of quotation
Yatta!	やった！	I did it!; Yippee!; Woohoo!
dokidoki (-suru)	ドキドキ（する）	nervous; excited (heart-pounding)
hotto-suru	ほっとする	feel relieved; feel comforted

GRAMMAR NOTE Expressing Thoughts

In Japanese, to say "I think...", you do so using the quotation particle /*to*/ followed
by the verb *omou* "think".

 I'i aidea da to omou. I think it's a good idea.
 I'i aidea ja nai to omoimasu. I don't think it's a good idea.

These expressions are complex structures in which a smaller sentence (e.g., "it's a good idea") is embedded in a larger sentence "I think it's a good idea". The embedded sentence reflects the actual thought as it occurs, thus the tense in the quotation remains as it was in the original thought. Compare the following.

Mēru ga kita to omotta.   I thought that an email had come.

Mēru ga kuru to omotta.   I thought that an email would come.

The predicate in the quoted sentence must always be in the Informal form. However, you can choose between the formal and informal form for the predicate of the larger sentence, and that determines the style of the entire sentence.

Formal sentence		Expressed as an opinion (Formal)	
Ame desu.	It is raining.	*Ame da to omoimasu.*	I think it's raining.
Ame deshita.	It was raining.	*Ame datta to omoimasu.*	I think it rained.
Ame ja nai desu.	It is not raining.	*Ame ja nai to omoimasu.*	I don't think it is raining.
Ame ja nai desu ka.	Isn't it raining?	*Ame ja nai ka to omoimasu.*	I wonder if it's not raining.

The sentences on the right above can be changed to the informal style by switching *omoimasu* to *omou*. Note that by expressing your thought in the form of a question, you can soften its impact and show politeness when you are disagreeing.

Chotto muzukashi'i ka to omoimasu. I wonder if it might be a bit difficult.

Fuben ja nai ka to omu kedo...   I wonder if it isn't inconvenient, and...

GRAMMAR NOTE Onomatopoeia

Dokidoki is an example of Japanese onomatopoeia (オノマトペ), like the sound your heartbeat makes. Onomatopoeia is abundant in Japanese, as you can see on the pages of comic books. The list on the next page are the most common.

Many Japanese onomatopoeias consist of four syllables with the first two syllables repeated twice, like *dokidoki*, and you find them written in either *hiragana* or *katakana*. Usually *shimasu* or *desu* follow them.

Dokidoki shimasu.   I'm nervous/thrilled.

Dokidoki deshita.   I was nervous/thrilled.

Onomatopoeias

pekopeko	ペコペコ	hungry
karakara	カラカラ	thirsty; dry
kutakuta	くたくた	tired
perapera	ペラペラ	fluent
hotto-suru	ホッとする	get relieved
gakkari-suru	がっかりする	get disappointed
iraira-suru	イライラする	irritated; frustrated
harahara-suru	ハラハラする	apprehensive
mukamuka-suru	ムカムカする	have a surge of anger; feel sick; queasy
kuyokuyo-suru	クヨクヨする	worry about a trivial matter; mope; brood
ukiuki-suru	ウキウキする	happy and excited; high spirited
mesomeso-suru	メソメソする	whimper and cry
nikoniko-suru	ニコニコする	smile; looking happy

PATTERN PRACTICE 1

Cue: *Kore wa i'i aidea desu ka.*
         Is this a good idea?
Response: *E'e, i'i aidea da to omoimasu.*
         Yes, I think so.
Cue: *Ano hito wa kimasen ka.*
         Will that person not be coming?
Response: *E'e, konai to omoimasu.*
         No, I don't think he will.

Repeat the drill with the following:
1. *Ano kodomo wa go-sai desu ka.*
2. *Shiken wa daijōbu desu ka.*
3. *Kaigi wa Getsu-yōbi deshita ka.*
4. *Ano gakusei wa apāto ni sunde imasu ka.*
5. *Mēru wa kimashita ka.*

PATTERN PRACTICE 2

Cue: *Takai to omoimasu ka.*
         Do you think it's expensive?
Response: *Ie, takai to wa omoimasen kedo…*
         No, I don't think it is, but…

Cue: ***Eigo perapera da to omoimasu ka.***
             Do you think he is fluent in English?
Response: ***Ie, perapera da to wa omoimasen kedo…***
             No, I do not think he is, but…

Repeat the drill using the following:
1. ***Kekkon-shitai desu ka.***
2. ***Oishikunai desu ka.***
3. ***Minna shitte imasu ka.***
4. ***Mō naremashita ka.***
5. ***Kodomo hoshi'i desu ka.***

EXERCISE 1
Say it in Japanese
You've been asked your opinions at an office meeting.
1. I think it's the best idea.
2. I don't think it's a good idea, but…
3. I wonder if it isn't difficult.
4. I thought it was a good idea before, but now I don't think so.
5. I think we talked about this last week.

EXERCISE 2
Role Play
1. You have just presented your proposal at a meeting. Ask everyone what they think.
2. Someone has expressed her disagreement at the meeting. Ask her the reason why she thinks that way.
3. You are about to have an interview. Express your nervousness to your friend. After the interview, express how relieved you are.
4. Express how you are feeling:
   1) hungry;
   2) thirsty;
   3) frustrated;
   4) tired;
   5) disappointed.
5. You have just closed a big business deal. Express your joy triumphantly to the following people:
   1) your co-workers;
   2) to your friend.

🔘 DIALOGUE 2 Being Sick

Yuki is worried because Mei looks sick.

Yuki: What's wrong?
Dō shita no?
どうしたの。

Mei: I just have a headache.
Chotto atama ga itai no.
ちょっと頭が痛いの。

Yūki: Are you alright? Have you taken medicine?
Daijōbu? Kusuri, nonda?
大丈夫。薬、飲んだ？

Mei: Yes. It may be a cold.
Un. Kaze ka mo shirenai.
うん。風邪かもしれない。

Yuki: You'd better go to a hospital.
Byōin ni itta hō ga i'i yo.
病院に行ったほうがいいよ。

Mei: No, it's not a big deal.
Iya, taishita koto nai kara.
いや、大したことないから。

VOCABULARY

atama	頭	head
itai	痛い	painful; hurt
kusuri	薬	medicine
kaze	風邪	a cold
ka mo shirenai	かもしれない	maybe
itta hō ga i'i	行ったほうがいい	better to go
taishita koto nai	大したことない	not a big deal

ADDITIONAL VOCABULARY

isha	医者	doctor
oisha-san	お医者さん	doctor (polite)
netsu ga aru	熱がある	have fever
seki o suru	咳をする	cough
kushami o suru	くしゃみをする	sneeze
kega o suru	けがをする	get injured
arerugī	アレルギー	allergy
tsuyoi	強い	strong

yowai	弱い	weak
tasukeru	助ける	rescue; save life
Tasukete!	助けて！	Help!
kyūkyū-sha	救急車	ambulance
Kyūkyūsha onegai-shimasu.	救急車、お願いします。	Please get an ambulance.

Body parts

karada	体	body
atama	頭	head
kami	髪	hair
kao	顔	face
me	目	eye
hana	鼻	nose
kuchi	口	mouth
mimi	耳	ear
kubi	首	neck
nodo	喉	throat
ha	歯	tooth
kata	肩	shoulder
se/senaka	背; 背中	back
onaka	お腹	belly; stomach
heso	へそ	belly button
mune	胸	chest; breast
ude	腕	arm
hiji	ひじ	elbow
te	手	hand
yubi	指	finger; toe
tsume	爪	nail
koshi	腰	lower back
ashi	足	leg; foot
hiza	膝	knee
ashi-kubi	足首	ankle
kakato	かかと	heel
shinzō	心臓	heart
hai	肺	lung
kanzō	肝臓	liver
i	胃	stomach (the organ)
chō	腸	intestine
jinzō	腎臓	kidney
hone	骨	bone
kin-niku	筋肉	muscle

GRAMMAR NOTE X–*shita hō ga i'i* **"It would be better if you do X"**

Earlier we learned that /*X no hō ga i'i* / means that X is better, in comparing two alternatives.

Dochira no hō ga i'i desu ka.   Which is better?
Kippu yori IC kādo no hō ga i'i desu.   IC cards are better than tickets.

You can also compare two actions, often doing or not doing something. And when you choose doing something as the better alternative, you can put it in the Informal Past form before *hō ga i'i*.

Byōin ni itta hō ga i'i.   You'd better go to the hospital.
Kusuri o nonda hō ga i'i desu.   You'd better take medicine.

If not doing something is the better choice, then you put the Informal Non-past Negative form before *hō ga i'i*.

Unten-shinai hō ga i'i.   You'd better not drive.
Sake nomanai hō ga i'i desu.   You'd better not drink Sake.

The less desirable alternative can be placed before *yori* "than" in the Informal form.

Sushi wa tsukuru yori katta hō ga i'i.   Buying sushi is better than making it.
Benkyō-shinai yori shita hō ga i'i.   Studying would be better than not
                                            studying.

You can also compare two states, being or not being a certain way, using adjectives and nouns.

Benri na hō ga i'i.   It's better if it is convenient.
Takai yori yasui hō ga i'i.   It's better if it's cheap than expensive.

GRAMMAR NOTE X *ka mo shirenai* = **"Might be" or "Possibly"**

Ka mo shirenai and its formal version *ka mo shiremasen* mean "might be" or "possibly". (Note that it's *shiREnai*, not *shiRAnai*.) They follow the Informal form of a predicate, and indicate uncertainty or possibility of the proposition.

Kaze ka mo shirenai.   I may have a cold.
Chotto muzukashi'i ka mo shiremasen yo.   It may be difficult.
Satō-san wa kaetta ka mo shirenai.   Ms. Sato may have gone home.

When the sentence has a noun predicate, *da* drops before *ka mo shirenai*, but *datta* stays.

Ame ka mo shirenai.   It may rain.
Ame datta ka mo shirenai.   It may have rained.

How is *ka mo shirenai* different from *deshō/darō* "probably"? Both indicate uncertainty, but *ka mo shirenai* usually indicates being less certain than *deshō/darō*. In fact, you can use both in order to express the different levels of certainty as follows.

> *Ashita wa i'i otenki deshō. Demo ame ka mo shiremasen.*
> It will probably be sunny tomorrow. However, it's possible that it will rain.

These expressions of uncertainty are often combined with *omou* "think" in order to express different shades of estimated uncertainty in subtler ways.

> *Byōin ni itta hō ga i'i ka mo shirenai to omou.*
> I think that it might be better if you go to the hospital.

PATTERN PRACTICE 3

Cue:	*Kusuri nomimasu ne.*	You'll take medicine, right?
Response:	*Hai, nonda hō ga i'i desu ne.*	Yes, it would be better, right?
Cue:	*Osake nomimasen ne.*	You won't drink alcohol, right?
Response:	*Hai, nomanai hō ga i'i desu ne.*	Right. It would be better not to, right?

Repeat the drill using the following:
1. *Byōin ni ikimasu ne.*
2. *Dekakemasen ne.*
3. *Okāsan ni wa hanashimasen ne.*
4. *Senpai ni kikimasu ne.*
5. *Kippu, yoyaku-shimasu ne.*

PATTERN PRACTICE 4

Cue:	*Byōki ja nai deshō?*	He is not sick, isn't he?
Response:	*Iya, byōki ka mo shiremasen yo.*	Well, he may be sick, you know.
Cue:	*Satō-san wa shitte iru deshō?*	Ms. Sato knows it, right?
Response:	*Iya, shiranai ka mo shiremasen yo.*	Well. She may not (know), you know.

Repeat the drill using the following:
1. *Kaze deshō?*
2. *Sakana wa suki ja nai deshō?*
3. *Minna sō omou deshō?*
4. *Kono kusuri nonda hō ga i'i deshō?*
5. *Hikōki wa mada tsuite inai deshō?*

EXERCISE 3
Say it in Japanese
You are in a doctor's office.
1. I have a headache and a fever.
2. I have a stomachache and have little appetite (do not want to eat much).
3. It may not be a big deal, but I cough a lot. Do you suppose I have a cold?
4. I've been taking medicine for a week, but it doesn't get better at all.
5. I have pain in my right shoulder and lower back.

A friend is sick. Offer your advice.
6. You'd better take medicine and rest.
7. You'd better go to the hospital, although it may not be serious (not a big deal).
8. You'd better not to go to work today.
9. You'd better eat something. I'll make something. Do you have any allergies (to food)?
10. You'd better not worry about anything (things). Get well soon.

EXERCISE 4
Role Play
1. Ask the following people what is wrong and ask if they are okay.
   1) a stranger;
   2) a friend
2. You have cold-like symptoms. Explain them to a co-worker and ask if he thinks you should see a doctor (go to a hospital).
3. Tell the doctor the following:
   1) your medical history;
   2) your family's medical history and
   3) general physical traits that run in your family.
4. A friend is struggling with a foreign language class. Offer her your advice as to how to improve proficiency.
5. A friend just collapsed and does not respond. Get help.

🔘 DIALOGUE 3 Emotions

Ms. Sato asks Michael about living alone.

Sato: Don't you get lonely, living alone?
           Hitori-gurashi wa sabishiku nai?
           一人暮らしは、寂しくない？

Michael: No, everyone is so kind, and I have a pet, too, so…
           Ie, minasan shinsetsu da shi, petto mo iru shi.
           いえ、みなさん親切だし、ペットもいるし。

Sato: What? Did you say a pet?
           E? Petto tte?
           え？ペットって。

Michael shows a picture of his pet to Ms. Sato.

Michael: I have a cat. Here. So therapeutic (to have it)!
           E'e, neko o katte iru n desu. Hora! Sugoku iyasaremasu yo.
           ええ、猫を飼っているんです。ほら。すごく癒されますよ。

Sato: So cute! What is its name?
           Kawai'i! Namae wa nan te iu n desu ka.
           かわいい！名前は何て言うんですか。

Michael: I'm a bit embarrassed, but it's called Tiger.
           Chotto hazukashi'i n desu kedo ne, "Taigā" tte iu n desu.
           ちょっと恥ずかしいんですけどね、「タイガー」っていうん
           です。

Sato: Wow!
           Sugoi!
           すごい！

VOCABULARY

hitori-gurashi	一人暮らし	living alone
sabishi'i	寂しい	lonely
shinsetsu (na)	親切（な）	kind
petto	ペット	pet
-shi	し	and (listing reasons)
neko	猫	cat
kau	飼う	keep (animal)
sugoku	すごく	awfully; very
iyasareru	癒される	therapeutic; get healed
iu	言う	say; tell
tte	て	Informal version of the quotation particle *to*
nan te iu	何ていう	what is it called?

| *hazukashi'i* | 恥ずかしい | embarrassed; feel shy |
| *sugoi* | すごい | superb; extraordinary; awful |

ADDITIONAL VOCABULARY

imi	意味	meaning
dō iu imi	どういう意味	what does it mean
naku	泣く・鳴く	cry; sounds made by animals
warau	笑う	laugh; smile
okoru	怒る	get angry; reprimand

Pets

inu	犬	dog
sakana	魚	fish
tori	鳥	bird
kingyo	金魚	goldfish
koi	鯉	Koi fish
usagi	うさぎ	rabbit
kame	かめ	turtle
hamusutā	ハムスター	hamster
konchū	昆虫	insect; bug
dōbutsu	動物	animals

Emotions

sabisi'i	寂しい	lonely
ureshi'i	嬉しい	delighted; glad
kanashi'i	悲しい	sad
hazukashi'i	恥ずかしい	embarrassed; feel shy
kurushi'i	苦しい	painful
natsukashi'i	懐かしい	feel nostalgic
tsurai	辛い	feel hardship; miserable
kowai	怖い	scared; afraid
shinpai (na)	心配（な）	worried
anshin (na)	安心（な）	feeling at ease; relief
shiawase (na)	幸せ（な）	happy; happiness
zan-nen (na)	残念（な）	regrettable; feel sorry

GRAMMAR NOTE Quotation X *to iu*

X *to i'imashita* means "someone said X". X represents the quote and is followed by the quotation particle *to* and the verb *i'imasu* (*iu*, a *U*-verb) "say, tell". In casual speech, the informal version of the quotation particle *tte* is often used. The quote X can end in either the Formal or Informal form depending on whether it is a direct

quote or indirect quote. The tense of the quoted sentence remains the same as in the original quote.

Shimasu to/tte i'imashita.	He said, "I'll do it".
Suru to/tte i'imashita.	He said that he would do it.
Shita to/tte i'imashita.	He said that he had done it.

In casual speech, the quote can end with *tte*.

Ashita ame da tte.	They say it will rain tomorrow.
Ame tte?	Did you say "rain"? or Did they say "rain"?

The particle *tte* can follow any word, and indicates that the preceding word is unfamiliar to you.

Iyasareru tte, dō iu imi desu ka.	What does *iyasareru* mean?
Konchū tte, nan desu ka.	What is *konchū*?
Satō-san tte, shinsetsu desu nē.	Ms. Sato is kind, isn't she?

(I recently discovered this about her.)

Use this pattern to quote anything, such as sounds, noises or foreign words.

"Thank you" *to i'imashita.*	He said, "Thank you."
Aka-chan ga mā to itta.	The baby said, "*Mā*."

When X in /*X to iu*/ or its formal version /*X to i'imasu*/ stands for the name of something or someone, it means "it is called X".

Kono ryōri wa nan to iu n desu ka.	What is this dish called?
Kore wa Eigo de nan to i'imasu ka.	What do you call this in English?

Similarly, /*X to iu Y*/ means "Y called X".

J-Net to iu kaisha	a company called J-Net
Oda-san to iu hito kara denwa desu.	It's a phone call from a person called Oda.
Nan to iu eki de oriru n desu ka.	

So, which station (a station called what) should we get off at?

You can ask what something means by saying:

Dō iu imi desu ka.	What does it mean?

When you want to clarify something, you can ask:

X tte, dō iu imi desu ka.	As for what is called X… what does it mean?

The verb *i'imasu* has two polite versions. *Osshaimasu* (*ossharu*, a Special Polite verb) is the honorific version (putting the person in a higher position) and *mōshimasu* (*mōsu*, a U-verb) is the humble version (where the speaker is putting him/herself in a lower position relative to the addressee). The honorific form refers

to someone above you and the humble form refers to yourself and your group. These expressions are very common in introductions.

Sumisu to mōshimasu. Dōzo yoroshiku. My name is Smith. How do you do?
Kochira, Honda-san to osshaimasu.   This person is called Mr./Ms. Honda.
Onamae wa nan to ossharu n desu ka.   What is your name?

GRAMMAR NOTE Expressing Emotions

Many words that express emotion are adjectives and others are *na*-nouns. They both appear in the double subject structure, where the first subject is the person who feels the emotion and the second subject is the cause of the emotion.

Watashi wa inu ga kowai.   I'm scared of dogs.
Nani ga kowai no?   What are you scared of?

Kowai can be translated either as "scared" or "scary" depending on the subject. Similarly, many of the emotion words have two English translations.

Ame ga shinpai desu.   "I'm worried about the rain" or "Rain worries me".
Namae ga hazukashi'i.   "I'm embarrassed by the name" or "The name is embarrassing."

Usually the emotion word expresses the speaker's feeling in a statement, and the addressee's in a question. When describing other people's feelings, it's common to attach /n desu/ to the emotion words. This is because one cannot state as fact exactly how others feel as a fact, and can only describe the situation in terms of how it appears.

Satō-san wa kanashi'i n desu.   Ms. Sato is sad (Lit., It's the case that Ms. Sato is sad.)

Alternatively, you can quote what others say regarding how they feel.

Satō-san wa kanashi'i tte.   Ms. Sato said that she is sad.

GRAMMAR NOTE Sentence + *shi*

Shi added to the end of a sentence indicates that the preceding sentence presents one reason among others that leads to the conclusion. Other reasons may follow.

Ame da shi.   Because it's raining, and… (so, I'm not going)

You can link more than two sentences using *shi*. The last sentence in the sequence can be either another reason or the conclusion. When asked about a restaurant for example, you may link three characteristics or two characteristics and a conclusion as follows.

Oishi'i shi, yasui shi, kirei desu yo.
The food is good, it's cheap and the place is clean.

Oishi'i shi, yasui shi, suki desu yo.
The food is good, and it's cheap, so I like it.

Since **shi** implies there are other reasons, it is often used to make a sentence sound inconclusive, thus polite in some cases, even when it is actually the only reason. You may notice younger speakers use **shi**-ending sentences a lot for this reason.

PATTERN PRACTICE 5

Cue: *Sabishi'i?* Are you lonely?
Response: *Mae wa sabishi katta kedo, mō sabishiku nai yo.*
                I was, but not anymore.
Cue: *Shinpai?* Are you worried?
Response: *Mae wa shinpai datta kedo, mō shinpai ja nai yo.*
                I was, but not anymore.

Repeat the drill using the following:
1. *Kanashi'i?*
2. *Anshin?*
3. *Natsukashi'i?*
4. *Tsurai?*
5. *Kowai?*

PATTERN PRACTICE 6

Cue: *Petto ga iru tte.*   He says he has a pet.
Response: *Dare ga iru tte itta no?*   Who said that he has one?
Cue: *Tabete kudasai tte.*   They said, "Please eat".
Response: *Dare ga tabete tte itta no?*   Who said, "Please eat"?

Repeat the drill using the following:
1. *Hazukashi'i tte.*
2. *Minasan shinsetsu da tte.*
3. *Petto ga shinda tte.*
4. *Denwa-shite kudasai tte.*
5. *Mada kekkon-shite inai tte.*

PATTERN PRACTICE 7

Cue: *Neko no namae wa Taigā desu ka.*
                Is the name of your cat Tiger?
Response: *Hai, Taigā to i'imasu.*
                Yes, it's called Tiger.

Cue: ***Ano kata no onamae wa Kimura-san desu ka.***
Is the name of that person Ms. Kimura?

Response: ***Hai, Kimura-san to osshaimasu.***
Yes, she is called Ms. Kimura.

Repeat the drill using the following:
1. ***Kaisha no namae wa J-Net desu ka.***
2. ***Kono mise no namae wa Voodoo (Bū Dū) Coffee desu ka.***
3. ***Senpai no okāsan no namae wa Sakura-san desu ka.***
4. ***Otaku no okosan no namae wa Yūki-kun desu ka.***
5. ***Ano ryōri no namae wa Mac and Cheese desu ka.***

EXERCISE 5
Say it in Japanese
Share with a friend the online reviews you read.
1. They say this restaurant is the best.
2. They say this tour is four hours long and is fun.
3. They say that this ***onsen*** is close to Mt. Fuji, beautiful and really therapeutic.
4. They say this movie is really scary and it's better for children not to see it.
5. They say that they recommend this book; they laughed a lot at first (***hajime***) and cried at the end (***owari***).

You've been asked how you feel about living in Japan.
6. Everyone is kind, I have good friends, so I'm blessed (***shiawase***).
7. I live alone and have no pet, so I sometimes feel a bit lonely.
8. My Japanese is poor, and I'm not used to life in Japan yet, so I'm bit embarrassed.
9. Everyone asks, "Aren't you lonely?" Actually I'm enjoying myself (***tanoshi'i***).
10. I usually don't think it's hard (***tsurai***), but I sometimes miss my family. In fact, my grandfather just passed away last month, and I'm terribly sad now.

EXERCISE 6
Role Play
1. Ask a co-worker if she has a pet. Ask what kind, its name and its age.
2. You are offered a dish you've never seen before. Ask the host what it is called.
3. Politely introduce yourself and Professor Kimura to a new business associate.
4. You thought that Ms. Sato has just said that she was going to get married. Confirm that she actually said that. Be sure to congratulate her.
5. Talk about some of your life's events and how they made you feel, using these four emotions—delighted or happy; sad or pained; worried or nervous; shy or embarrassed.

🔘 DIALOGUE 4 Politeness

Michael is nervous about an upcoming appointment with a business associate.

Michael: In this kind of situation, would it be better to use polite language?
Konna ba'ai wa, keigo o tsukatta hō ga i'i desu ka.
こんな場合は、敬語を使ったほうがいいですか。

Sato: Of course. After all, the other person is someone above you, so…
Mochiron desu. Yappari aite wa me-ue no hito desu kara.
もちろんです。やっぱり相手は目上の人ですから。

Michael: What do you think would be a good gift?
Omiyage wa nani ga i'i to omoimasu ka.
お土産は何がいいと思いますか?

Sato: Well, it's the thought that matters, so...
Mā, kimochi no mondai desu kara nē.
まあ、気持ちの問題ですからねえ。

Michael: It's so hard!
Muzukashi'i nā!
難しいなあ。

VOCABULARY

ba'ai	場合	case; situation
keigo	敬語	honorific language; polite language
mochiron	もちろん	of course
yappari	やっぱり	after all; as assumed
aite	相手	the other party; partner
me-ue	目上	superior; senior
omiyage	お土産	gift; souvenir
kimochi	気持ち	feeling; frame of mind
mondai	問題	matter; problem; issue
kimochi no mondai	気持ちの問題	a matter of how you feel
nā	なあ	Informal form of *nē*

ADDITIONAL VOCABULARY

teinei (na)	丁寧	polite; careful
teinei-go	丁寧語	polite language
kenjō-go	謙譲語	humble language
tame-go	ため語	casual language (between equals)
me-shita	目下	subordinate; junior
ageru	上げる	give

GRAMMAR NOTE **The Politeness System of Japanese**

When you look at the system of polite language (***keigo*** 敬語) in Japanese, it's important to recognize two axes, one horizontal and the other vertical, that are intertwined. The horizontal one shows the distance between the speaker and the addressee, which typically results in the choice between the Formal forms (***teinei-go*** 丁寧語) and the Informal forms (***tame-go*** タメ語) (e.g., ***shimasu*** vs. ***suru***), and between the plain and polite versions of some words (***teinei-go*** 丁寧語) (e.g., ***dare*** vs. ***donata***, ***genki*** vs. ***ogenki***, ***arimasu*** vs. ***gozaimasu***).

The vertical axis shows the relative hierarchy between the speaker and the subject of the sentence, which results in choosing between the plain, Honorific, and Humble forms of the predicates (e.g., ***i'imasu***, ***osshaimasu***, and ***mōshimasu***).

Honorifics (***sonkei-go*** 尊敬語) raise the subject person(s), typically someone in the speaker's out-group or above the speaker (***me-ue*** 目上) such as bosses, customers, strangers, seniors, etc. You NEVER raise yourself. The humble form (***kenjō-go*** 謙讓語) lower the subject person(s), typically the speaker him/herself or someone considered as the speaker's in-group member such as family, friends, co-workers, etc.

Humble speech is not used to downgrade subordinates (***me-shita*** 目下) in a discriminatory way. Remember it is still part of the politeness system. Both Honorifics and Humble speech are used to linguistically indicate the relative hierarchy between the speaker and the other party. Whether you raise the other party or lower yourself, the result is the same, a vertical gap.

The In-group/Out-group distinction is not absolute. The same person can be in your Out-group or In-group depending on the situation. For example, when you ask your boss what she said, you use the Honorific form—***Nan to osshaimashita ka***. But if you ask a business associate from another company (Out-group) what your boss (In-group) said, you use the humble form—***Nan to mōshimashita ka***. You do not use Honorifics to describe a co-worker's action when talking to him, but you may want to use them when talking to his parent about him, since they are in one group to which you don't belong. The only person you can always count on as your In-group is yourself.

The chart below shows the special Honorific and Humble forms.

	Plain	Honorific	Humble
say	*iu*	*ossharu*	*mōsu*
go; come	*iku; kuru*	*irassharu*	*mairu*
be	*iru*	*irassharu*	*oru*
eat	*taberu*	*meshiagaru*	*itadaku*
drink	*nomu*	*meshiagaru*	*itadaku*

	Plain	Honorific	Humble
give to me	*kureru*	*kudasaru*	-
do	*suru*	*nasaru*	*itasu*
look; see	*miru*	*goran ni naru*	*haiken-suru*
know	*shitte iru*	*gozonji da*	*zonjite iru*

The honorific verbs *ossharu, irassharu, kudasaru, nasaru*, and polite verb *gozaru* constitute the verb group called Special Polite Verbs. They follow the inflection rules for *U*-verbs except that before *masu*, the /r/ ending drops, and /u/ becomes /i/.

   Ossharu → *osshaimasu*

For the other verbs, there are the Honorific formula and the Humble formula.

   The Honorific formula: *O* + verb stem + *ni naru*

          kaku → *okaki ni naru*   "write"

          matsu → *omachi ni naru*   "wait"

   The Humble formula: *O* + verb stem + *suru*

          kaku → *okaki-suru*   "write"

          matsu → *omachi-suru*   "wait"

CULTURAL NOTE | **Politeness in Japanese Culture**

While considerations of politeness play an important role in Japanese culture, the linguistic skill to handle polite language correctly does not come naturally to all native speakers. Many native speakers study the system and learn how to use polite language, just as foreign learners do. In fact, polite language is taught at school as part of the Japanese language curriculum.

   For those entering the job market or are newly hired, it's also not uncommon to receive some training on how to speak professionally, focusing on correctly using polite language. This explains why, besides a knowledge of Kanji characters, a command of polite language is often taken as a sign of one's educational and intellectual level in Japanese society. Being a sophisticated, mature speaker of the language contributes to one's success in the society.

CULTURAL NOTE | **Gift Giving**

Gift giving is an important part of Japanese life. It's customary to bring small food items such as cake or sweets when visiting homes or offices, and to bring back local items from places you visit as gifts for those back home. These are called *omiyage* (お土産). Slightly more substantial or expensive gifts should be given twice a year, during the summer and in December, to business associates, teachers, and others to whom you are indebted. These are called *ochūgen* (お中元) and *oseibo* (お歳暮), respectively.

It is polite to reciprocate the sentiment (*kimochi* 気持ち) and give something of slightly less value as a token in return (*okaeshi* お返し) when you have a chance. To downplay the value of your gift, you can say, "It's just my thought (or a small token)" *Hon no kimochi desu.* (ほんの気持ちです。)

In business situations, this custom should not be confused with bribery. Gifts should not be too lavish but of good quality, and always wrapped (The stores in Japan will likely wrap them for you if you say it's a gift—and the traditional way of wrapping is quite unique). These can be bought from department stores all around the country. Gift sets usually contain five or 10 pieces. Avoid four or nine as these are unlucky numbers. Bring a number of small gifts to Japan to distribute to new and existing contacts.

PATTERN PRACTICE 8

Cue:	*So i'imashita.*	I said so.
Response:	*Ā, sensei mo sō osshaimashita yo.*	Oh, the teacher said so, too.
Cue:	*Kakimasu.*	I'll write it.
Response:	*Ā, sensei mo okaki ni narimasu yo.*	Oh, the teacher will write it, too.

Repeat the drill using the following:
1. *Tabemashita.*
2. *Machimasu.*
3. *Mimasu.*
4. *Shimasu.*
5. *Ikimasu.*

PATTERN PRACTICE 9

Cue:	*Kaite kudasai.*	Please write it.
Response:	*Hai, okaki-shimashō.*	Sure, I'll write it (for you.)
Cue:	*Matte kudasai.*	Please wait.
Response:	*Hai, omachi-shimashō.*	Sure, I'll wait (for you.)

Repeat the drill using the following:
1. *Susumete kudasai.*
2. *Mite kudasai.*
3. *Kite kudasai.*
4. *Ki'ite kudasai.*
5. *Tsukutte kudasai.*

EXERCISE 7
Say it in Japanese
You are preparing for an important meeting. Ask a co-worker for advice.
1. In this case, which would be better, to email or to call?
2. In that situation, what kind of gift would be good?
3. In case it rains, would it be better to call?
4. Which is higher in rank (*me-ue*), Ms. Sato or Ms. Suzuki?

EXERCISE 8
Role Play
1. Ask a co-worker in what kind of situations one uses Honorifics.
2. You are visiting a company. Ask the receptionist if Mr. Ito is in. You have a 2:00 appointment with him.
3. Politely ask a business associate the following questions:
   1) what is wrong (she looks sick);
   2) if she saw the schedule;
   3) how she came here today (by which transportation);
   4) if she has had lunch already.
4. Discuss what kind of gift would be good from your home country for the following people:
   1) a person above you;
   2) a friend;
   3) a child.
5. Present the following gifts to the following people. Downplay its value.
   1) a birthday gift to a friend;
   2) a gift from your business trip to everyone in your office to share.

REVIEW QUESTIONS
1. a) What does X *to omou* mean?
   b) How about X *to i'imashita*?
2. What forms of the predicate occur before *to omou*?
3. What is the difference in meaning among the following?
   1) *Suru to omou.*
   2) *Shita to omou.*
   3) *Suru to omotta.*
   4) *Shita to omotta.*
4. a) How do you say "you'd better take medicine" in Japanese?
   b) How about "you'd better NOT take medicine"?

5.   What is the difference in meaning between the following?
    1) *Ame darō.*
    2) *Ame ka mo shirenai.*
6.   What is the difference in meaning between the following?
    1) *Ame desu.*
    2) *Ame da tte.*
7.   What is the difference in meaning between the following?
    1) *Nan to iu kaisha desu ka.*
    2) *Dō iu kaisha desu ka.*
8.   What is the difference in meaning between the following?
    1) *Ame da kara…*
    2) *Ame da shi…..*
9.   What is the difference in meaning between the following?
    1) *Satō to i'imasu.*
    2) *Satō to mōshimasu.*
    3) *Satō-san to osshaimasu.*
10. a) How do you make the Honorific form of a verb?
    b) How about the Humble form?
11. What does *Kimochi no mondai* mean?

LESSON 10
Do's and Don'ts

🔘 **DIALOGUE 1** **Please Enter Your Password**

Mei needs help reading the words on the screen at an ATM

Yuki: What's wrong? Is there a problem?
Dō shita no? Nani ka mondai?
どうしたの。何か問題。

Mei: I cannot read this.
Kore, yomenai no.
これ、読めないの。

Yuki : Oh, it says, "Please enter your password".
Ā, pasuwādo o irete kudasai tte.
ああ「パスワードを入れてください」って。

Mei: Okay. Don't look.
Okkē. Minai de yo.
オッケー。見ないでよ。

Yuki: I'm not gonna look.
Minai yo.
見ないよ。

VOCABULARY

yomeru	読める	can read
yomenai	読めない	cannot read
pasuwādo	パスワード	password
ireru	入れる	enter; put it in
minai yo	見ないよ	Don't look

ADDITIONAL VOCABULARY

wasureru	忘れる	forget
oboeru	覚える	remember; commit to memory
honyaku	翻訳	translation
honyaku-suru; yakusu	翻訳する; 訳す	translate
tsūyaku	通訳	interpretation; interpreter
tsūyaku-suru	通訳する	interpret

GRAMMAR NOTE Making a Verb a Potential Form = "Can Do"

The verb *suru* "do" has a special potential form *dekiru* "can do". For all the other verbs, there are conjugation rules for Potential forms for each verb group.

U-Verbs: Change *u* to *eru*
The resulting form is a *RU*-verb. To make the negative form, change *ru* to *nai*.

nomu	→	*nomeru*	→	*nomenai*
drink		can drink		cannot drink
kau	→	*kaeru*	→	*kaenai*
buy		can buy		cannot buy

RU-Verbs: Change *ru* to *rareru* (or *reru* for the newly emerging version)

taberu	→	*taberareru (tabereru)*	→	*taberarenai (taberenai)*
eat		can eat		cannot eat

Irregular Verbs (Note: There is no potential form for *aru* "to be")

kuru	→	*korareru (koreru)*	→	*korarenai (korenai)*
come		can come		cannot come
suru	→	*dekiru*	→	*dekinai*
do		can do		cannot do
iku	→	*ikeru*	→	*ikenai*
go		can go		cannot go

Special Polite Verbs
Follow the same rule as Group 1—change *u* to *eru*

irassharu	→	*irasshareru*	→	*irassharenai*
be/come/go		can be/come/go		cannot be/come/go

Note that the object of Potential verbs can be marked either by the particle *o* or *ga*, just like we saw before with the verb *-tai* forms.

Kādo o/ga tsukaeru.   You can use a credit card.
Nihongo o/ga hanaseru.   I can speak Japanese.

GRAMMAR NOTE Negative Requests

Earlier, we learned that the *-te* form of verbs are used to make a request.

Casual:	*Tabete.*	Eat.
Formal:	*Tabete kudasai.*	Please eat.
More polite:	*Tabete itadakemasen ka.*	Could you please eat?

To make a negative request (asking someone not to do something), you add *de* to the Informal negative form of the verb.

Casual:	*Tabenai de.*	Don't eat.
Formal:	*Tabenai de kudasai.*	Please don't eat.
More polite:	*Tabenai de itadakemasen ka.*	Could you please not eat?

Some sentence particles can follow these requests with an added meaning.

Tabenai de ne?	Don't eat, okay? (softer)
Tabenai de yo.	Don't eat, I'm telling you. (more demanding)

PATTERN PRACTICE 1

Cue:	*Yomu?*	Will you read it?
Response:	*Sumimasen. Yomenai n desu.*	Sorry. I can't read it.
Cue:	*Taberu?*	Will you eat it?
Response:	*Sumimasen. Taberarenai n desu.*	Sorry. I cannot eat it.

Repeat the drill using the following:
1. *Aruku?*
2. *Tsukuru?*
3. *Tetsudau?*
4. *Kaeru?*
5. *Kuru?*

PATTERN PRACTICE 2

Cue:	*Kētai, tsukaimasu yo.*	I'll use a cellphone.
Response:	*A, tsukawanai de kudasai.*	Oh, please don't use it.
Cue:	*Kore, tabemasu yo.*	I'll eat this.
Response:	*A, tabenai de kudasai.*	Oh, please don't eat it.

Repeat the drill using the following:
1. *Shashin, torimasu yo.*
2. *Omiyage, kaimasu yo.*
3. *Pasuwādo, kakimasu yo.*
4. *Fairu, mimasu yo.*
5. *Okane, iremasu yo.*

EXERCISE 1
Say it in Japanese
You've been asked about your various skills during an interview.
1. As for Japanese, I can speak a little, but I cannot read very much.
2. Of course, I can use Word, Excel, etc. No problem. (*wādo*, *ekuseru*)
3. I can make simple dishes, but cannot make difficult ones.
4. I can work in the evenings and on weekends, too.
5. I cannot do interpretation, but can do translation.

Give the following instructions to an intern in your office.
6. Don't email this file. Send the PDF.
7. Don't use your cellphone here. Use it outside.
8. Don't forget the password. Don't write it down. Remember it.
9. Don't go home yet. Work hard (good luck!)
10. Don't eat here. Eat in the dining hall.

EXERCISE 2
Role Play
1. Your team is about to take on a new project. Tell everyone not to forget the deadline and work hard.
2. Your supervisor is reading your report. Ask if there is any problem.
3. Let a friend know that you have a problem:
   1) you forgot the password;
   2) you cannot use the Internet in this hotel;
   3) you cannot memorize *kanji*;
   4) you cannot talk to your parents about this;
   5) you cannot forget an ex-boy/girlfriend.
4. A friend offers to cook something for you. Tell him what you do or do not want in the dish. How about in your coffee?
5. Compare what you can and cannot do at work in Japan and in your home country.

🔘 DIALOGUE 2 No Smoking

During a visit to a historic temple

Guide: No smoking here.
Koko wa kin'en desu.
ここは禁煙です。

Michael: What does "kin-en" mean?
Kin'en tte dō iu imi?
禁煙って、どういう意味。

Sato: It means "please do not smoke".
Tabako wa suwanai de tte iu imi.
タバコは吸わないでっていう意味。

Michael: Is it okay if I take pictures?
Shashin, totte mo i'i desu ka.
写真、撮ってもいいですか。

Guide: Sure. But no flash pictures please.
Dōzo. De mo furasshu wa goenryo kudasai.
どうぞ。でも、フラッシュはご遠慮ください。

VOCABULARY

kin'en	禁煙	no smoking
dō iu imi	どういう意味	what does it mean
tabako	タバコ	tobacco; cigarette
su'u	吸う	smoke; inhale
toru	取る,撮る	take
totte mo	撮っても	even if you take (pictures)
totte mo i'i	撮ってもいい	it's okay even if you take (pictures)
furasshu	フラッシュ	flash
enryo	遠慮	holding back, decline
go-enryo	ご遠慮	holding back (polite)
go-enryo kudasai	ご遠慮ください	Please refrain from …

ADDITIONAL VOCABULARY

shitsumon	質問	question
shitsumon-suru	質問する	ask a question
kinshi	禁止	forbidden; prohibited
chūsha	駐車	parking
chūsha kinshi	駐車禁止	No Parking
enu-jī	NG	no good, not allowed

GRAMMAR NOTE Expressing Permission

Earlier, we learned that when the context is clear, we can ask for permission by simply saying *I'i desu ka*. For example, if someone raises her camera and says *I'i desu ka*, it's clear that she wants permission to take pictures. If the context is not clear, you should be more specific and use the *-te* form of the verb.

    Shashin totte i'i desu ka.   Is it okay if I take pictures?

It is common to add *mo* to the V-*te* form, which means "EVEN if you do V".

    e.g., *Shashin totte mo i'i desu ka.*   Is it okay even if I take pictures?

The other *te*-forms—/adjective-*kute*/ and /noun *de*/—are also used in this pattern with or without /*mo*/.

    Takakute mo i'i desu.   It's okay even if it's expensive.
    Eigo de mo i'i desu.   It's okay even if it's English.

CULTURAL NOTE The Virtue of Holding Back

Enryo means hesitating out of politeness, which is one of the most highly valued virtues in Japan. When offered something, you are usually expected to show some *enryo* before accepting it. Thus, sometimes "no" may not mean "no" and indicate *enryo* instead. To play it right, pay attention to tone of voice and facial expressions. You can urge someone not to worry about being polite by saying:

    Enryo shinai de.
    Enryo shinai de kudasai.
    Dōzo, goenryo nasaranai de kudasai.

To accept the offer, the expression *enryo naku* "without hesitation" is commonly used, e.g., *Sō desu ka. Jā, enryo naku itadakimasu.* "Are you sure? Then, I'll accept it without hesitation."

    On the other hand, *enryo-shimasu* indicates that you are politely declining an invitation, e.g., *Sumimasen kedo, enryo shimasu.* "I'm sorry, but no thank you."

    X wa goenryo kudasai is a polite expression—more so than X *kinshi*—commonly used to ask someone to refrain from doing X.

    Otabako wa goenryo kudasai.   Please refrain from smoking.
    Kētai wa goenryo kudasai.   Please refrain from using cellphones.

PATTERN PRACTICE 3

Cue:	*Shashin, toritai n desu kedo.*	I'd like to take pictures.
Response:	*Totte mo i'i desu yo.*	It's okay to take pictures.
Cue:	*Kētai, tsukaitai n desu kedo.*	I'd like to use my cellphone.
Response:	*Tsukatte mo i'i desu yo.*	It's okay to use a cellphone.

Repeat the drill using the following:
1. *Ashita yasumitai n desu kedo.*
2. *Hayaku kaeritai n desu kedo.*
3. *Toire ni ikitai n desu kedo.*
4. *Hirugohan, katte kitai n desu kedo.*
5. *Pawāpointo, tsukaitai n desu kedo.*

PATTERN PRACTICE 4

Cue:	*Shashin totte mo i'i desu ka.*	Is it okay if I take pictures?
Response:	*A, toranai de kudasai.*	Oh, please don't take them.
Cue:	*Kētai, tsukatte mo i'i desu ka.*	Is it okay if I use my cellphone?
Response:	*A, tsukawanai de kudasai.*	Oh, please don't use it.

Repeat the drill using the following:
1. *Tabako, suttē mo i'i desu ka.*
2. *Koko ni chūsha-shite mo i'i desu ka.*
3. *Kyōkasho, mite mo i'i desu ka.*
4. *Are, minna ni itte mo i'i desu ka.*
5. *Konban, dekakete mo i'i desu ka.*

EXERCISE 3
Say it in Japanese
You are on a group tour. Ask for permission as follows.
1. Can I get on the bus?
2. Can I go and buy *omiyage* at that store?
3. Can I ask you a question?
4. Can I use a flash (camera)?
5. Can I enter here?

You've just heard a Japanese word that you do not know. Ask a co-worker to explain using the statements below.
6. What does *enryo* mean in English?
7. What does *dentōteki* mean in English?
8. What does *dota kyan* mean? (*dota kyan* = last-minute cancelation)

9. What does *ikemen* mean? (*ikemen* = good looking guy)
10. What does *yabai* mean? (*yabai* = bad)

EXERCISE 4
Role Play
1. At a restaurant, ask a waiter:
    1) if smoking is prohibited here;
    2) what this (description on the menu) means.
2. You've been shown a sample product. Ask if you can take a picture.
3. You are in a park. Check if the following items are prohibited.
    1) pets,
    2) drinks,
    3) bicycles
4. Politely ask visitors to refrain from taking pictures here.
5. As a host, offer your guests food and drinks. Tell your guests not to hesitate and help themselves.
6. As a guest, be polite and hesitate from helping yourself. After being urged, accept politely.

🔘 DIALOGUE 3 Recycling

Mrs. Yamamoto sees Mei throwing away her trash and explains recycling to her.

Yamamoto: Wait a second! You shouldn't throw those away.
 Chotto matte! Sore wa sutete wa ikemasen yo.
 ちょっと待って！それは、捨ててはいけませんよ。

Mei: Do you mean these bottles and cans, too?
 Kono bin ya kan mo.
 このビンや缶も。

Yamamoto: Same. It would be wasteful, wouldn't it?
 Onaji desu. Mottainai deshō.
 同じです。もったいないでしょう。

Mei: You recycle everything, don't you?
 Nan de mo risaikuru-suru n desu nē.
 何でもリサイクルするんですねえ。

VOCABULARY

matsu	待つ	wait
suteru	捨てる	throw away, discard
ikenai	いけない	won't do; bad; mustn't do
sutete wa ikenai	捨ててはいけない	should not throw away
bin	ビン	bottle; jar
kan	缶	can
onaji	同じ	same

(/*no*/ or /*na*/ is NOT required to modify a noun: *onaji namae* "same name")

mottainai	もったいない	wasteful; sacrilegious
X de mo	Xでも	even X
nan demo	何でも	anything
risaikuru	リサイクル	recycle

ADDITIONAL VOCABULARY

petto botoru	ペットボトル	plastic bottle
gomi	ごみ	trash
gomibako	ゴミ箱	trash can
chigau	違う	is different; is wrong

(an *U*-verb: ***chigaimasu***, ***chigawanai***, ***chigatta***: ***chigau namae*** "different name")

GRAMMAR NOTE Expressing Prohibition

When X-*te* + *wa* "if you do X" is followed by *ikenai/ikemasen* "it cannot go" or "it won't do", it expresses prohibition "it's not good to do X" or "you must not do X".

Sutete wa ikemasen.	It's not good to throw it away.
Shashin o totte wa ikenai.	It's not good to take pictures.

In addition to *ikenai*, other negative expressions such as *dame*, *yoku nai*, *shitsurei*, etc., sometimes follow the -*te wa* pattern.

Mada mite wa dame.	You must not look yet.
Osoku denwa-shite wa shitsurei desu.	It's rude to call (so) late.

In casual speech, the following sound contractions often occur:

te wa → *cha(a)* and *de wa* → *ja(a)*

sutete wa ikenai → *sutecha(a) ikenai*	You must not throw it away.
nonde wa ikenai → *nonja(a) ikenai*	You must not drink it.

Note that permission and prohibition are the "yin and yang" of the rule, so to speak. In many contexts, the /-*te mo i'i*/ and /-*te wa ikenai*/ express opposite sides of the same rule.

Tabako sutte mo i'i desu ka.	May I smoke?
-Iya, sutte wa ikemasen.	No, you mustn't.

To be more polite when prohibiting someone from doing something, use more indirect patterns including *chotto*, *sumimasen kedo...*, and negative requests.

Tabako sutte mo i'i desu ka.	May I smoke?
-Chotto...	It's just...
-Anō, sumimasen kedo...	Umm, I'm sorry, but...

-Sumimasen kedo, suwanai de itadakemasen ka.
I'm sorry, but can you please not smoke?
-Sumimasen kedo, goenryo kudasaimasen ka.
I'm sorry, but can you please refrain from smoking?

GRAMMAR NOTE The Noun *Demo* = Even X

Demo placed before a sentence means "however" or "but", and comes from "*Sō de mo*", which literally means "even if it is so." This is the noun version of the -*te mo* pattern, which is introduced in Dialogue 2. *Demo* can be attached to a noun like a particle, and X *de mo* means "even X".

Kodomo de mo wakarimasu.	Even children can understand it.
Obentō de mo i'i desu yo.	I'm fine with *bentō*.

When combined with a question word, it means "any X" or "every X".

Nan de mo risaikuru-shimasu.	We recycle anything (and everything.)
Dare demo shitte imasu.	Everyone knows it.
Itsu de mo i'i desu yo.	Anytime is fine.

This pattern contrasts with Question word + *ka*, which was introduced earlier and means "some X".

some X		any and every X	
nani ka	something	*nan de mo*	anything
dare ka	someone	*dare demo*	anyone
doko ka	somewhere	*doko demo*	anywhere
itsu ka	sometime	*itsu demo*	anytime

Nani ka tabe ni ikanai?	Would you like to go and eat something?
-Un, nan de mo i'i yo.	Sure. Anything is fine.
Itsu ka denwa shimasu.	I'll call you sometime.
-Itsu de mo shite kudasai.	Please call me anytime.

CULTURAL NOTE **The Concept of** *Mottainai* **and Recycling in Japan**

Mottainai is an expression of regret regarding waste—used when a useful object is thrown away, misused or underused. This expression may have originated from the Shinto animist concept—that all things have a soul and should be respected—and the Buddhist transmigration of soul philosophy, resulting in the desire to maintain a harmonious relationship with nature. To achieve this, Japan has embarked on several efforts at energy conservation (*shō-ene* 省エネ), preserving the environment (*kankyō* 環境) and ecology (*eko* エコ), among other things. Naturally, recycling is strictly enforced in Japan.

Public trashcans are rare in Japan, and you will usually see several bins arranged together, each dedicated to different items. You should strictly follow the garbage disposal system in your local area.

Waste disposal (*gomi-shūshū* ゴミ収集) is carried out at the municipal level and each city has a completely different system. You will need to note the day, container, disposal location, and put out the right garbage on that day or your garbage will not be picked up. Get a booklet from your municipal office or have your landlord/property manager explain the rules to you. *Ganbatte kudasai!*

Recycling Materials in Japan

Paper (紙 *Kami*)	Plastic (プラ *Pura*)
Aluminum (アルミ *Arumi*)	PET bottles (ペットボトル *Pettobotoru*)

https://en.wikipedia.org/wiki/Recycling_in_Japan

PATTERN PRACTICE 5

Cue: *Sutete mo i'i desu ka.*   May I throw it away?
Response: *Ie, sutte wa ikemasen yo.*   No, you must not.
Cue: *Tabako, sutte mo i'i desu ka.*   May I smoke?
Response: *Ie, sutte wa ikemasen yo.*   No, you must not.

Repeat the drill with the following:
1. *Chūsha-shite mo i'i desu ka.*
2. *Osake, nonde mo i'i desu ka.*
3. *Chotto, okurete mo i'i desu ka.*
4. *Pasuwādo, itte mo i'i desu ka.*
5. *Issho ni shukudai shite mo i'i desu ka.*

PATTEN PRACTICE 6

Cue: *Nani o risaikuru-suru n desu ka.*   What do you recycle?
Response: *Nan de mo risaikuru-shimasu yo.*   We recycle everything.
Cue: *Itsu taberaremasu ka.*   When can we eat?
Response: *Itsu de mo taberaremasu yo.*   We can eat anytime.

Repeat the drill with the following:
1. *Dare ga tsukuremasuka.*
2. *Donna shigoto ga dekimasu ka.*
3. *Nan-nin shōkai-shimasu ka.*
4. *Itsu isogashi'i desu ka.*
5. *Doko no rāmen ga suki desu ka.*

EXERCISE 5

Say it in Japanese

Tell an intern the following:
1. It's not good if you are late for the appointment.
2. It's not good if you forget the name of the *senpai*.
3. It's not good if you go home earlier than everyone.
4. It's not good if you take more days off.
5. It's not good if you drink any more beer.

You are visiting a factory. Tell your group what the tour guide said.

6. We must not take pictures inside.
7. We must not smoke inside. Go outside to smoke.
8. We must not use cellphones inside.
9. We must not park in front of the building. Park in the back.
10. We must not litter. Use the garbage can at the exit.

EXERCISE 6
Role Play

1. Ask a landlord how to dispose of the garbage. How about cans, bottles, and plastic bottles?
2. A co-worker is about to throw away all the extra bento from the lunch meeting. What would you say?
3. You are discussing when and where the office party should be held. Express your preference or non-preference regarding the time and place.
4. Discuss the recycling policies in your community; the laws regarding drinking, driving, and drinking and driving in your country.
5. Discuss what you were prohibited from doing as a child. How about now?

🔘 DIALOGUE 4 Clothing

Michael and Ms. Sato are discussing the dress code for an event.

Michael:　It's probably okay if I don't wear a suit, right?
　　　　　Sūtsu kinakute mo i'i darō.
　　　　　スーツ着なくてもいいだろう。

Sato:　　No, it would be bad if you don't.
　　　　　Iya, kinakucha mazui desu yo.
　　　　　いや、着なくちゃまずいですよ。

On the day of the event, Michael shows up in a suit.

Sato:　　Wow! Cool!
　　　　　Wā, oshare desu nē!
　　　　　わあ、おしゃれですねえ！

Michael:　Isn't this tie too loud?
　　　　　Kono nekutai hade-suginai?
　　　　　このネクタイ、派手すぎない。

Sato:　　No, it looks good on you.
　　　　　Iya, yoku niaimasu yo.
　　　　　いや、よく似合いますよ。

Michael:　Then, let's go!
　　　　　Ja, ikimashō!
　　　　　じゃ、行きましょう！

VOCABULARY

sūtsu	スーツ	suit
kiru	着る	put on, wear (on upper body)
kinakute mo	着なくても	even if you don't wear (it's ok)
kinakucha	着なくちゃ	if you don't wear (it's not ok)
mazui	まずい	not good; awkward; bad-tasting
oshare (na)	おしゃれ（な）	stylish; fashionable; fashion
nekutai	ネクタイ	necktie
hade (na)	派手（な）	flashy; showy
niau	似合う	becoming; look good

ADDITIONAL VOCABULARY

haku	はく	put on; wear (on lower body)
kaburu	かぶる	put on; wear (on head)
nugu	ぬぐ	take off
jimi (na)	地味（な）	quiet (style, color)

Clothing
Items for the Verb *kiru*

kimono	着物	kimono
burausu	ブラウス	blouse
doresu	ドレス	dress
shatsu	シャツ	shirt
jaketto	ジャケット	jacket
uwagi	上着	jacket, outerwear
shitagi	下着	underwear
kōto	コート	coat
sētā	セーター	sweater

Items for the Verb *haku*

zubon	ズボン	trousers; pants
pantsu	パンツ	pants
jīnzu	ジーンズ	jeans
sukāto	スカート	skirt
kutsu	靴	shoes
kutsushita	靴下	socks
sokkusu	ソックス	casual (school) socks; white socks

Item for the Verb *kaburu*

bōshi	帽子	hat, cap

Items for the Verb *suru*

nekutai	ネクタイ	necktie
nekkuresu	ネックレス	necklace
ringu	リング	ring
iyaringu	イヤリング	earrings
sukāfu	スカーフ	scarf
beruto	ベルト	belt
megane	眼鏡	eye glasses
tokei	時計	watch
mēku	メーク	make-up

GRAMMAR NOTE **Expressing Negative Permission "Do Not Have To"**

We use the negative /-*nakute mo*/ in negative permission patterns, i.e., "It's okay NOT to do X" or "You do not have to do X".

Matanakute mo i'i desu yo.   You don't have to wait.

Mō ganbaranakute mo i'i desu.
You don't have to try so hard anymore (that is, it's okay not to work so hard).

Hon'yaku-shinakute mo i'i desu ka. Is it okay if I don't translate it?

Combine more than one permission pattern together to indicate options.

> ***Kite mo konakute mo i'i desu.***   It's okay whether you come or not.
> ***Eigo de mo, Nihon-go de mo i'i.***
> It doesn't matter if it's (in) English or Japanese.
> ***Mēru-site mo denwa-shite mo i'i yo.***   It's okay to email or call.

GRAMMAR NOTE Expressing Necessities "must"

In Dialogue 3, we discussed the affirmative /-*te wa*/ in prohibition patterns. Now we consider the negative /-***nakute wa***/ in necessity patterns. Necessity means "you must do X" or "it's no good if you do NOT do X". The sound changes of /*te wa*/to /*cha*/ and /*de wa*/ to /*ja*/ occur with this pattern as well. In addition to ***ikenai***, other negative expressions can follow this pattern.

> ***Benkyō-shinakute wa ikemasen.***   You must study.
> ***Sūtsu kinakucha mazui yo.***   It's not good if you do not wear
>   a suit.
>
> ***Shigoto ni ikanakute wa dame na n desu...***   I must go to work, so…

We have seen all the four patterns involving the -*te* form—permissions, prohibitions, negative permissions, and necessities. Now let's see how they complement each other.

> ***Tabako sutte mo i'i desu ka.***   Is it okay if I smoke?
> ***Iya, sutte wa ikemasen yo.***   No, it's not good if you do.
> ***Kore yomanakute mo i'i desu ka.***   Is it okay if I do not read this?
> ***Iya, yomanakute wa ikemasen yo.***   No, it's not good to not read this.

To be more polite, use the softer or indirect patterns including apologies, requests, ***chotto***, ***kedo***, ***n desu***, ***shi***, etc., instead.

> ***Tabako sutte mo i'i desu ka.***   Is it okay if I smoke?
> ***Iya, sumimasen kedo, kodomo ga imasu shi….***
> Well, sorry, but (there are) children here, and…
>
> ***Chotto, soto de onegai-dekimasen ka.***   Can I just ask you to do it outside?
> ***Asoko ni kin'en tte...***   Over there it says "no smoking"…
>
> ***Kore yomanakute mo i'i desu ka.***   Is it okay if I do not read this?
> ***Iya, kore wa yonde hoshi'i n desu kedo...***   I'd like you to read this at least, and…
> ***Iya, yonde kudasai. Onegai-shimasu.***   Please read, if you don't mind.

GRAMMAR NOTE X–*sugiru*

The verb ***sugiru*** means "past (something)". It can be attached to a verb stem (verb ***masu***-form without ***masu***), adjective root (adjective *i*-form without *i*) or *na*-nouns to make a compound verb that means "overly so" or "too much for X". The resulting compound form is a ***RU***-verb.

With Verb Stem: *Chotto tabe-sugimashita.*   I ate a little too much.

With Adj. Root: *Taka-sugiru kara, kawanai.*

I won't buy it because it's too expensive.

With *Na*-Noun: *Koko wa fuben sugiru.*   It is too inconvenient here.

When *-ru* of *sugiru* is dropped, it becomes a noun and often used in a casual speech.

Ano hito kakko yo-sugi!   He is too cool!

Chotto, nomi-sugi ja nai no?   Aren't you drinking a little too much?

GRAMMAR NOTE Verbs of Dressing

There are different verbs in Japanese for the English verb "put on (pieces of clothing)" or "wear", depending on where you put on the item. *Kiru* is used for the upper body, *haku* for the lower body, *kaburu* for on the head, and *suru* for smaller items such as accessories and ties. Note the difference in meaning among the following.

Shatsu o kiru.   I'll put on a shirt. (Action)

Shatsu o kite iru.   I'm wearing a shirt / I'm dressed in a shirt. (State)

Nekutai o shinai.   I'll not put on a tie. (Action)

Nekutai o shite inai.   I have no tie on. (State)

PATTERN PRACTICE 7

Cue: *Sūtsu, kimashō ka.*   Shall I wear a suit?

Response: *Ie, kinakute mo i'i desu yo.*   No, you don't have to.

Cue: *Bōshi, kaburimashō ka.*   Shall I wear a hat?

Response: *Ie, kaburanakute mo i'i desu yo.*   No, you don't have to.

Repeat the drill using the following:

1. *Nekutai shimashō ka.*
2. *Chiketto, kaimashō ka.*
3. *Okane haraimashō ka.*
4. *Pasuwādo, iremashō ka.*
5. *Chikatetsu ni norikaemashō ka.*

PATTERN PRACTICE 8

Cue: *Shukudai, shinai?*   Why don't we do the homework?

Response: *Shinakucha ikenai no?*   Do we have to?

Cue: *Furui shashin, sutenai?*   Why don't we throw away the old pictures?

Response: *Sutenakucha ikenai no?*   Do we have to?

Repeat the drill using the following:
1. *Byōin ni ikanai?*
2. *Shiryō, yomanai?*
3. *Ryōshin ni awanai?*
4. *Arukanai?*
5. *Pawāpointo, tsukawanai.*

PATTERN PRACTICE 9

Cue:	*Chotto hade desu nē.*	It's a little loud, isn't it?
Response:	*E'e hade-sugimasu nē.*	Right. It's too loud.
Cue:	*Yoku nomimashita nē.*	We drank a lot, didn't we?
Response:	*E'e, nomisugimashita nē.*	Right. We drank too much.

Repeat the drill using the following:
1. *Kono hoteru, takai desu nē.*
2. *Nihon-jin, yoku hatarakimasu nē.*
3. *Ano shachō, sugoi desu nē.*
4. *Omiyage, takusan kaimashita nē.*
5. *Ano obāsan, genki desu nē.*

EXERCISE 7
Say it in Japanese
Ask the supervisor about the project.
1. Do we have to translate the document?
2. Do we have to use these pictures?
3. Do we have to visit the company?
4. Do we have to do this by next week?
5. Do we have to recycle everything?

Ask a co-worker about the dress code for an event.
6. Do we have to wear a suit?
7. Men don't have to wear a tie, do they?
8. We must not wear jeans, right?
9. Is any color okay?
10. Do women have to wear a dress? Can we wear pants?

EXERCISE 8
Role Play
1. Describe the following:
   1) how your classmates are dressed today;
   2) how to dress for different occasions such as weddings and funerals in your country.
2. Discuss the dos and don'ts in the workplace in your country such as dress code, rules on eating and drinking, punctuality, etc.
3. Compliment a friend on his suit, mentioning how becoming it is on him.
4. Send your colleagues off to a party. Warn them not to drink too much.
5. With freedom, comes responsibility. Explain what the responsibilities are for:
   1) driving;
   2) being a foreigner in Japan;
   3) working from home (*tere-wāku* "telework")

REVIEW QUESTIONS
1. Explain how to make potential forms for each of the four verb groups.
2. Is a potential verb form a *U*-verb or *RU*-verb?
3. Explain how to make a negative request.
4. Explain how to express the following:
   - Permission   "it's okay to do X" or "you can do X".
   - Prohibition   "it's not good if you do X" or "you must not do X".
   - Negative permission "it's okay not to do X" or "you do not have to do X".
   - Necessity   "it's not good if you do not do X" or " you must do X".
5. a) What does *enryo* mean?
   b) How is it used?
6. What is the difference in meaning between:
   Nani ka arimasu.
   Nan de mo arimasu.
7. a) What are the Japanese equivalents of the English word "wear"?
   b) How are they used?
8. a) What is -*sugiru* attached to in order to make a compound word?
   b) What does it mean?
9. In what way is the noun *onaji* unique?

ENGLISH–JAPANESE DICTIONARY

A

a little while ago ***sakki*** さっき
a lot ***yoku*** よく
about ***~goro*** ごろ
above ***ue*** 上
absence ***yasumi*** 休み
academic term ***gakki*** 学期
accept (humble) ***itadakimasu*** いただきます
accessories ***akusesari'i*** アクセサリー
accident ***jiko*** 事故
acquaintance ***shiriai*** 知り合い
actually ***jitsu wa*** 実は
administrative assistant ***hisho*** 秘書
adult ***otona*** 大人
afraid ***kowai*** 怖い
after all ***yappari*** やっぱり
after this ***kono ato*** この後
again ***mata*** また
Again! ***Mata!*** また！
ah ***ā*** ああ
ahead ***saki*** 先
air conditioner ***eakon*** エアコン
airplane ***hikōki*** 飛行機
airport ***kūkō*** 空港
all ***minna*** みんな
allergy ***arerugī*** アレルギー
already ***mō*** もう
alternative ***hō*** 方
always ***itsumo*** いつも
apartment ***apāto*** アパート
amazing ***sugoi*** すごい
ambulance ***kyūkyū-sha*** 救急車
American ***Amerika-jin*** アメリカ人
ankle ***ashi-kubi*** 足首
and ***sore kara; to; ~shi*** (listing reasons) それから; と; し
animal ***dōbutsu*** 動物
animation ***anime*** アニメ
anything ***nan de mo*** なんでも
appetizing ***oishi-sō*** おいしそう
apple ***appuru; ringo*** アップル; りんご
application ***apuri*** アプリ
appointment ***apo*** アポ
apprehensive ***harahara*** ハラハラ
approximately ***yaku*** 約
April ***Shi-gatsu*** 四月
area ***hen*** 辺
area map ***eria mappu*** エリアマップ
arm ***ude*** 腕
arrive ***tsukimasu; tsuku*** 着きます; 着く
as assumed ***yappari*** やっぱり
as for X ***wa*** は
ask ***kikimasu; kiku*** 聞きます; 聞く
at ***ni*** (particle of location) に
attorney ***bengoshi*** 弁護士
August ***Hachi-gatsu*** 八月
aunt ***oba; oba-san*** 叔母；伯母
autumn ***aki*** 秋

B

baby ***akachan*** 赤ちゃん
back ***ushiro; se; senaka*** 後ろ; 背；背中
bad ***warui*** 悪い
bad tasting ***mazui*** まずい
bag ***kaban*** かばん
bamboo ***take*** 竹
banana ***banana*** バナナ
bank ***ginkō*** 銀行
bank employee ***ginkō-in*** 銀行員
baseball ***yakyū*** 野球
basement ***chika*** 地下
basketball ***basuke; basuketto bōru*** バスケ; バスケットボール
be ***arimasu; aru/imasu; iru/gozaimasu*** (polite) あります; ある/います; いる/ございます
be born ***umaremasu; umareru*** 生まれます; 生まれる
become ***narimasu; naru*** なります; なる
become empty ***sukimasu; suku*** すきます; すく
become late ***osoku naru*** 遅くなる
become tired ***tsukaremasu; tsukareru*** 疲れます; 疲れる
becoming ***niaimasu; niau*** 似合います; 似合う
bed ***beddo*** ベッド
beef ***gyū-niku*** 牛肉
beer ***bīru*** ビール
before ***mae*** 前
beginning ***hajime*** はじめ
behind ***ushiro*** 後ろ

belly button *heso* へそ

below *shita* 下

belt *beruto* ベルト

bench *benchi* ベンチ

best *ichi-ban; saikō* 一番; 最高

between *aida* 間

bicycle *jitensha* 自転車

big *ōki'i* 大きい

bird *tori* 鳥

birthday *tanjōbi* 誕生日

black *kuroi; kuro* 黒い; 黒

black tea *kōcha* 紅茶

blink of time, a *atto iu ma* あっという間

blouse *burausu* ブラウス

blue *aoi; ao* 青い; 青

boat *fune* 船

body *karada* 体

bone *hone* 骨

book *hon* 本

bookshelf *hon-dana* 本棚

boring *tsumara-nai* つまらない

boss *jōshi* 上司

bottle *bin* ビン

bowl *donburi* 丼

box *hako* 箱

boxed meal *bentō; o-bentō* 弁当; お弁当

bread *pan* パン

break *yasumi* 休み

break up *wakaremasu; wakareru* 別れます; 別れる

breakfast *asa-gohan* 朝ご飯

bridge *hashi* 橋

broken *dame* ダメ

brothers *kyōdai; go-kyōdai* 兄弟; ご兄弟

brown *chairoi; chairo* 茶色い; 茶色

buckwheat noodle *soba* そば

Buddhist temple *tera; o-tera* 寺; お寺

bugs *konchū* 昆虫

building *biru; tatemono* ビル; 建物

bullet train *shinkansen* 新幹線

bus *basu* バス

business card *meishi* 名刺

business owner *keiei-sha* 経営者

businessman *bijinesu-man* ビジネスマン

busy *isogashi'i* 忙しい

but *demo, kedo* でも; けど

buy *kaimasu; kau* 買います; 買う

by *made ni* までに

by foot *toho* 徒歩

by means of *de* で

by walking *aruite* 歩いて

bye *ja(a); baibai* じゃ(あ); バイバイ

C

C'mon! *Mata!* また！

cabinet *kyabinetto* キャビネット

café *kafe* カフェ

cake *kēki* ケーキ

can *kan* 缶

can do *dekimasu; dekiru* できます; できる

Can I have X? *Itadakemasen ka* いただけませんか

cap *bōshi* 帽子

car *kuruma* 車

careful *teinei; go-teinei* 丁寧; ご丁寧

case *ba'ai* 場合

cash *gen'kin* 現金

castle *shiro; o-shiro* 城; お城

casual (school) socks *sokkusu* ソックス

casual language (between equals) *tame-go* タメ語

casual title for boys, subordinates *~kun* 君

cat *neko* 猫

cellphone *kētai* ケータイ

certainly *kashikomari-mashita* かしこまりました

chair *isu* 椅子

cheap *yasui* 安い

check in *chekkuin* チェックイン

check out *chekkuauto* チェックアウト

Cheers! *Kanpai!* 乾杯!

cherry *sakura* 桜

chest *mune* 胸

chicken *tori; tori-niku* 鳥; 鶏肉

child *ko; kodomo* 子; 子供

China *Chūgoku* 中国

Chinese person *Chūgoku-jin* 中国人

Chinese food *Chūka* 中華

chocolate *chokorēto* チョコレート

chopsticks *hashi; ohashi* 箸; お箸

Christian church *kyōkai* 教会

chrysanthemum *kiku* 菊

cigarette *tabako* タバコ

civil servant *kōnu-in* 公務員

class *jugyō* 授業

cleaning *sōji* 掃除

climb *noborimasu; noboru* 登ります; 登る

clock *tokei* 時計

close *chikai* 近い

cloth *fuku* 服

co-worker *dōryō* 同僚

coat *kōto* コート

coffee shop *kissaten* 喫茶店

cola *kōra* コーラ

cold *samui; tsumetai* (to touch) 寒い; 冷たい

cold, a *kaze* 風邪

colleague *dōryō* 同僚

college *daigaku* 大学

come *kimasu; kuru* 来ます; 来る

comfortable *raku* 楽

comics *manga* マンガ

commit to memory *oboemasu; oboeru* 覚えます; 覚える

commute to school *tsūgaku* 通学

commute to work *tsūkin* 通勤

company *kaisha* 会社

company employee *kaisha-in* 会社員

company president *shachō* 社長

complete meal *teishoku* 定食

completed, is *dekimasu; dekiru* できます; できる

computer *konpyūtā* コンピューター

condominium *manshon* マンション

conference *kaigi* 会議

Congratulations! *Omedetō!* おめでとう!

consulate *ryōjikan* 領事館

consultant *konsarutanto* コンサルタント

convenience store *konbini* コンビニ

convenient *benri* 便利

cook *ryōri* 料理

cooked rice *gohan* ご飯

cookie *kukkī* クッキー

cool *suzushi'i* 涼しい

corner *kado* 角

cosmetics *keshō-hin* 化粧品

cost *kakarimasu; kakaru* かかります; かかる

cough *seki* 咳

Could you please give me X? *Kudasaimasen ka.* くださいませんか。

counter for animals *~hiki; ~piki; ~biki* 匹

counter for bound things *~satsu* 冊

counter for concrete items *~ko* 個

counter for days of the month *~ka; ~nichi* 日

counter for flat things *~mai* 枚

counter for floors/stories *~kai* 階

counter for human age *~sai* オ; 歳

counter for long things *~hon; ~pon; ~bon* 本

counter for months *~kagetsu* ヶ月

counter for people *~nin* 人

counter for people *~mei; ~mei-sama* 名; 名様

counter for years *~nen* 年

country *kuni* 国

country side *inaka* 田舎

credit card *kādo* カード

cross *watarimasu; wataru* 渡ります; 渡る

cry *nakimasu; naku* 泣きます; 泣く/鳴きます; 鳴く

culture *bunka* 文化

cup *koppu; kappu* コップ; カップ

curry *karē* カレー

D

dance *odorimasu; odoru/ dansu* 踊ります; 踊る/ ダンス

dangerous *abunai* 危ない

dating *kōsai* 交際

daughter *musume; musume-san; o-jō-san* 娘; 娘さん; お嬢さん

day off *yasumi* 休み

deadline *shimekiri* 締め切り

decease *nakunarimasu; nakunaru* なくなります; なくなる

December *Jū-ni-gatsu* 十二月

decline *enryo; go-enryo* 遠慮; ご遠慮

deep-fried items *furai* フライ

delicious *oishi'i* おいしい

delighted *ureshi'i* 嬉しい

department store *depāto* デパート

desk *tsukue* 机

did *shimashita* しました

die *shinimasu; shinu* 死にます; 死ぬ

different *chigaimasu; chigau* 違います; 違う

difficult *taihen; muzuka-shi'i* 大変; 難しい

diner; dining hall *shokudō* 食堂

dinner *ban-gohan* 晩ご飯

direction, the *hō* 方

discard *sutemasu; suteru* 捨てます; 捨てる

disease *byōki* 病気

dish (food) *ryōri* 料理

dislike *kirai* 嫌い

division chief *buchō* 部長

divorce *rikon* 離婚

do *shimasu; suru/ yarimasu; yaru* (casual) します; する/やります; やる

doesn't work *mazui* まずい

dog *inu* 犬

dollar *doru* ドル

don't mention it *dō itashimashite* どういたしまして

door *doa* ドア

dormitory *ryō* 寮

draft beer *nama* 生

draw *kakimasu; kaku* 書きます; 書く

drawer *hikidashi* 引き出し

dress *doresu* ドレス

drink *nomimasu; nomu* 飲みます; 飲む

drinks *nomimono* 飲み物

driver *unten-shu* 運転手

driving *unten* 運転

dry *karakara* カラカラ

E

ear *mimi* 耳

earring *iyaringu* イヤリング

early *hayai* 速い; 早い

east *higashi* 東

east exit *higashi-guchi* 東口

easy *raku; yasashi'i* 楽; 優しい

eat *tabemasu; taberu* 食べます; 食べる

edamame *edamame* 枝豆

egg *tamago* 卵

eight *hachi* 八

eight units *yat-tsu* 八つ

eighth day of the month; eight days *yō-ka* 八日

either *mo* も

elbow *hiji* ひじ

elder brother *ani; onī-san* 兄; お兄さん

elder sister *ane; onē-san* 姉; お姉さん

elementary school *shō-gakkō* 小学校

elevator *erebētā* エレベーター

email *mēru* メール

embarrassed *hazuka-shi'i* 恥ずかしい

embassy *taishikan* 大使館

emotions *kimochi* 気持ち

ending *owari* 終わり

energetic *genki* 元気

engagement *kon-yaku* 婚約

England *Igirisu* イギリス

English *Eigo* 英語

enjoyable *tanoshi'i* 楽しい

enter *iremasu; ireru* 入れます; 入れる

entering school *nyūgaku* 入学

entrance *iriguchi* 入り口

entrepreneur *keiei-sha* 経営者

escalator *eskarētā* エスカレーター

ethnic food *esunikku* エスニック

evening *ban* 晩

every day *mainichi* 毎日

every month *mai-tsuki* 毎月

every now and then *tama ni* たまに

every week *mai-shū* 毎週

every year *mai-toshi* 毎年

everyone *minna; minasan* (polite) みんな; みなさん

exam *shiken* 試験

excited *dokidoki* ドキドキ

excuse me *shitsurei; shitsurei-shimasu/ gomen* (casual); *gomen nasai* (casual, gentle) 失礼; 失礼します/ごめん; ごめんなさい

excuse me for doing something rude *shitsurei; shitsurei-shimasu* 失礼; 失礼します

exist *arimasu; aru/ imasu; iru* あります; ある/います; いる

exist (polite) *gozaimasu* ございます

exit *deguchi* 出口

expensive *takai* 高い

eye *me* 目

eye glasses *megane* メガネ

F

face *kao* 顔

Facebook *Feisubukku* フェイスブック

family *kazoku; go-kazoku* 家族; ご家族

family restaurant *famirī resutoran; fami-resu* ファミリーレストラン; ファミレス

famous *yūmei* 有名

far *tōi* 遠い

fashionable *oshare* おしゃれ

fast *hayai* 速い; 早い

father *chichi; otō-san* 父; お父さん

February *Ni-gatsu* 二月

feel hardship *tsurai* 辛い

feel nostalgic **natsuka-shi'i** 懐かしい

feel relieved **hotto-shimasu/suru** ホッとします/する

feel shy **hazuka-shi'i** 恥ずかしい

feel sorry **zan-nen** 残念

feeling **kimochi** 気持ち

feeling at ease **anshin** 安心

female; woman **onna** 女

festival **matsuri; o-matsuri** 祭り; お祭り

fever **netsu** 熱

fifth day of the month, five days **itsu-ka** 五日

find out **shirimasu; shiru** 知ります; 知る

fine **daijōbu** 大丈夫

finger **yubi** 指

first day of the month **tsuitachi** 一日

first-year student; freshman **ichi-nen-sei** 一年生

fish **sakana** 魚

five **go** 五

five units **itsu-tsu** 五つ

flash **furasshu** フラッシュ

flashy **hade** 派手

flower **hana** 花

fluent in a language **perapera** ペラペラ

food **tabemono** 食べ物

foot **ashi** 足

for now **toriaezu** とりあえず

for the most part **daitai** だいたい

for the purpose of X **ni** に

forbidden **kinshi** 禁止

foreign country **gaikoku** 外国

foreign student **ryūgakusei** 留学生

forget **wasuremasu; wasureru** 忘れます; 忘れる

fork **fōku** フォーク

four **shi; yo; yon** 四

four floors, fourth floor **yon-kai** 4階

four units **yot-tsu** 四つ

fourth day of the month, four days **yok-ka** 四日

fourth-year student senior **yo-nen-sei** 四年生

France **Furansu** フランス

free of charge **tada; muryō** ただ; 無料

French food **Furenchi** フレンチ

French language **Furansu-go** フランス語

French person **Furansu-jin** フランス人

Friday **Kin-yōbi** 金曜日

fried chicken **kara-age** 唐揚げ

friend **tomodachi** 友達

from **kara** から

front **mae** 前

fruit **kudamono** 果物

full **ippai** いっぱい

fun **tanoshi'i** 楽しい

furniture **kagu** 家具

G

game **gēmu** ゲーム

gardening **gādeningu** ガーデニング

gas station **gasorin sutando** ガソリンスタンド

Germany **Doitsu** ドイツ

German language **Doitsu-go** ドイツ語

German person **Doitsu-jin** ドイツ人

get accustomed **naremasu; nareru** なれます; なれる

get angry **okorimasu; okoru** 怒ります; 怒る

get disappointed **gakkari-suru** がっかりする

get healed **iyasaremasu; iyasareru** 癒されます; 癒される

get off **orimasu; oriru** 降ります; 降りる

get on (a vehicle) **norimasu; noru** 乗ります; 乗る

get out **demasu; deru** 出ます; 出る

get up **okimasu; okiru** 起きます; 起きる

getting employed **shūshoku** 就職

gift **omiyage** お土産

girl/boyfriend **koibito** 恋人

glad **ureshi'i** 嬉しい

glass **koppu** コップ

go **ikimasu; iku** 行きます; 行く

Go (game) **Igo; Go** 囲碁; 碁

go home **kaerimasu; kaeru** 帰ります; 帰る

go in **hairimasu; hairu** 入ります; 入る

go out **dekakemasu; dekakeru** 出かけます; 出かける

going out **odekake** お出かけ

goldfish **kingyo** 金魚

golf **gorufu** ゴルフ

good **i'i** いい

good at **jōzu** 上手

goodbye **sayo(u)nara** さよ(う)なら

Good evening **Kon'ban'wa** こんばんは

Good morning **Ohayō** おはよう

Good night **Oyasumi**
おやすみ

good weather **i'i tenki**
いい天気

Google **Gūguru** グーグル

graduate school **daigaku-
in** 大学院

graduation **sotsugyō** 卒業

grandchild **mago; o-mago-
san** 孫; お孫さん

grandfather **sofu; ojī-san**
祖父；おじいさん

grandmother **sobo; obā-
san** 祖母；おばあさん

grapes **budō** ぶどう

grass **kusa** 草

Great Britain **Igirisu**
イギリス

green **midori** 緑

green tea **ocha** お茶

gray **hai-iro** 灰色

grow up **sodachimasu;
sodatsu** 育ちます; 育つ

H

Hachi, the local dog
monument **Hachi-kō**
ハチ公

hair **kami** 髪

half **han** 半

Hamamatsu **Hamama-
tsu-chō** 浜松町

hamburger **hanbāgā** ハ
ンバーガー

hamster **hamusutā** ハム
スター

hand **te** 手

handbag **hando baggu**
ハンドバッグ

Haneda Airport **Haneda
kūkō** 羽田空港

happiness; happy
shiawase 幸せ

happy (anticipating good
news) **ukiuki** ウキウキ

hat **bōshi** 帽子

Have a nice day **itte
rasshai** 行ってらっし
ゃい

have difficulty
komarimasu; komaru
困ります; 困る

having a surge of anger
mukamuka ムカムカ

head **atama** 頭

healthy **genki** 元気

heart **shinzō** 心臓

Hello **Kon'nichi'wa**
こんにちは

here **koko** ここ

here you go **hai** はい

high **takai** 高い

high school **kōkō** 高校

hike **haikingu** ハイキング

hill **yama** 山

hobby **shumi** 趣味

holding back **enryo;
go-enryo** 遠慮; ご遠慮

hometown **shusshin** 出身

homework **shukudai** 宿題

honorific language **keigo**
敬語

hospital **byōin** 病院

hot **atsui** 暑い；熱い

hot coffee **hotto** ホット

hot spring **onsen** 温泉

hour **~ji** 時

hours **jikan** 時間

house **ie** 家

how **dō; dō yatte; ikaga**
(polite) どう; どうやっ
て; いかが

How do you do?
Hajime-mashite 初めま
して。

how long **dono gurai** ど
のぐらい

how many people **nan-
mei-sama** 何名様

how much **ikura** いくら

however **demo** でも

Huh? **Are?** あれ

humble language **kenjō-go**
謙譲語

hundred **hyaku** 百

hungry **pekopeko** ペコ
ペコ

hurry **isogimasu; isogu**
急ぎます; 急ぐ

hurt **kurushi'i; itai** 苦し
い; 痛い

husband **shujin; go-shujin**
主人; ご主人

I

I **watashi; boku** (male
speaker) 私; 僕

I guess **Mā** まあ

I see **Naruhodo** なるほど

I tell you (particle indicating
new information) **yo** よ

I'm here **Hai** はい

I'm home **Tadaima** ただ
いま

I'm sorry **Sumimasen; dō
mo** すみません; どうも

IC card **aishī kādo** ICカ
ード

ice cream **aisu kurīmu**
アイスクリーム

iced coffee **aisu kōhī**
アイスコーヒー

idea **aidea** アイデア

in every way **dō mo**
どうも

in progress **~chū** 中

in that way **ā; sō** ああ;
そう

in the middle of **~chū** 中

in the vicinity **soba** そば

in this way **kō** こう

inconvenient **fuben** 不便

India **Indo** インド

inexpensive **yasui** 安い

information booth
an'nai-jo 案内所

inhale **suimasu; sū** 吸い
ます; 吸う

injury *kega* 怪我
insects *konchū* 昆虫
inside *naka* 中
interest *kyōmi* 興味
interesting *omoshiroi* 面白い
Internet *Netto* ネット
interpreter *tsūyaku* 通訳
intestine *chō* 腸
irritated *iraira* イライラ
is *desu* です
is not *ja nai desu* じゃないです
isn't it *nē; nā* (casual) ねえ；なあ
it's the case *no* の
Italian food *Itarian* イタリアン
Italian language *Itaria-go* イタリアン
Italian person *Itaria-jin* イタリアン
Italy *Itaria* イタリア

J
jacket *jaketto; uwagi* ジャケット；上着
January *Ichi-gatsu* 一月
Japan *Nihon* 日本
Japan Railway (JR) *Jeiāru* JR
Japanese calligraphy *sho-dō* 書道
Japanese chess *shōgi* 将棋
Japanese flower arrangement *ka-dō* 華道
Japanese food *washoku* 和食
Japanese language *Nihongo* 日本語
Japanese tea ceremony *sa-dō* 茶道
jar *bin* ビン
jeans *jīnzu* ジーンズ
joke *jōdan* 冗談

journalist *jānarisuto* ジャーナリスト
juice *jūsu* ジュース
July *Shichi-gatsu* 七月
June *Roku-gatsu* 六月
junior *san-nen-sei* 三年生
junior in rank *me-shita* 目下
junior member of a group *kōhai* 後輩
just now *sakki* さっき
interpreter *tsūyaku* 通訳

K
Kabuki Theater *Kabuki* 歌舞伎
Karaoke *karaoke* カラオケ
keep (animal) *kaimasu; kau* 飼います；飼う
key *kagi* 鍵
kidding *jōdan* 冗談
kidney *jinzō* 腎臓
kimono *kimono* 着物
Kimura (family name) *Kimura* 木村
kind *shinsetsu* 親切
kind-hearted *yasashi'i* 優しい
knee *hiza* 膝
knife *naifu* ナイフ
know *shirimasu; shiru* 知ります；知る
koi fish *koi* 鯉
Korea *Kankoku* 韓国
Korean language *Kankoku-go* 韓国語
Korean person *Kankoku-jin* 韓国人
Korean BBQ *yaki-niku* 焼肉

L
language *kotoba* 言葉
laptop *pasokon* パソコン
last month *sen-getsu* 先月

last night *yūbe* タベ
last term *sen-gakki* 先学期
last week *sen-shū* 先週
last year *kyonen* 去年
late *osoi* 遅い
later *ato* 後
laugh *waraimasu; warau* 笑います；笑う
leave *demasu; deru* 出ます；出る
left *hidari* 左
leg *ashi* 足
Let me see (hesitation noise) *etto* えっと
library *toshokan* 図書館
lie *uso* うそ
like *suki* 好き
limited to *dake* だけ
limousine *rimujin* リムジン
Line *Rain* ライン
listen *kikimasu; kiku* 聞きます；聞く
little *chotto* ちょっと
live *sumimasu; sumu* 住みます；住む
liver *kanzō* 肝臓
living *seikatsu* 生活
living alone *hito-ri-gurashi* 一人暮らし
lock *kagi* 鍵
lonely *sabishi'i* 寂しい
look delicious *oishi-sō* おいしそう
look good *niaimasu; niau* 似合す；似合う
Look! *Hora!* ほら！
loud *hade* 派手
laundry *sentaku* 洗濯
lower back *koshi* 腰
lunch *hiru-gohan; o-hiru; ranchi* 昼ご飯；お昼；ランチ
lung *hai* 肺

M

magazine *zasshi* 雑誌

make *tsukurimasu; tsukuru* 作ります; 作る

make an error *machigaemasu; machigaeru* 間違えます; 間違える

make a turn *magarimasu; magaru* 曲がります; 曲がる

make-up *mēku* メーク

male; man *otoko* 男

management *keiei* 経営

manager *manējā* マネージャー

Mandarin-Chinese *Chūgoku-go* 中国語

mandarin orange *mikan* みかん

many *ippai* いっぱい

map *chizu* 地図

March *San-gatsu* 三月

marriage *kekkon* 結婚

May *Go-gatsu* 五月

maybe *kamo shirenai* かもしれない

me *watashi; boku* (male speaker) 私; 僕

meal, a *gohan* ご飯

meaning *imi* 意味

meat *niku* 肉

medical doctor *isha* 医者

medicine *kusuri* 薬

meet *aimasu; au* 会います; 会う

meeting *kaigi; uchiawase* (for planning) 会議; 打ち合わせ

middle school *chūgaku* 中学

milk *gyūnyū; miruku* 牛乳; ミルク

minutes *~fun; ~pun* 分

miserable *tsurai* 辛い

miso *miso* みそ

miso soup *miso-shiru* 味噌汁

Monday *Getsu-yōbi* 月曜日

money *okane* お金

monorail *monorēru* モノレール

month before the last *sensen-getsu* 先々月

month after the next *sarai-getsu* 再来月

more *mō; motto* もう; もっと

morning *asa* 朝

most of the time *taitei* たいてい

mother *haha; okā-san* 母; お母さん

motorcycle *baiku* バイク

mountain *yama* 山

mouth *kuchi* 口

move (residence) *hikkoshimasu; hikkosu* 引っ越します; 引っ越す

movie *eiga* 映画

movie theater *eigakan* 映画館

Ms., Mr. *san* さん

Mt. Fuji *Fuji-san* 富士山

muscle *kin-niku* 筋肉

museum *bijutsu-kan* 美術館

music *ongaku* 音楽

my home *uchi* 家

N

nail *tsume* 爪

name *namae* 名前

Narita Airport *Narita Kūkō* 成田空港

navy *kon-iro* 紺色

near *soba; chikai* そば; 近い

neck *kubi* 首

necklace *nekkuresu* ネックレス

necktie *nekutai; tai* ネクタイ; タイ

neighboring *tonari* 隣

nephew *oi; oigo-san* 甥; 甥御さん

nervous *dokidoki* ドキドキ

new *atarashi'i* 新しい

news *nyūsu* ニュース

newspaper *shinbun* 新聞

next *tsugi* 次

next month *rai-getsu* 来月

next term *rai-gakki* 来学期

next to *tonari* 隣

next week *rai-shū* 来週

next year *rainen* 来年

no good *enu jī* NG

nice to meet you *yoroshiku* よろしく

niece *mei; meigo-san* めい; めい御さん

night *ban* 晩

nine *ku; kyū* 九

nine o'clock *ku-ji* 九時

nine units *kokono-tsu* 九つ

ninth day of the month; nine days *kokono-ka* 九日

no *ie, i'ie, iya* いえ、いいえ、いや

no good *dame* ダメ

no longer *mō* もう

No parking *Chūsha-kinshi* 駐車禁止

No smoking *Kin'en* 禁煙

noon *o-hiru* お昼

north *kita* 北

north exit *kita-guchi* 北口

nose *hana* 鼻

not a big deal *taishita koto nai* 大したことない

not at all *zenzen* 全然

not particularly *betsu ni* 別に

not quite *ima-ichi* いまいち

not very much *amari* あまり

not yet *mada* まだ

November *Jū-ichi-gatsu* 十一月

now hiring *boshū-chū* 募集中

number one *ichi-ban* 一番

number; # *~ban* 番

O

ocean *umi* 海

October *Jū-gatsu* 十月

of course *mochiron* もちろん

office clerk *jimu-in* 事務員

often *yoku* よく

oh *ā* ああ

OK *Okkē* オッケー

okay *daijōbu* 大丈夫

Okinawa *Okinawa* 沖縄

old *furui* 古い

one *ichi* 一

one hour *ichi-jikan* 一時間

one more time *mō ichi-do* もう一度

one time *ichi-do* 一度

one unit *hito-tsu* 一つ

one week *is-shūkan* 一週間

one year *ichi-nen* 一年

only *dake* だけ

only child *hito-ri-kko* 一人っ子

oolong tea *ūron-cha* ウーロン茶

opposite *hantai* 反対

opposite side *hantai-gawa* 反対側

orange *orenji* オレンジ

order *chūmon* 注文

other party *aite* 相手

other side *mukō* 向こう

outerwear *uwagi* 上着

outside *soto* 外

over there *asoko; mukō* あそこ; 向こう

P

Pachinko (pinball game) *pachinko* パチンコ

painful *kurushi'i; itai* 苦しい; 痛い

painting *e* 絵

pants *pantsu; zubon* パンツ; ズボン

park *tomemasu; tomeru; kōen* 止めます; 止める; 公園

parking *chūsha* 駐車

parking lot *chūsha-jō* 駐車場

particle for location of activity *de* で

particle indicating subject *ga* が

particle of contrast *wa* は

particle of empathy *nē* ねえ

particle of quotation *to* と

partner *aite* 相手

PASMO *pasumo* PASMO

password *pasuwādo* パスワード

pastry *pan* パン

PC *pasokon* パソコン

pedestrian bridge *hodō-kyō* 歩道橋

pedestrian crossing *ōdan-hodō* 横断歩道

pepper *koshō* コショウ

persevere *ganbarimasu; ganbaru* がんばります; がんばる

person *hito* 人

person in a higher position *jōshi* 上司

person of what nationality *nani-jin* 何人

pet *petto* ペット

phone *denwa* 電話

photocopier *kopī* コピー

photography *shashin* 写真

pine *matsu* 松

pink *pinku* ピンク

pizza *piza* ピザ

plan *yotei* 予定

plastic bottle *petto botoru* ペットボトル

plate *sara; o-sara* 皿; お皿

play *asobimasu; asobu* 遊びます; 遊ぶ

please (offering) *dōzo* どうぞ

please give me *kudasai* ください

plum *ume* 梅

police box *kōban* 交番

polite *teinei; go-teinei* 丁寧; ご丁寧

poor at *heta* 下手

pork *buta-niku* 豚肉

pork cutlet *tonkatsu* とんかつ

practice *renshū* 練習

printer *purintā* プリンター

private railroad *shitetsu* 私鉄

probably (informal) *darō* だろう

problem *mondai* 問題

Professor *sensei* 先生

prohibited *kinshi* 禁止

purple *murasaki* 紫

put in *iremasu; ireru* 入れます; 入れる

put on *kaburimasu; kaburu* (on head)/ *kimasu; kiru* (clothes)/

hakimasu; haku (on lower body) かぶります; かぶる/着ます; 着る/はきます; はく

Q

question *shitsumon* 質問
question-marker *ka* か
quickly *hayaku* 早く

R

rabbit *usagi* うさぎ
rain *ame* 雨
ramen *rāmen* ラーメン
ramen shop *rāmen-ya* ラーメン屋
read *yomimasu; yomu* 読みます; 読む
reading *dokusho* 読書
Really? *Hē?* へえ?
recommend *susumemasu; susumeru* 勧めます; 勧める
recommendation *osusume* おすすめ
recruiting *boshū* 募集
recycle *risaikuru* リサイクル
red *akai; aka* 赤い; 赤
refrigerator *reizōko* 冷蔵庫
regrettable *zan-nen* 残念
relatives *shinseki; go-shinseki* 親戚; ご親戚
relief *anshin* 安心
remember *oboemasu; oboeru* 覚えます; 覚える
request *onegai* お願い
rescue *tasukeru* 助ける
reservation *yoyaku* 予約
rest *yasumimasu; yasumu* 休みます; 休む
restaurant *resutoran* レストラン
restaurant bar *izaka-ya* 居酒屋

return *kaerimasu; kaeru* 帰ります; 帰る
rice ball *onigiri* おにぎり
rice bowl *chawan* 茶碗
right *migi* 右
ring *ringu* リング
ritual expression before eating/drinking *itadakimasu* いただきます
road *michi* 道
rose *bara* バラ
running *hashirimasu; hashiru; ran'nin'gu* 走ります; 走る/ランニング
Russia *Roshia* ロシア

S

sacrilegious *mottai nai* もったいない
sad *kanashi'i* 悲しい
sake (alcohol) *sake* 酒
salad *sarada* サラダ
Salisbury Steak *hanbāgu* ハンバーグ
salmon *sake* 鮭
salt *shio* 塩
same *onaji* 同じ
sandwich *sando* サンド
sashimi *sashimi* 刺身
Saturday *Do-yōbi* 土曜日
save life *tasukeru* 助ける
say *i'imasu; iu* 言います; 言う
scared *kowai* 怖い
schedule *sukejūru* スケジュール
school *gakkō* 学校
sea *umi* 海
season *kisetsu* 季節
seat *seki* 席
Seattle *Shiatoru* シアトル
seaweed *nori* のり
second day of the month, two days *futsu-ka* 二日

second-year student, sophomore *ni-nen-sei* 二年生
secretary *hisho* 秘書
section chief *kachō* 課長
See you *Itte rasshai* (response to *Itte kimasu*) 行ってらっしゃい
See you later (leaving home) *Itte kimasu* 行ってきます
self introduction *jikoshōkai* 自己紹介
senior citizen *shinia* シニア
senior in rank *me-ue* 目上
senior member of group *senpai* 先輩
September *Ku-gatsu* 九月
service area *sābisu eria* サービスエリア
service counter *sābisu kauntā* サービスカウンター
seven *shichi; nana* 七
seven units *nana-tsu* 七つ
seventh day of the month, seven days *nano-ka* 七日
Shanghai *Shanhai* 上海
Shinto shrine *Jinja* 神社
ship *fune* 船
shirt *shatsu* シャツ
shoes *kutsu* 靴
shop *mise* 店
shopping *kaimono* 買い物
shopping mall *mōru* モール
short break *kyūkei* 休憩
shoulder *kata* 肩
shrimp *ebi* エビ
siblings *kyōdai; go-kyōdai* 兄弟; ご兄弟
sick *byōki* 病気
side *~gawa; yoko* ～側; 横
sightseeing *kankō* 観光

sing **utaimasu; utau** 歌います; 歌う

singing **uta** 歌

single (unmarried) **dokushin** 独身

sit **suwarimasu; suwaru** 座ります; 座る

situation **ba'ai** 場合

six **roku** 六

six units **mut-tsu** 六つ

sixth day of the month; six days **mui-ka** 六日

skewered chicken BBQ **yaki-tori** 焼き鳥

ski **sukī** スキー

skirt **sukāto** スカート

Skype **Sukaipu** スカイプ

sleep **nemasu; neru/ yasumimasu; yasumu** 寝ます; 寝る/休みます; 休む

slow **osoi** 遅い

slowly **yukkuri** ゆっくり

small **chi'isai** 小さい

small (soup) bowl **owan** お椀

smartphone **sumaho** スマホ

smile **nikoniko** ニコニコ

smoke **suimasu; sū** 吸います; 吸う

snacks **okashi** お菓子

sneeze **kushami** くしゃみ

snow **yuki** 雪

so **sō** そう

soba restaurant **soba-ya** そば屋

soccer **sakkā** サッカー

socks **kutsushita** 靴下

sofa **sofā** ソファー

someone **dare ka** だれか

sometimes **tama ni; tokidoki** たまに; 時々

son **musuko; musuko-san; botchan** 息子; 息子さん; 坊ちゃん

song **uta** 歌

soon **sugu; mō sugu; hayaku** すぐ; もうすぐ; 早く

sorry **gomen** (casual)**; gomen nasai** (casual, gentle) ごめん; ごめんなさい

south **minami** 南

south exit **minami-guchi** 南口

souvenir **omiyage** お土産

soy sauce **shōyu** しょう油

Spain **Supein** スペイン

Spanish language **Supein-go** スペイン語

Spanish person **Supein-jin** スペイン人

speak **hanashimasu; hanasu** 話します; 話す

spirited **genki** 元気

split **wakaremasu; wakareru** 別れます; 別れる

spoon **supūn** スプーン

sports **supōtsu** スポーツ

spring **haru** 春

staircase **kaidan** 階段

start, to **toriaezu** とりあえず

station **eki** 駅

station building **eki-biru** 駅ビル

stationery **bunbōgu** 文房具

steak **sutēki** ステーキ

still **mada** まだ

stir-fried noodles **yaki-soba** 焼きそば

stomach **I; onaka** 胃; お腹

stop **tomemasu; tomeru** 止めます; 止める

store clerk **ten-in** 店員

strawberry **ichigo** いちご

street **michi** 道

strong **tsuyoi** 強い

student **gakusei** 学生

student discount **gakuwari** 学割

study **benkyō** 勉強

stylish **oshare** おしゃれ

subsection chief **kakarichō** 係長

subtle (style, color) **jimi** 地味

subway **chikatetsu** 地下鉄

sushi **sushi** 寿司

sugar **satō** 砂糖

Suica (IC card for JR) **suika** Suica

suit **sūtsu** スーツ

summer **natsu** 夏

summer vacation **natsu-yasumi** 夏休み

Sunday **Nichi-yōbi** 日曜日

supermarket **sūpā** スーパー

sushi restaurant **sushi-ya** 寿司屋

sweater **sētā** セーター

sweets **okashi; suītsu** お菓子; スイーツ

swim **oyogimasu; oyogu** 泳ぎます; 泳ぐ

swimming **suiei** 水泳

T

table **tēburu** テーブル

tablet **taburetto** タブレット

take **kakarimasu; kakaru/ torimasu; toru** かかります; かかる/取ります; 取る/撮ります; 撮る

take (a bath) **hairimasu; hairu** 入ります; 入る

take off (clothes, shoes) **nugimasu; nugu** 脱ぎます; 脱ぐ

take time off **yasumimasu; yasumu** 休みます; 休む

take up residence **sumimasu; sumu** 住みます; 住む

talk **hanashimasu; hanasu** 話します; 話す

taxi **takushī** タクシー

tea **ocha** お茶

teacher **sensei** 先生

teacher (in a school) **kyōshi** 教師

tell **i'imasu; iu** 言います; 言う

Tempura **tenpura** 天ぷら

ten **jū** 十

ten minutes **jup-pun** 十分

ten thousand **ichi-man** 一万

tennis **tenisu** テニス

tenth day of the month; ten days **tō-ka** 十日

ten units **tō** 十

text message **mēru** メール

thank you **arigatō; dō mo; sumimasen; sankyū; ~yori** (complimentary close) ありがとう; どうも; すみません; サンキュー; ～より

thank you for the food/ drink **gochisō-sama** ごちそうさま

thank you for waiting **omatase-itashimashita** お待たせいたしました

thank you in advance **yoroshiku** よろしく

thanks for your work **otsukare** (casual); **otsukare-sama** お疲れ; お疲れ様

that (away from us) **are** あれ

that (near you) **sore** それ

that makes sense **naruhodo** なるほど

that X **ano; sono** あの; その

that's incorrect **ie; i'ie, iya** いえ、いいえ、いや

that's correct **hai** はい

then **de wa** では

therapeutic **iyasaremasu; iyasareru** 癒されます; 癒される

there **kochira; soko** こちら; そこ

think **omoimasu; omou** 思います; 思う

third day of the month; three days **mik-ka** 三日

third-year student junior **san-nen-sei** 三年生

thirsty **karakara** カラカラ

thirty minutes past the hour **han** 半

this **kore** これ

this month **kon-getsu** 今月

this morning **kesa** 今朝

this side **temae** 手前

this term **kon-gakki** 今学期

this way **kochira** こちら

this week **kon-shū** 今週

this X **kono X** このX

this year **kotoshi** 今年

thousand **sen** 千

three **san** 三

three units **mit-tsu** 三つ

throat **nodo** 喉

throw away **sutemasu; suteru** 捨てます; 捨てる

Thursday **Moku-yōbi** 木曜日

ticket **kippu** 切符

time **jikan** 時間

time when **toki** 時

tired **kutakuta** くたくた

to **made** まで

tobacco **tabako** タバコ

today **kyō** 今日

toe **yubi** 指

toilet **toire** トイレ

Tokyo Station **Tōkyō-eki** 東京駅

tomorrow **ashita** 明日

tonight **konban** 今晩

too **mo** も

tooth **ha** 歯

top **ue** 上

tour **tsuā** ツアー

toy **omocha** おもちゃ

tradition **dentō** 伝統

traditional **dentō-teki** 伝統的

traffic light **shingō** 信号

train **densha** 電車

train station attendant **eki-in** 駅員

transfer **norikaemasu; norikaeru** 乗り換えます; 乗り換える

translate **yakushimasu; yakusu** 訳します; 訳す

translation **hon-yaku** 翻訳

transportation **norimono** 乗り物

trash **gomi** ゴミ

trash can **gomi bako** ゴミ箱

travel **ryokō** 旅行

tree **ki** 木

trip abroad **kaigai ryokō** 旅行

trousers **zubon** ズボン

true, truth **hontō** 本当

try hard **ganbarimasu; ganbaru** がんばります; がんばる

Tuesday **Ka-yōbi** 火曜日

turtle **kame** 亀

TV **terebi** テレビ

tweet **tsuīto** ツイート

twentieth day of the month, twenty days **hatsu-ka** 二十日

twenty years old **hatachi** 二十歳

two **ni; ni-hon** (long things) 二; 二本

two parents **ryōshin; go-ryōshin** 両親; ご両親

two people **futa-ri** 二人

two units **futa-tsu** 二つ

U

Udon (noodle) **udon** うどん

umbrella **kasa** 傘

umm (hesitation noise) **anō** あのう

uncle **oji; oji-san** 叔父; 伯父

under **shita** 下

underpants **pantsu** パンツ

understand **wakarimasu; wakaru** わかります; わかる

underwear **shitagi** 下着

unit (counter for things) **~tsu** つ

university **daigaku** 大学

unmarried **dokushin** 独身

until **made** まで

USA **Amerika** アメリカ

use **tsukaimasu; tsukau** 使います; 使う

usually **taitei** たいてい

V

vacuum cleaner **sōji-ki** 掃除機

vegetable **yasai** 野菜

vehicle **norimono** 乗り物

very much **taihen** 大変

video **bideo; dōga** (Internet) ビデオ; 動画

Vietnam **Betonamu** ベトナム

Vietnamese language **Betonamu-go** ベトナム語

Vietnamese person **Betonamu-jin** ベトナム人

W

wait **machimasu; matsu** 待ちます; 待つ

waitress **wētoresu** ウェートレス

wake up **okimasu; okiru** 起きます; 起きる

walk **arukimasu; aruku/ sanpo** 歩きます; 歩く/ 散歩

want **hoshi'i** 欲しい

wanted **boshū** 募集

warm **atatakai** 暖かい

was **deshita; datta** (informal form of **deshita**) でした; だった

Waseda **Waseda** 早稲田

washer **sentaku-ki** 洗濯機

wasteful **mottai nai** もったいない

watch **tokei** 時計

water (cold) **mizu** 水

weak **yowai** 弱い

wear **kimasu; kiru/ kaburimasu; kaburu** (on head)/**hakimasu; haku** (on lower body) 着ます; 着る/かぶります; かぶる/はきます; はく

weather **tenki; otenki** 天気; お天気

Wednesday **Sui-yōbi** 水曜日

weed **kusa** 草

week **shū; shūkan** 週; 週間

week after next **sarai-shū** 再来月

week before the last **sensen-shū** 先々週

Welcome home **Okaeri nasai** おかえりなさい

Welcome to our business **Irasshaimase** いらっしゃいませ

well **mā; yoku** まあ; よく

well then **ja(a)** じゃ(あ)

West **Nishi** 西

West exit **Nishi-guchi** 西口

Western food **Yōshoku** 洋食

what color **nani iro** 何色

what day of the week **nan-yōbi** 何曜日

what kind **don na** どんな

what kind of **dō iu** どういう

what language **nani-go** 何語

what month **nan-gatsu** 何月

what time **nan-ji** 何時

when **itsu** いつ

where **doko** どこ

where one is from **shusshin** 出身

which one **dore** どれ

which X **dono** どの

whimper and cry **mesomeso** メソメソ

white collar worker **sararī-man** サラリーマン

who **dare; donata** (polite) だれ; どなた

Whoa! **Wā!** わあ!

why **dōshite; nande** (casual) どうして; なんで

wife **kanai; oku-san** 家内; 奥さん

will do **kashikomari-mashita** かしこまりました

window **mado** 窓

wine *wain* ワイン

winter *fuyu* 冬

Woohoo! *Yatta!* やった！

word *kotoba* 言葉

work *hatarakimasu; hataraku/shigoto* 働きます；働く/仕事

worried *shinpai* 心配

worry about trivial matters *kuyokuyo* クヨクヨ

write *kakimasu; kaku* 書きます；書く

wrong *chigaimasu; chigau* 違います；違う

X

X-in-law *giri no X* 義理のX

X or Y *ka* か

X, Y and others *toka* とか

Y

year after the next *sarainen* 再来年

year before the last *ototoshi* おととし

yellow *ki'iroi; ki'iro* 黄色い；黄色

Yen *en* 円

yesterday *kinō* 昨日

Yippee! *Yatta!* やった！

yoga *yoga* ヨガ

you're welcome *dō itashimashite* どういたしまして

younger brother *otōto; otōto-san* 弟, 弟さん

younger sister *imōto; imōto-san* 妹, 妹さん

your home (polite) *otaku* お宅

YouTube *Yūchūbu* ユーチューブ

JAPANESE–ENGLISH DICTIONARY

A

ā ああ ah; in that way; oh

abunai 危ない dangerous

aida 間 between

aidea アイデア idea

aimasu; au 会います; 会う meet

aishī kādo ICカード IC card

aisu kōhī アイスコーヒー iced coffee

aisu kurīmu アイスクリーム ice cream

aite 相手 the other party; partner

akachan 赤ちゃん baby

akai; aka 赤い; 赤 red

aki 秋 autumn

akusesa-ri'i アクセサリー accessories

amari あまり not very much

ame 雨 rain

Amerika アメリカ USA

Amerika-jin アメリカ人 American

an'nai-jo 案内所 information booth

ane 姉 elder sister

ani 兄 elder brother

anime アニメ animation

anō あのう umm (hesitation noise)

ano あの that X

anshin 安心 feeling at ease; relief

aoi; ao 青い; 青 blue

apāto アパート apartment

apo アポ appointment

Appuru アップル Apple

apuri アプリ application

are あれ that (away from us)

Are? あれ？ Huh?

arerugī アレルギー allergy

arigatō ありがとう thank you

arimasu; aru あります; ある be; exist

aruite 歩いて by walking

arukimasu; aruku 歩きます; 歩く walk

asa 朝 morning

asa-gohan 朝ご飯 breakfast

ashi 足; 脚 foot; leg

ashi-kubi 足首 ankle

ashita 明日 tomorrow

asobimasu; asobu 遊びます; 遊ぶ play

asoko あそこ over there

atama 頭 head

atarashi'i 新しい new

atatakai 暖かい warm

ato 後 later

atsui 暑い; 熱い hot

atto iu ma あっという間 blink of the eye (time)

B

ba'ai 場合 case; situation

baibai バイバイ bye

baiku バイク motorcycle

ban 晩 evening; night

ban-gohan 晩ご飯 dinner

~ ban ～番 number; #

banana バナナ banana

bara バラ rose

basu バス bus

basuke; basuketto-bōru バスケ; バスケットボール basketball

beddo ベッド bed

benchi ベンチ bench

bengoshi 弁護士 attorney

benkyō 勉強 study

benri 便利 convenient

bentō; o-bentō 弁当; お弁当 boxed meal

beruto ベルト belt

Betonamu ベトナム Vietnam

Betonamu-go ベトナム語 Vietnamese language

Betonamu-jin ベトナム人 Vietnamese person

betsu ni 別に not particularly

bideo ビデオ video

bijinesu-man ビジネスマン businessman

bijutsu-kan 美術館 museum

bin ビン bottle; jar

biru ビル building

bīru ビール beer

boku 僕 I; me (by male speaker)

bōshi 帽子 cap; hat

boshū 募集 recruiting; wanted

boshū-chū 募集中 now hiring

botchan 坊ちゃん son

buchō 部長 division chief

budō ぶどう grapes

bunbōgu 文房具 stationery

bunka 文化 culture

burausu ブラウス blouse

buta-niku 豚肉 pork

byōin 病院 hospital

byōki 病気 disease; sick

C

chairoi; cha-iro 茶色い; 茶色 brown

chawan 茶碗 rice bowl

chekkuin チェックイン check in

chekkuauto チェックアウト check out

chi'isai 小さい small

chichi 父 father

chigaimasu; chigau 違います; 違う different; wrong

chika 地下 basement

chikai 近い close; near

chikatetsu 地下鉄 subway

chizu 地図 map

chō 腸 intestine

chokorēto チョコレート chocolate

chotto ちょっと little

~ chū ～中 in progress; in the middle of

chūgaku 中学 middle school

Chūgoku 中国 China

Chūgoku-go 中国語 Mandarin-Chinese (language)

Chūgoku-jin 中国人 Chinese person

Chūka 中華 Chinese food

chūmon 注文 order

chūsha 駐車 parking

chūsha-jō 駐車場 parking lot

chūsha-kinshi 駐車禁止 no parking

D

daigaku 大学 college; university

daigaku-in 大学院 graduate school

daijōbu 大丈夫 fine; okay

daitai だいたい for the most part

dake だけ limited to; only

dame ダメ broken; no good

dansu ダンス dance

dare だれ who

dare ka だれか someone

darō だろう probably (informal)

datta だった was (informal form of *deshita*)

de で by means of; particle indicating location of activity

de wa では then

deguchi 出口 exit

dekakemasu; dekakeru 出かけます; 出かける go out

dekimasu; dekiru できます; できる can do; completed, is

demasu; deru 出ます; 出る get out; leave

demo でも but; however

densha 電車 train

dentō 伝統 tradition

dentō-teki 伝統的 traditional

denwa 電話 phone

depāto デパート department store

deshita でした was

desu です is

dō どう how

dō itashimashite どういたしまして don't mention it; you're welcome

dō iu どういう what kind of

dō mo どうも I'm sorry; in every way; thank you

dō yatte どうやって how

Do-yōbi 土曜日 Saturday

doa ドア door

dōbutsu 動物 animal

dōga 動画 video (on Internet)

Doitsu ドイツ Germany

Doitsu-go ドイツ語 German language

Doitsu-jin ドイツ人 German person

dokidoki ドキドキ excited; nervous

doko どこ where

dokushin 独身 single; unmarried

dokusho 読書 reading

don na どんな what kind

donata どなた who (polite)

donburi 丼 bowl

dono どの which X

dono gurai どのぐらい how long

dore どれ which one

doresu ドレス dress

doru ドル dollar

dōryō 同僚 co-worker; colleague

dōshite どうして why

dōzo どうぞ please (offering)

E

e 絵 painting

eakon エアコン air conditioner

ebi エビ shrimp

edamame 枝豆 edamame (soyabean)

eiga 映画 movie

eigakan 映画館 movie theater

Eigo 英語 English

eki 駅 station

eki-biru 駅ビル station building

eki-in 駅員 train station attendant

en 円 Yen

enryo; go-enryo 遠慮; ご遠慮 decline; holding back

enu jī NG NG; no good

erebētā エレベーター elevator

eria mappu エリアマップ area map

eskarētā エスカレーター escalator

esunikku エスニック ethnic food

etto えっと Let me see (hesitation noise)

F

famirī resutoran; fami-resu ファミリーレストラン; ファミレス family restaurant

Feisubukku フェイスブック Facebook

fōku フォーク fork

fuben 不便 inconvenient

Fuji-san 富士山 Mt. Fuji

fuku 服 cloth

~fun; ~pun 〜分 minutes

fune 船 boat; ship

furai フライ deep-fried items

Furansu フランス France

Furansu-go フランス語 French language

Furansu-jin フランス人 French person

furasshu フラッシュ flash

Furenchi フレンチ French food

furui 古い old

futa-ri 二人 two people

futa-tsu 二つ two units

futsu-ka 二日 second day of the month; two days

fuyu 冬 winter

G

ga が particle indicating subject

gādeningu ガーデニング gardening

gaikoku 外国 foreign country

gakkari-suru がっかりする get disappointed

gakki 学期 academic term

gakkō 学校 school

gakusei 学生 student

gakuwari 学割 student discount

ganbarimasu; ganbaru がんばります; がんばる persevere; try hard

gasorin sutando ガソリンスタンド gas station

~ gawa 〜側 side

gēmu ゲーム game

gen'kin 現金 cash

genki 元気 energetic; healthy; spirited

Getsu-yōbi 月曜日 Monday

ginkō 銀行 bank

ginkō-in 銀行員 bank employee

giri no X 義理のX X-in-law

go 碁 Go (game)

go 五 five

Go-gatsu 五月 May

go-kyōdai ご兄弟 brothers; siblings

Gochisō-sama ごちそうさま Thank you for the food/drink

gohan ご飯 cooked rice; meal

gomen ごめん excuse me; sorry (casual)

gomen nasai ごめんなさい excuse me; sorry (casual, gentle)

gomi ゴミ trash

gomi bako ゴミ箱 trash can

~ goro 〜ごろ about

gorufu ゴルフ golf

gozaimasu ございます be; exist (polite)

Gūguru グーグル Google

gyū-niku 牛肉 beef

gyūnyū 牛乳 milk

H

ha 歯 tooth

hachi 八 eight

Hachi-gatsu 八月 August

Hachi-kō ハチ公 Hachi, the local dog statue at Shibuya station

hade 派手 flashy; loud

haha; okā-san 母; お母 さん mother

hai はい here you go; I'm here; that's correct

hai 肺 lung

hai-iro 灰色 gray

haikingu ハイキング hike

hairimasu; hairu 入りま す; 入る go in; take (a bath)

hajime はじめ beginning

Hajime-mashite 初めま して How do you do?

hakimasu; haku はきま す; はく put on; wear (on lower body)

hako 箱 box

Hamama-tsu-chō 浜松町 Hamamatsu

hamusutā ハムスター hamster

han 半 half; thirty minutes past the hour

hana 花 flower

hana 鼻 nose

hanashimasu; hanasu 話 します; 話す speak; talk

hanbāgā ハンバーガー hamburger

hanbāgu ハンバー グ Salisbury Steak (hamburger without buns)

hando baggu ハンドバ ッグ handbag

Haneda kūkō 羽田空港 Haneda Airport

hantai 反対 opposite

hantai-gawa 反対側 opposite side

harahara ハラハラ apprehensive

haru 春 spring

hashi 橋 bridge

hashi; ohashi 箸; お箸 chopsticks

hashirimasu; hashiru 走 ります; 走る running

hatachi 二十歳 twenty years old

hatarakimasu; hataraku 働きます; 働く work

hatsu-ka 二十日 the twentieth day of the month; twenty days

hayai 速い; 早い early; fast

hayaku 早く quickly; soon

hazuka-shi'i 恥ずかしい embarrassed; feel shy

Hē? へえ Really?

hen 辺 area

heso へそ belly button

heta 下手 poor at

hidari 左 left

higashi 東 east

higashi-guchi 東口 east exit

hiji ひじ elbow

~hiki; ~piki; ~biki ～匹 counter for animals

hikidashi 引き出し drawer

hikkoshimasu; hikkosu 引っ越します; 引っ越 す move (residence)

hikōki 飛行機 airplane

hiru-gohan 昼ご飯 lunch

hisho 秘書 administrative assistant; secretary

hito 人 person

hito-ri-gurashi 一人暮ら し living alone

hito-ri-kko 一人っ子 only child

hito-tsu 一つ one unit

hiza 膝 knee

hō 方 alternative; direction

hodō-kyō 歩道橋 pedestrian bridge

hon 本 book

hon-dana 本棚 bookshelf

hon-yaku 翻訳 translation

~hon; ~pon; ~bon ～本 counter for long things

hone 骨 bone

hontō 本当 true; truth

hora ほら Look!

hoshi'i 欲しい want

hotto ホット hot coffee

hotto-shimasu/suru ホッとします/する feel relieved

hyaku 百 hundred

I

i 胃 stomach

i'i いい good

i'i tenki いい天気 good weather

i'imasu; iu 言います; 言う say; tell

ichi 一 one

ichi-ban 一番 best; number one

ichi-do 一度 one time

Ichi-gatsu 一月 January

ichi-jikan 一時間 one hour

ichi-man 一万 ten thousand

ichi-nen 一年 one year

ichi-nen-sei 一年生 first-year student; freshman

ichigo いちご strawberry

ie 家 house

ie; i'ie; iya いえ; いいえ; いや no; that's incorrect

Igirisu イギリス England; Great Britain

Igo 囲碁 Go (game)

ikaga いかが how (polite)

ikimasu; iku 行きます; 行く go

ikura いくら how much

ima-ichi いまいち not quite

imasu; iru います; いる be; exist

imi 意味 meaning

imōto 妹 younger sister

imōto-san 妹さん younger sister

inaka 田舎 country side

Indo インド India

inu 犬 dog

ippai いっぱい full; many

iraira イライラ irritated

Irasshaimase いらっしゃいませ Welcome to our business

iremasu; ireru 入れます; 入れる enter; put in

iriguchi 入り口 entrance

is-shūkan 一週間 one week

isha 医者 medical doctor

isogashi'i 忙しい busy

isogimasu; isogu 急ぎます; 急ぐ hurry

isu 椅子 chair

Itadakemasen ka いただけませんか Can I have X?

itadakimasu いただきます accept (humble); ritual expression before eating/drinking

itai 痛い hurt; painful

Itaria イタリア Italy

Itaria-go イタリア語 Italian language

Itaria-jin イタリア人 Italian person

Itarian イタリアン Italian food

itsu いつ when

itsu-ka 五日 the fifth day of the month; five days

itsu-tsu 五つ five units

itsumo いつも always

Itte kimasu 行ってきます See you later (on leaving home)

Itte rasshai 行ってらっしゃい Have a nice day; See you

iyaringu イヤリング earring

iyasaremasu; iyasareru 癒されます; 癒される get healed; therapeutic

Izaka-ya 居酒屋 restaurant bar

J

ja nai desu じゃないです is not

ja(a) じゃ(あ) bye; well then

jaketto ジャケット jacket

jānarisuto ジャーナリスト journalist

Jeiāru JR Japan Railway (JR)

~ji ～時 hour

jikan 時間 hours; time

jiko 事故 accident

jikoshōkai 自己紹介 self introduction

jimi 地味 quiet (style, color)

jimu-in 事務員 office clerk

jinja 神社 Shinto shrine

jinzō 腎臓 kidney

jīnzu ジーンズ jeans

jitensha 自転車 bicycle

jitsu wa 実は actually

jōdan 冗談 joke; kidding

jōshi 上司 boss; person in a higher position

jōzu 上手 good at

jū 十 ten

Jū-gatsu 十月 October

Jū-ichi-gatsu 十一月 November

Jū-ni-gatsu 十二月 December

jugyō 授業 class

jup-pun 十分 ten minutes

jūsu ジュース juice

K

ka か question-marker; X or Y

ka-dō 華道 Japanese flower arrangement

Ka-yōbi 火曜日 Tuesday

~ ka ～日 counter for days of the month

kaban かばん bag

Kabuki 歌舞伎 Kabuki Theater

kaburimasu; kaburu かぶります; かぶる put on; wear (on head)

kachō 課長 section chief

kado 角 corner

kādo カード credit card

kaerimasu; kaeru 帰ります; 帰る go home; return

kafe カフェ café

~kagetsu ～ヶ月 counter for months

kagi 鍵 key; lock

kagu 家具 furniture

~ kai ～階 counter for floors/stories

kaidan 階段 staircase

kaigai ryokō 旅行 trip abroad

kaigi 会議 conference; meeting

kaimasu; kau 買います; 買う buy

kaimasu; kau 飼います; 飼う keep (animal)

kaimono 買い物 shopping

kaisha 会社 company

kaisha-in 会社員 company employee

kakarichō 係長 subsection chief

kakarimasu; kakaru か かります; かかる cost; take

kakimasu; kaku 書きま す; 書く draw; write

kame 亀 turtle

kami 髪 hair

kamo shirenai かもしれ ない maybe

kan 缶 can

kanai; oku-san 家内; 奥 さん wife

kanashi'i 悲しい sad

kankō 観光 sightseeing

Kankoku 韓国 Korea

Kanpai 乾杯 Cheers!

kanzō 肝臓 liver

kao 顔 face

kappu カップ cup (tea; coffee)

kara から from

kara-age 唐揚げ fried chicken

karada 体 body

karakara カラカラ dry; thirsty

karaoke カラオケ karaoke

karē カレー curry

kasa 傘 umbrella

kashiko-marimashita かしこまりました certainly; will do

kata 肩 shoulder

kaze 風邪 cold, a

kazoku; go-kazoku 家族; ご家族 family

kedo けど but

kega 怪我 injury

keiei 経営 management

keiei-sha 経営者 business owner; entrepreneur

keigo 敬語 honorific language

kēki ケーキ cake

kekkon 結婚 marriage

kenjō-go 謙譲語 humble language

kesa 今朝 this morning

keshō-hin 化粧品 cosmetics

kētai ケータイ cellphone

ki 木 tree

ki'iroi; ki-iro 黄色い; 黄色 yellow

kikimasu; kiku 聞きま す; 聞く ask; listen

kiku 菊 chrysanthemum

kimasu; kiru 着ます; 着る put on (clothes); wear

kimasu; kuru 来ます; 来る come

kimochi 気持ち emotions; feeling

kimono 着物 kimono

Kimura 木村 Kimura (family name)

kin-niku 筋肉 muscle

Kin-yōbi 金曜日 Friday

kin'en 禁煙 no smoking

kingyo 金魚 goldfish

kinō 昨日 yesterday

kinshi 禁止 forbidden; prohibited

kippu 切符 ticket

kirai 嫌い dislike

kisetsu 季節 season

kissaten 喫茶店 coffee shop

kita 北 north

kita-guchi 北口 north exit

ko; kodomo 子; 子供 child

kō こう in this way

~ ko ～個 counter for concrete items

kōban 交番 police box

kōcha 紅茶 black tea

kochira こちら these; this way

kōen 公園 park

kōhai 後輩 junior member of a group

koi 鯉 Koi fish

koibito 恋人 girl/boyfriend

koko ここ here

kōkō 高校 high school

kokono-ka 九日 ninth day of the month; nine days

kokono-tsu 九つ nine units

komarimasu; komaru 困ります; 困る have difficulty

Kon'ban'wa こんばんは Good evening

Kon'nichi'wa こんにちは Hello

kon-gakki 今学期 this term

kon-getsu 今月 this month

kon-iro 紺色 navy (color)

kon-shū 今週 this week

kon-yaku 婚約 engagement

konban 今晩 tonight

konbini コンビニ convenience store

konchū 昆虫 bugs; insects

kono この this X

kono ato この後 after this

konpyūtā コンピューター computer

konsarutanto コンサルタント consultant

kōnu-in 公務員 civil servant

kopī コピー photocopier

koppu コップ cup; glass

kōra コーラ cola

kore これ this

kōsai 交際 dating

koshi 腰 lower back

koshō コショウ pepper

kōto コート coat

kotoba 言葉 language; word

kotoshi 今年 this year

kowai 怖い afraid; scared

Ku-gatsu 九月 September

ku-ji 九時 nine o'clock

ku; kyū 九 nine

kubi 首 neck

kuchi 口 mouth

kudamono 果物 fruit

kudasai ください please give me

Kudasaimasen ka. くださいませんか。 Could you please give me X?

kukkī クッキー cookie

kūkō 空港 airport

~ kun ～君 casual title for boys and subordinates

kuni 国 country

kuroi; kuro 黒い; 黒 black

kuruma 車 car

kurushi'i 苦しい hurt; painful

kusa 草 grass; weed

kushami くしゃみ sneeze

kusuri 薬 medicine

kutakuta くたくた tired

kutsu 靴 shoes

kutsushita 靴下 socks

kuyokuyo クヨクヨ worry about trivial matters

kyabinetto キャビネット cabinet

kyō 今日 today

kyōdai 兄弟 brothers; siblings

Kyōkai 教会 Christian church

kyōmi 興味 interest

kyonen 去年 last year

kyōshi 教師 teacher (in a school)

kyūkei 休憩 short break

kyūkyū-sha 救急車 ambulance

M

mā まあ I guess; well

machigaemasu; machigaeru 間違えます; 間違える make an error

machimasu; matsu 待ちます; 待つ wait

mada まだ (not) yet; still

made まで to; until

made ni までに by

mado 窓 window

mae 前 before; front

magarimasu; magaru 曲がります; 曲がる make a turn

mago; o-mago-san 孫; お孫さん grandchild

mai-shū 毎週 every week

mai-toshi 毎年 every year

mai-tsuki 毎月 every month

~ mai ～枚 counter for flat things

mainichi 毎日 every day

manējā マネージャー manager

manga マンガ comics

manshon マンション condominium

mata また again

Mata! また！ Again!; C'mon!

matsu 松 pine

matsuri; o-matsuri 祭り; お祭り festival

mazui まずい bad-tasting; doesn't work

me 目 eye

me-shita 目下 junior in rank

me-ue 目上 senior in rank

megane 眼鏡 eyeglasses

~ mei; ~ mei-sama ～名；名様 counter for people

mei; meigo-san めい; めい御さん niece

meishi 名刺 business card

mēku メーク make-up

mēru メール email; text message

mesomeso メソメソ whimper and cry

michi 道 road; street

midori 緑 green

migi 右 right

mik-ka 三日 the third day of the month; three days

mikan みかん mandarin orange

mimi 耳 ear

minami 南 south

minami-guchi 南口 south exit

minasan みなさん everyone (polite)

minna みんな all; everyone

miruku ミルク milk

mise 店 shop

miso みそ miso

miso-shiru 味噌汁 miso soup

mit-tsu 三つ three units

mizu 水 water (cold)

mo も either; too

mō もう already; no longer; more

mō ichi-do もう一度 one more time

mō sugu もうすぐ soon

mochiron もちろん of course

Moku-yōbi 木曜日 Thursday

mondai 問題 problem

monorēru モノレール monorail

mōru モール shopping mall

mottai nai もったいない sacrilegious; wasteful

motto もっと more

mui-ka 六日 the sixth day of the month; six days

mukamuka ムカムカ having a surge of anger

mukō 向こう the other side; over there

mune 胸 chest

murasaki 紫 purple

muryō 無料 free of charge

musuko; musuko-san 息子; 息子さん son

musume; musume-san 娘; 娘さん daughter

mut-tsu 六つ six units

muzuka-shi'i 難しい difficult

N

nā なあ isn't it (casual)

naifu ナイフ knife

naka 中 inside

nakimasu; naku 泣きます; 泣く/鳴きます; 鳴く cry

nakunarimasu; nakunaru なくなります; なくなる decease

nama 生 draft beer

namae 名前 name

nan de mo なんでも anything

nan-gatsu 何月 what month

nan-ji 何時 what time

nan-mei-sama 何名様 how many people

nan-yōbi 何曜日 what day of the week

nana-tsu 七つ seven units

nande なんで why (casual)

nani iro 何色 what color

nani-go 何語 what language

nani-jin 何人 person of what nationality

nano-ka 七日 the seventh day of the month; seven days

naremasu; nareru なれます; なれる get accustomed

narimasu; naru なります; なる become

Narita Kūkō 成田空港 Narita Airport

naruhodo なるほど I see; that makes sense

natsu 夏 summer

natsu-yasumi 夏休み summer vacation

natsuka-shi'i 懐かしい feel nostalgic

nē ねえ isn't it; particle of empathy

nekkuresu ネックレス necklace

neko 猫 cat

nekutai; tai ネクタイ; タイ necktie

nemasu; neru 寝ます; 寝る sleep

~ nen ～年 counter for years

netsu 熱 fever

netto ネット Internet

ni に for the purpose of X; at (particle of location)

ni 二 two

Ni-gatsu 二月 February

ni-hon 二本 two (long things)

ni-nen-sei 二年生 second-year student; sophomore

niaimasu; niau 似合います; 似合う becoming; look good

Nichi-yōbi 日曜日 Sunday

~ nichi ～日 counter for days of the month

Nihon 日本 Japan

Nihongo 日本語 Japanese language

nikoniko ニコニコ smile

niku 肉 meat

~ nin ～人 counter for people

nishi 西 west

nishi-guchi 西口 west exit

no の it's the case; one (pronoun)

noborimasu; noboru 登ります; 登る climb

nodo 喉 throat

nomimono 飲み物 drinks

nomimasu; nomu 飲みます; 飲む drink

nori のり seaweed

norikaemasu; norikaeru 乗り換えます; 乗り換える transfer

norimasu; noru 乗ります; 乗る get on (a vehicle)

norimono 乗り物 transportation; vehicle

nugimasu; nugu 脱ぎます; 脱ぐ take off (clothes, shoes)

nyūgaku 入学 entering school

nyūsu ニュース news

O

o-hiru お昼 lunch; noon

o-jō-san お嬢さん daughter

oba; oba-san 叔母; 伯母 aunt

oboemasu; oboeru 覚えます; 覚える commit to memory; remember

ocha お茶 green tea; tea

ōdan-hodō 横断歩道 pedestrian crossing

odekake お出かけ going out

odorimasu; odoru 踊ります; 踊る dance

Ohayō おはよう Good morning

oi; oigo-san 甥; 甥御さん nephew

oishi-sō おいしそう appetizing; look delicious

oishi'i おいしい delicious

oji; oji-san 叔父; 伯父 uncle

Okaeri nasai おかえり なさい Welcome home

okane お金 money

okashi お菓子 snacks; sweets

ōki'i 大きい big

okimasu; okiru 起き ます; 起きる get up; wake up

Okinawa 沖縄 Okinawa

okkē オッケー OK

okorimasu; okoru 怒り ます; 怒る get angry

Omatase-itashimashita お待たせいたしました Thank you for waiting

Omedetō! おめでとう! Congratulations!

omiyage お土産 gift; souvenir

omocha おもちゃ toy

omoimasu; omou 思いま す; 思う think

omoshiroi 面白い interesting

onaji 同じ same

onaka お腹 stomach

onē-san お姉さん elder sister

onegai お願い request

ongaku 音楽 music

onī-san お兄さん elder brother

onigiri おにぎり rice ball

onna 女 female; woman

onsen 温泉 hot spring

orenji オレンジ orange

orimasu; oriru 降りま す; 降りる get off

oshare おしゃれ fashionable; stylish

osoi 遅い late; slow

osoku naru 遅くなる become late

osusume おすすめ recommendation

otaku お宅 your home (polite)

otō-san お父さん father

otoko 男 male; man

otona 大人 adult

otōto; otōto-san 弟, 弟さ ん younger brother

ototoshi おととし year before last

otsukare (casual); *otsukare-sama* お疲れ; お疲れ様 thanks for your work

owan お椀 small (soup) bowl

owari 終わり ending

oyasumi おやすみ good night

oyogimasu; oyogu 泳ぎ ます; 泳ぐ swim

P

pachinko パチンコ Pachinko (pinball game)

pan パン bread; pastry

pantsu パンツ pants

pasokon パソコン laptop

pasumo PASMO PASMO (IC card for private railroad)

pasuwādo パスワード password

pekopeko ペコペコ hungry

perapera ペラペラ fluent in a language

petto; petto botoru ペット; ペットボトル pet, plastic bottle (PET)

pinku ピンク pink

piza ピザ pizza

purintā プリンター printer

R

rai-gakki 来学期 next term

rai-getsu 来月 next month

rai-shū 来週 next week

Rain ライン Line

rainen 来年 next year

raku 楽 comfortable; easy

rāmen ラーメン ramen

rāmen-ya ラーメン屋 ramen shop

ran'nin'-gu ランニング running

ranchi ランチ lunch

reizōko 冷蔵庫 refrigerator

renshū 練習 practice

resutoran レストラン restaurant

rikon 離婚 divorce

rimujin リムジン limousine

ringo りんご apple

ringu リング ring

risaikuru リサイクル recycle

roku 六 six

Roku-gatsu 六月 June

Roshia ロシア Russia

ryō 寮 dormitory

ryōjikan 領事館 consulate

ryokō 旅行 travel

ryōri 料理 cook; dish (food)

ryōshin; ryōshin 両親; ご両親 two parents

ryūgaku-sei 留学生 foreign student

S

sa-dō 茶道 Japanese tea ceremony

sabishi'i 寂しい lonely

sābisu eria サービスエリア service area

sābisu kauntā サービスカウンター service counter

~sai ～才; ～歳 counter for human age

saikō 最高 best

sakana 魚 fish

sake 酒 sake

sake 鮭 salmon

saki 先 ahead

sakkā サッカー soccer

sakki さっき a little while ago; just now

sakura 桜 cherry

samui 寒い cold

san さん Ms, Mr

san 三 three

San-gatsu 三月 March

san-nen-sei 三年生 junior; third-year student

sando サンド sandwich

sankyū サンキュー thank you

sanpo 散歩 walk

sara; o-sara 皿; お皿 plate

sarada サラダ salad

sarai-getsu 再来月 month after next; week after next

sarainen 再来年 year after next

sararī-man サラリーマン white collar worker

sashimi 刺身 sashimi

satō 砂糖 sugar

~satsu ～冊 counter for bound things

sayo(u)nara さよ(う)なら goodbye

se; senaka 背; 背中 back

seikatsu 生活 living

seki 咳 cough

seki 席 seat

sen 千 thousand

sen-gakki 先学期 last term

sen-getsu 先月 last month

sen-shū 先週 last week

senpai 先輩 senior member of a group

sensei 先生 professor; teacher

sensen-getsu 先々月 month before last

sensen-shū 先々週 week before last

sentaku 洗濯 laundry

sentaku-ki 洗濯機 washer

sētā セーター sweater

shachō 社長 company president

Shanhai 上海 Shanghai

shashin 写真 photography

shatsu シャツ shirt

Shi-gatsu 四月 April

shi; yo; yon 四 four

~shi ～し and (listing reasons)

Shiatoru シアトル Seattle

shiawase 幸せ happiness; happy

Shichi-gatsu 七月 July

shichi; nana 七 seven

shigoto 仕事 work

shiken 試験 exam

shimashita しました did

shimasu; suru します; する do

shimekiri 締め切り deadline

shinbun 新聞 newspaper

shingō 信号 traffic light

shinia シニア senior citizen

shinimasu; shinu 死にます; 死ぬ die

Shinkansen 新幹線 bullet train

shinpai 心配 worried

shinseki; go-shinseki 親戚; ご親戚 relatives

shinsetsu 親切 kind

shinzō 心臓 heart

shio 塩 salt

shiriai 知り合い acquaintance

shirimasu; shiru 知ります; 知る find out; know

shiro; o-shiro 城; お城 castle

shita 下 below; under

shitagi 下着 underwear

shitetsu 私鉄 private railroad

shitsumon 質問 question

shitsurei; shitsurei-shimasu 失礼; 失礼します excuse me for doing something rude

sho-dō 書道 Japanese calligraphy

shō-gakkō 小学校 elementary school

Shōgi 将棋 Japanese chess

shokudō 食堂 diner; dining hall

shōyu しょう油 soy sauce

shū; shūkan 週; 週間 week

shujin; go-shujin 主人; ご主人 husband

shukudai 宿題 homework

shumi 趣味 hobby

shūshoku 就職 getting employed

shusshin 出身 hometown; where one is from

sō そう in that way; so

soba そば buckwheat noodle

soba そば in the vicinity; near

soba-ya そば屋 soba restaurant

sobo; obā-san 祖母; おばあさん grandmother

sodachimasu; sodatsu 育ちます; 育つ grow up

sofā ソファー sofa

sofu; ojī-san 祖父; おじいさん grandfather

sōji 掃除 cleaning

sōji-ki 掃除機 vacuum cleaner

sokkusu ソックス casual (school) socks

soko そこ there

sono その that X

sore それ that near you

sore kara それから and

soto 外 outside

sotsugyō 卒業 graduation

sugoi すごい amazing

sugu すぐ soon

Sui-yōbi 水曜日 Wednesday

suiei 水泳 swimming

Suika Suica Suica (IC card for JR)

suimasu; sū 吸います; 吸う inhale; smoke

suītsu スイーツ sweets

Sukaipu スカイプ Skype

sukāto スカート skirt

sukejūru スケジュール schedule

sukī スキー ski

suki 好き like

sukimasu; suku すきます; すく become empty

sumaho スマホ smartphone

sumimasen すみません I'm sorry; thank you

sumimasu; sumu 住みます; 住む live; take up residence

sūpā スーパー supermarket

Supein スペイン Spain

Supein-go スペイン語 Spanish language

Supein-jin スペイン人 Spanish person

supōtsu スポーツ sports

supūn スプーン spoon

sushi 寿司 sushi

sushi-ya 寿司屋 sushi restaurant

susumemasu; susumeru 勧めます; 勧める recommend

sutēki ステーキ steak

sutemasu; suteru 捨てます; 捨てる discard; throw away

sūtsu スーツ suit

suwarimasu; suwaru 座ります; 座る sit

suzushi'i 涼しい cool

T

tabako タバコ cigarette; tobacco

tabemasu; taberu 食べます; 食べる eat

tabemono 食べ物 food

taburetto タブレット tablet

tada ただ free of charge

tadaima ただいま I'm home

taihen 大変 difficult; very much

taishikan 大使館 embassy

taishita koto nai 大したことない not a big deal

taitei たいてい most of the time; usually

takai 高い expensive; high

take 竹 bamboo

takushī タクシー taxi

tama ni たまに every now and then; sometimes

tamago 卵 egg

tame-go タメ語 casual language (between equals)

tanjōbi 誕生日 birthday

tanoshi'i 楽しい enjoyable; fun

tasukeru 助ける rescue; save life

tatemono 建物 building

te 手 hand

tēburu テーブル table

teinei; go-teinei 丁寧; ご丁寧 careful; polite

teishoku 定食 complete meal

temae 手前 this side

ten-in 店員 store clerk

tenisu テニス tennis

tenki; otenki 天気; お天気 weather

tenpura 天ぷら Tempura

tera; o-tera 寺; お寺 Buddhist temple

terebi テレビ TV

to と and; particle of quotation

tō 十 ten units

tō-ka 十日 the tenth day of the month; ten days

toho 徒歩 by foot

tōi 遠い far

toire トイレ toilet

toka とか X, Y and others

to 計 clock; watch

toki 時 time when

tokidoki 時々 sometimes

Tōkyō-eki 東京駅 Tokyo Station

tomemasu; tomeru 止めます; 止める park; stop

tomodachi 友達 friend

tonari 隣 neighboring; next to

tonkatsu とんかつ pork cutlet

tori 鳥 bird; chicken

tori-niku 鶏肉 chicken

toriaezu とりあえず for now; to start

torimasu; toru 取ります; 取る/撮ります; 撮る take

toshokan 図書館 library

~ tsu ~つ unit (counter for things)

tsuā ツアー tour

tsūgaku 通学 commute to school

tsugi 次 next

tsuitachi 一日 first day of the month

tsuīto ツイート tweet

tsukaimasu; tsukau 使います; 使う use

tsukaremasu; tsukareru 疲れます; 疲れる become tired

tsukimasu; tsuku 着きます; 着く arrive

tsūkin 通勤 commute to work

tsukue 机 desk

tsukurimasu; tsukuru 作ります; 作る make

tsumaranai つまらない boring

tsume 爪 nail

tsumetai 冷たい cold (to touch)

tsurai 辛い feel hardship; miserable

tsūyaku 通訳 interpreter

tsuyoi 強い strong

U

uchi 家 my home

uchiawase 打ち合わせ meeting (for planning)

ude 腕 arm

udon うどん Udon (noodle)

ue 上 above; top

ukiuki ウキウキ happy (anticipating good news)

umaremasu; umareru 生まれます; 生まれる be born

ume 梅 plum

umi 海 ocean; sea

unten 運転 driving

unten-shu 運転手 driver

ureshi'i 嬉しい delighted; glad

ūron-cha ウーロン茶 oolong tea

usagi うさぎ rabbit

ushiro 後ろ back; behind

uso うそ lie

uta 歌 singing; song

utaimasu; utau 歌います; 歌う sing

uwagi 上着 jacket; outer wear

W

wa は as for X; particle of contrast

Wā! わあ! Whoa!

wain ワイン wine

wakaremasu; wakareru
別れます; 別れる
break up; split

wakarimasu; wakaru
わかります; わかる
understand

waraimasu; warau 笑い
ます; 笑う laugh

warui 悪い bad

Waseda 早稲田 Waseda

washoku 和食 Japanese
food

wasuremasu; wasureru
忘れます; 忘れる forget

watarimasu; wataru 渡
ります; 渡る cross

watashi 私 I; me

wētoresu ウェートレス
waitress

Y

yaki-niku 焼肉 Korean
BBQ

yaki-soba 焼きそば
stir-fried noodles

yaki-tori 焼き鳥
skewered chicken BBQ

yaku 約 approximately

yakushimasu; yakusu 訳
します; 訳す translate

yakyū 野球 baseball

yama 山 hill; mountain

yappari やっぱり after
all; as assumed

yarimasu; yaru やりま
す; やる do (casual)

yasai 野菜 vegetable

yasashi'i 優しい easy;
kind-hearted

yasui 安い cheap;
inexpensive

yasumi 休み absence;
break; day off

yasumimasu; yasumu
休みます; 休む
rest; sleep; take time off

yat-tsu 八つ eight units

Yatta! やった！
Woohoo!; Yippee!

yo よ I tell you
(particle indicating new
information)

yō-ka 八日 the eighth day
of the month; eight days

yo-nen-sei 四年生
fourth-year student;
senior

yoga ヨガ yoga

yok-ka 四日 the fourth
day of the month; four
days

yoko 横 side

yoku よく a lot; often;
well

yomimasu; yomu 読みま
す; 読む read

yon-kai 4階 four floors;
fourth floor

~ yori ～より than
(particle of comparison)

yoroshiku よろしく
nice to meet you; thank
you in advance

yōshoku 洋食 Western
food

yot-tsu 四つ four units

yotei 予定 plan

yowai 弱い weak

yoyaku 予約 reservation

yūbe 夕べ last night

yubi 指 finger; toe

Yūchūbu ユーチューブ
YouTube

yuki 雪 snow

yukkuri ゆっくり
slowly

yūmei 有名 famous

Z

zan-nen 残念 feel sorry;
regrettable

zasshi 雑誌 magazine

zenzen 全然 not at all

zubon ズボン pants;
trousers

AUDIO TRACK LIST

How to Download the Audios for this Book.

1. You must have an Internet connection.
2. Type the URL below into your web browser.

http://www.tuttlepublishing.com/easy-japanese-downloadable-cd-content

For support email us at info@tuttlepublishing.com.